INNOVATION IN SOCIAL SERVICES

Innovation in Social Services

The Public-Private Mix in Service Provision, Fiscal Policy and Employment

Edited by

TOMÁŠ SIROVÁTKA
Masaryk University, Czech Republic

BENT GREVE
Roskilde University, Denmark

ASHGATE

Published by
Ashgate Publishing Limited
Wey Court East
Union Road
Farnham
Surrey, GU9 7PT
England

Ashgate Publishing Company
110 Cherry Street
Suite 3-1
Burlington, VT 05401-3818
USA

www.ashgate.com

British Library Cataloguing in Publication Data
A catalogue record for this book is available from the British Library

The Library of Congress has cataloged the printed edition as follows:
Innovation in social services : the public-private mix in service provision, fiscal policy and employment / [edited] by Tomáš Sirovátka and Bent Greve.
    pages cm
Includes bibliographical references and index.
ISBN 978-1-4094-6347-4 (hardback) – ISBN 978-1-4094-6348-1 –
ISBN 978-1-4724-0759-7 (print) 1. Social service – Europe. 2. Public-private sector cooperation – Europe. 3. Europe – Social policy. 4. Welfare state – Europe.
    I. Sirovátka, Tomáš . II. Greve, Bent.

HV238.I56 2014
361.94068'4–dc23

2013043990

ISBN 9781409463474 (hbk)
ISBN 9781409463481 (ebk – PDF)
ISBN 9781472407597 (ebk – ePUB)

MIX
Paper from
responsible sources
FSC
www.fsc.org   FSC® C013985

Printed in the United Kingdom by Henry Ling Limited,
at the Dorset Press, Dorchester, DT1 1HD

Contents

List of Tables, Annexes and Boxes

Tables

Annexes

Boxes

List of Abbreviations

ADM	Public administration and defence; compulsory social security
ADL	Activities of daily living, Personal care
ALMP	Active labour market policies
ARGE	*Arbaitsagenturen* [Employment agencies]
APSS	*Asociace poskytovatelů sociálních služeb* [Association of social services providers]
BEPA	Bureau of European Policy Advisers
BMFSFJ	*Bundesministeriums für Familie, Senioren, Frauen und Jugend,* [Federal Ministry of Family Affairs, Senior Citizens, Women and Youth]
CASS	Consolidation Act on Social Services
CCCABC	Coalition of Child Care Advocates of British Columbia
CEDEFOP	European Centre for the Development of Vocational Training
CZ	the Czech Republic
CZK	*česká koruna* [Czech crown (currency)]
CZSO	Czech Statistical Office
DA	The Confederation of Danish Employers
DK	Denmark
DKK	*dansk krone* [Danish crown (currency)]
DG ECFIN	Directorate General for Economic and Financial Affairs
DWP	The Department for Work and Pensions
EC	European Commission
ECEC	Early Childhood Education and Care
ECJ	European Court of Justice
ECS	European Company Survey
EEC	European Economic Community
EES	European Employment Strategy
EMU	Economic and Monetary Union
ESF	European Social Fund
ESPROSS	European system of integrated social protection statistics
ESWT	Establishment Survey on Working Time and Work-Life Balance
EU	European Union
EU-12	European Union 12 Member States (1 November 1993–31 December 1994)
EU-15	European Union 15 Member States (1 January 1995–30 April 2004)
EU-27	European Union 27 Member States (1 January 2007–30 June 2013)

EUR   Euro (currency)
Eurofound   European Foundation for the Improvement of Living and
               Working Conditions
Eurostat   Statistical Office of the European Communities
EWCS   European Working Conditions Survey
FOA   *Fag og Arbejde* [Danish Union of Public Employees]
GER   Germany
GDP   Gross domestic product
HC   Health care
HSW   Health and Social Work
IADL   Instrumental activities of daily living, practical assistance
IAQ   *Institut Arbeit und Qualifikation*
ICT   Information and Communication Technology
ILO   International Labour Organisation
ISCED   The International Standard Classification of Education
ISCO88   The International Standard Classification of Occupations
               (Revision 1988)
ISCO08   The International Standard Classification of Occupations
               (Revision 2008)
ICT   Information and Communication Technologies
IT   Information Technology
LCFD   Long-Term Care Further Development Act
LTA   Long Term Act
LTC   Long-Term Care
LTCI   Long-Term Care Insurance scheme
LFS   Labour Force Survey
LO   Trade Unions
MLSA   Ministry of Labour and Social Affairs (of the Czech Republic)
NACE   *Nomenclature statistique des activités économiques dans la*
               Communauté européenne [statistical classification of economic
               activities in the European Community]
NGO   non-governmental organization
NPM   new public management
OECD   The Organisation for Economic Co-operation and Development
OMC   Open Method of Co-ordination
PES   Public Employment Service(s)
PPP   Public Private Partnerships
PST   pre-school teachers
PST act.   professional, scientific and technical activities
RAS   The register-based labour force statistics
SES   Structure of Earnings Survey
STATBANK   StatBank, statistical database of Denmark
VAT   value added tax
UI   unemployment insurance

ÚIV	*Ústav pro informace ve vzdělávání* [Institute for information on education]
UN	United Nations
UNECE	United Nations Economic Commission for Europe
UNESCO	United Nations Educational, Scientific and Cultural Organization
UNICEF IRC	United Nations Children's Fund Innocenti Research Centre
UNIFEM	United Nations Development Fund for Women
ÚZIS	*Ústav zdravotnických informací a statistiky ČR* [Institute of health information and statistics of the Czech Republic]
WTE	whole time equivalent, full-time equivalent
WZ	*Klassifikation der Wirtschaftszweige* [Classification of Economic Activities]

Preface

The aim of this book is to fill the gap of knowledge within the European context on how the interplay between the public and private mix of social service might help in creating jobs, as well as how this can serve as a way of coping with citizens' needs and expectations concerning higher levels of services in the core areas of the welfare state. It is, further, our ambition to present a combination of theoretical and empirical data on different welfare service regimes in order to explore and develop knowledge on service in welfare states.

Historically, service has been a neglected area in welfare state studies. The book thus offers an in-depth examination on a topic which we consider to be of increasing importance within the current socio-economic context. EU member states have seen high levels of unemployment in recent years, and, especially youth unemployment in several member states. At the same time, the fiscal crisis of the welfare states has made it difficult to invest in new jobs and economic growth. The EU has had a focus on how to support member state development of employment policy with the aim of higher levels of participation, lower levels of unemployment and a more gender-equal approach. Nevertheless, the EU and member states have been less focused on the interplay and mix between the public/private provision of social service as a way to both support and enhance employment and the important welfare services, especially in light of the on-going demographic transition in Europe.

This book has been written during our work within the NEUJOBS 7th Framework research project 'Creating and adapting jobs in the context of socio-ecological transition' (No. 266833). The objective of the project has been to analyse the current and possible future developments of the European labour market(s) under the main assumption that European societies are now facing or preparing for socio-ecological transitions that will have a major impact on employment, in particular certain groups in the labour force or sectors of the economy. The authors of the book have been focused on the Work-Package 7 Public-Private Mix in service provision, fiscal policy and employment.

We are thankful to many colleagues for their valuable suggestions and comments that we obtained during the NEUJOBS conferences and workshops. Special thanks must go to the project coordinators and supervisory committee, especially Miroslav Beblavý, Illaria Masselli, Elisa Martelucci, Iain Begg. We are also grateful to the colleagues who helped us by commenting on the manuscripts of some chapters: Irene Dingeldey, Adrian Sinfield, Richard Parry and Sharon Wright.

Finally, the authors would like to give thanks to the European Commission, which financed the project under the 7th Framework Programme, and to the Czech

Grant Agency for the support of the national project 'Modernisation of Czech Social Policy' (No. 404/11/0086), which was started earlier and enabled us to analyse and elaborate on most of the topics covered in this book at a national level beforehand (Chapters 3, 6 and 8).

Tomáš Sirovátka and Bent Greve

Notes on Contributors

Tomáš Sirovátka is Professor of Social Policy at the Faculty of Social Studies, Masaryk University, closely cooperating with the Research Institute of Labour and Social Affairs. He has carried out a number of national as well as international research projects on social policy and employment policy. He publishes regularly in international journals (including special issues) such as the *Journal of Comparative Policy Analysis, European Journal of Social Security, International Review of Sociology, International Journal of Sociology and Social Policy, Social Policy and Administration, Journal of Marriage and the Family, Czech Sociological Review, Prague Economic Papers* and *Central European Journal of Public Policy*. He has contributed to several comparative books on employment and social policy, co-edited *The Governance of Active Welfare States in Europe*, published by Palgrave/Macmillan in 2011, as well as having published numerous monographs in Czech.

Bent Greve is Professor of Social Science with an emphasis on welfare state analysis at the University of Roskilde, Denmark. His research interests focus on the welfare state, and social and labour market policy, often from a comparative perspective. He has published extensively on social and labour market policy, social security, tax expenditures, public sector expenditures and the financing of the welfare state. He is Regional and Special Issues Editor of *Social Policy & Administration*. Recent books include the *Routledge Handbook of the Welfare State* (2013), *The Times They are Changing* (2012), *Happiness* (2011), *Choice* (2010), *Social Policy and Happiness in Europe* (2009) and *Occupational Welfare* (2007).

Ondřej Hora (PhD) is Assistant Professor at the Department of Social Policy and Social Work, Faculty of Social Studies, Masaryk University, Czech Republic and research worker at the Research Institute of Labour and Social Affairs. He focuses on social policy, especially the labour market, employment and unemployment, job quality, employment policy (evaluation) and social protection. He has participated in several projects and published numerous articles, book chapters and research reports. He has recently co-edited the book *Rodina, děti a zaměstnání v české společnosti* [*Family, Children and Employment in Czech Society*] and has contributed to the book *Regulating the Risk of Unemployment* (Oxford University Press, 2011) edited by J. Clasen and D. Clegg.

Pavel Horák (PhD) is Assistant Professor at the Faculty of Social Studies, Masaryk University. In 2007, he received PhD in social policy and social work for a dissertation thesis entitled 'Changing goals of state social programs during their implementation by street-level bureaucrats'. His research deals with the topics of labour market policy implementation, discretion of street-level bureaucrats, the governance of public policy and organizational flexibility. He teaches the courses 'Labour market policy and work with the unemployed', 'Public policy, Sociology for social policy and social work' and 'Social deviance'. He is a regular contributor to Czech journals in the field of political science, public and social policy and social work, authoring over forty papers in reviewed periodicals and edited monographs. Some papers have been published in international journals such as *International Journal of Sociology and Social Policy*, *Czech Sociological Review* and *Slovak Sociological Review*.

Markéta Horáková (PhD) works as Assistant Professor at the Faculty of Social Studies, Masaryk University and as a researcher in the Research Institute of Labour and Social Affairs. She teaches courses dealing with social policy, employment services, theories of labour market policy and education policy. She has published about forty papers primarily devoted to unemployment, active labour market policy and education and human resource development in a knowledge society. She has had several papers published in *Slovak Sociological Review*, *International Journal of Sociology and Social Policy* and *Czech Sociological Review*.

Chapter 1

Introduction

Tomáš Sirovátka and Bent Greve

The Aim of the Book

Modern welfare states lack jobs and the ability to sustainably finance the welfare state and fulfil the expectations of their citizens. This combination raises new issues and new problems for welfare states in their ability to supply the expected welfare services, find the qualified persons to do the jobs in times of changing labour force supply and fiscal constraints. This book fills a gap by combining a clear-cut presentation of existing problems with ways to sustainably cope with them. As a consequence of the pressure on financing the welfare state and the ambition of ensuring high quality services and employment, the central issues point to how the welfare state can continue to be a social investment welfare state.

In the wake of the financial crisis and due to expected change in demography, there are also on-going debates about how to innovate and develop welfare states in a sustainable way and how to solve the present and expected financial pressure on the welfare states in the near future. This book tries to answer how governance, financing, social innovation and sustainability are interlinked issues in modern societies. This chapter will provide an outline of the book as well as some methodological choices, including a selection of countries serving as specific cases, allowing a comparative analysis presenting knowledge that can be interpreted in a broader European welfare state debate. The focus is on problems associated with social services in contemporary welfare states.

How fiscal constraints create pressure on the welfare states will be shown, including the continuing restructuring of welfare states in light of the financial crisis. We will discuss how these ongoing changes look, including changes in our perception and understanding of the public sector's role in welfare states. These changes will have an impact on the public/private mix in service provision in core welfare state areas such as health, education and welfare service.

An overview of recent changes will be presented as well as the difficulties in measuring these changes, especially their effect on employment due to the direct/ indirect impact on employment and the statistical difficulties in the division of responsibilities and activities between the public and private sectors. This also implies the need for a discussion of qualitative changes in policies concerning who is delivering the goods and services – especially any changes towards a higher degree of market delivery. This relates to the ongoing discussion on the healthcare and social service sector and the question of when a welfare good is open for competition in the private sector. Furthermore, there are discussions about how to ensure that the public sector innovates so as to deliver goods and services in the most effective way as well as how the governance ensures that evidence is included in the decision-making.

Central Issues

The intention, from a theoretical and comparative case-based approach, is to explore patterns of employment in social services and the public sector in different EU member states in the broader context of labour market and welfare state development. The analysis will explore how EU countries pursue their fiscal policies in social services, how they develop modes of governance and the change in the public/private mix in social services, and what the new patterns of employment in social services are, in light of the main challenges facing welfare states: the recent fiscal pressures and the expected demographic changes. This double challenge has repercussions on the way welfare states are governed and thus on how to ensure the sustainable development of the welfare state.

There are several reasons for investigating these issues. Comparative analysis of the welfare state has only recently concentrated more explicitly on social services (for example Seeleib-Kaiser 2008, Wollmann and Marcou 2010). Part of the reason for this is that the welfare state was historically developed with the intention of covering specific risks, thus ensuring economic security in the case of certain contingencies that would occur (unemployment, sickness, work-accident, retirement). For this reason, most investigations, including comparative analyses, have traditionally focused mainly on contributory and non-contributory benefit schemes. Similarly, patterns of employment and their changes in social services in different welfare states have not been intensively studied. This is so despite the fact that the development of several types of social services represents a key issue with respect to job creation in many welfare states, as well as to the expectations directed towards the welfare state effort and what citizens can expect to receive, including the reconciliation of work and family life (for example affordable and high quality day-care).

Social services are further expected to respond to the changing demography and new social risks. As such, they are becoming central pillars in the 'welfare state architecture'. It seems that social services like health, elderly people's services, child care, employment and life-long learning have become central to ensuring effective social protection, social justice/equity, social inclusion and cohesion. Thus finding ways to finance, steer and innovate these types of services in different kinds of welfare state is central.

At the same time, since social services are labour-intensive, they also meet the expectations of job creation, thereby potentially providing ways to cope with the lack of jobs and the high levels of unemployment in many countries. However, job creation is not only dependent on the overall effective labour demand, but also relies on how to ensure the sufficient sustainable financing of social services. Under the conditions of European and globalised economies, ageing societies and fiscal pressures on welfare states – all aggravated by the economic crisis, the sustainable financing of social services and their provision – have become more problematic and might thus work against the development of new social services unless new innovative solutions are examined.

One of the key perspectives is to analyse the inter-relationship between the two issues that are central to welfare state and labour market development: the financing and governance of social services, on the one hand, and employment in social services, on the other. This question has been investigated only marginally up until now. The approach in itself is thus innovative in the sense that it integrates two streams of literature. One of them deals with social services as such: their financing, governance and performance (accessibility, scope, quality and the effects/outputs/consequences for their beneficiaries). The other deals with employment in social services and labour market performance: job creation, scope and structure of employment in social services in the public sector, implications for unemployment, labour market mobility and so on.

Preliminarily, it can be assumed that the size and forms of financing social services and their governance can have strong implications for the scope and structure of employment in social services. At the same time, the existing patterns of employment in social services and the public sector may represent an important background for the development of their financing and governance. The complexity of the relationship between the financing and governance of social services, on the one hand, and employment patterns in social services, on the other, represents a challenge.

Furthermore, the complexity arising from the multiple roles/functions of social services in contemporary societies is having the effect that all the possible outcomes resulting from the input will be less clear. Therefore, another central issue also concerns whether the potential for job creation in social services is possible in light of the contemporary developments in financing and the organisation of service delivery, and the potential for sustainable employment and social innovation in social services. Sustainability in the financing of the welfare state is thus also central.

Summing up, the above ideas imply that the following key questions will be covered:

1. What are the ways and trends in financing the welfare state, especially under the fiscal pressures emerging from Europeanisation, globalisation and financial crises?
2. What are the trends in the governance of social services associated with change in the fiscal regime and with other policy changes?
3. What are the consequences of the changing fiscal regime and governance for employment in social services and job creation in social services – either public or private, and for the performance of contemporary labour markets?

4. What are the consequences for the 'production' of the services in terms of their scope, accessibility and in meeting social needs and expectations?
5. What is the impact of these changes of the welfare mix on the understanding of welfare states, including issues related to the convergence/divergence of welfare states in Europe?

Methodological Considerations

A combination of desk-top studies, quantitative data and case analyses is used to depict changes and developments regarding the five central questions presented above.

The approach thus combines several streams of literature in different fields: first, literature on the overall development of the welfare state and its regimes; second, literature on the economics of the welfare state and public finance; third, literature on the governance and recent shifts in governance in social services and innovations in their financing and delivery; and fourth, literature on the dynamics of employment and labour markets with explicit focus on social services. This broad approach is necessary in view of the research issues outlined.

In order to provide an in-depth analysis, there is a focus on the situations in four countries that represent examples of various welfare state regimes: the Czech Republic (post-communist/Central-East European), Denmark (Scandinavian), Germany (conservative) and the UK (liberal). The book thus also uses welfare regimes as a heuristic device to paint a broader picture of the developments in European welfare states (compare Greve 2013). To put the information into a wider framework, Chapters 2 to 7 include data for all EU-27 member states, whereas Chapters 8 to 11 focus on data for the four member states, comparing them with each other as well as with the EU-27. This methodological approach is preferred as it allows the use of both quantitative and qualitative data, ensuring an overview of the similarities and differences in the various types of welfare state.

The empirical data will be based upon the following:

1. Aggregate information on the development of employment in social services 2000–2010; the changes of employment structures in health and social services – divided by gender, age, education; and the structure of financing (expenditure in specific fields of social services).
2. Information on the level, structure and change in the financing of social services (expenditures and sources of financing including user fees) during 2000–2010.

Finally, governance structures and mechanisms will be examined in selected fields of social services (long-term care, child care and employment services) in four selected countries (Czech Republic, Denmark, Germany and United Kingdom).

These different choices will be elaborated throughout, presenting arguments for the understanding and interpretation of the data.

Delimitations

There are multiple functions of social services in contemporary society and of their role in meeting the social needs of people, raising the quality of life and securing the principles of human rights, social citizenship, social justice and cohesion. These central purposes of social services are not the core of the analysis; nevertheless, they may be relevant for governance, financing and employment in social services.

The quality of the services will be included in the analysis only to a certain extent due to the limitations of data and to the lack of a clear concept and understanding of what quality actually means in several areas. However, as the quality of welfare services is important, some elements related to quality will be included.

Overview of the Book

The book tries to grasp the interrelated central issues related to the above-mentioned core questions. This also reflects the way the book has been organised. Chapter 2 focuses on the theoretical debate about what social service actually means, as well as what its role is now and what it is expected to be in the future. This includes the following question: How can social service and sustainability in the delivery and financing of the welfare state be understood from a theoretical perspective?

This involves a review of literature on the key aspects of the dynamics of social services, including various explanations for growth in services. Especially three different types of explanation will be highlighted:

1. Demand-side explanation.
2. Supply-side interpretation.
3. Structural explanations.

Types of governance and service delivery in selected fields of social services (for example employment services, care of the elderly, child care) are also included due to their centrality with regard to the analyses of changes.

The chapter will include a short discussion on the chosen methodological approach, including arguments for the choice of the four countries. This was based upon their welfare state typologies, including the fact that work and de-commodification, on the one hand, have been central and, on the other hand, that having a job has come more into focus in dealing with welfare state developments. The welfare typology debate will be touched upon very briefly.

Given the importance of employment, financing and governance, the next three chapters deal with these issues. Chapter 3 focuses on the actual current knowledge about employment in social services. The main issues and discussion points relate to who is employed in the area and the types of employment, as well as how they influence employment levels in societies in general and the possible options for future sustainable development.

The financial crisis and expected fiscal pressures on the welfare states in the near future are core issues that will determine how to proceed and develop sustainability in the financing of welfare states, including the creation of new jobs (which is discussed in Chapter 4). The fiscal pressure due to globalisation and changes in demography is one issue; another is the expected outcome of the fiscal crisis leading to an even more prudent fiscal policy than earlier. This chapter will first present some theoretical positions on how to finance the welfare state and then proceed to a discussion on how to ensure and cope in a sustainable way with the fiscal pressure on the welfare state. The chapter will further analyse whether convergence in the choice of instruments and changes in financing have taken place within the EU since 2000. This will relate to a discussion on how to ensure the sustainable financing of the European welfare states both now and in the future in light of the impact of increasingly open economies and global economic development.

Chapter 5 discusses the changes in governance and innovation in the public sector. This includes changes in the boundaries between state, market and civil society, which have for a long time been undergoing change. This chapter will briefly outline what social innovation is and how it may influence development in the social services.

Building especially on the presentation of the concepts in Chapters 3 and 5, Chapter 6 focuses on the role of employment in social service and the expectations regarding different types of jobs in the future. A central question is asked: What are the factors influencing the development of social service and especially employment in social services? This chapter also links the issue of change in governance, especially the new social risks involving possible development in employment in the social services in the future.

The analyses in the first six chapters generally reflect on nation states. However, in recent years there has been an increase in the focus on whether welfare and the delivery of welfare are national prerogatives alone. Chapter 7 looks into the concept of Europeanisation. Some core issues involve the free movement of workers and how social services (compare regulation on the free movement of goods and services and the service directive) are regulated, as well as the delimitation between the role of the nation state and the supranational institutions. There is a focus on how governance, financing and regulation can be implemented in the border areas between the various actors, as well as how this might have an impact on the nation states' options and possibilities for sustainable development in social services, or on the welfare states generally. There is an analysis of whether supranational development changes the role of national welfare states, including pressures on the ability to finance the welfare state (thereby continuing the discussion from Chapter 4) given the conditions of global and regional economic integration. The chapter thus scrutinises the development of supranational and national welfare states in the contested field of social services.

The following chapters contain four case analyses representing four countries. These four chapters (8 to 11) on the Czech Republic, Denmark, Germany and the United Kingdom highlight the restructuring and changes in the public/private mix in the four countries with a focus on the impact on employment. National data are used to supplement comparative data from the EU and OECD. There is a focus on social services especially (child care, elderly care and employment services). The choice of these four countries covers four distinct clusters of 'worlds of welfare services' as distinguished by Stoy (2012). The three areas of social services were selected to reflect those which are widely used by different groups in society in order to achieve some complexity of the overview.

The case studies depict changes in the financing of welfare services such as the degree of user fees, the change in impact of insurance, development in employment and information on changes in governance: regulation, delivery and providers (that is public/private/non-government non-profit).

Chapter 12 systematically compares the four national cases by using quantitative as well as qualitative data on financing, governance, service provision and employment for the four countries. Chapter 13 summarises the findings and concludes on the possible development: how this has an impact on the governance and public/private mix in social services in different kinds of welfare states and the consequences for employment in social services.

Chapter 2

Social Services and the Public Sector

Tomáš Sirovátka and Bent Greve

Introduction

This chapter focuses on what social service actually is and its role in the modern welfare state. The focus is on how social service can be delivered and financed in a sustainable way mainly from a theoretical perspective (for example empirical issues are left to Chapters 4 and 8 to 11). In Chapter 3 employment will be in focus and in Chapter 4 more emphasis will be given to the issue of financing welfare states in the EU from a sustainable perspective. The central explanation of why social services have been increasing will be presented, as they also form the basis for the expectation of future growth in social services and for the need for innovation in the area.

The chapter is organised so that it starts with how to define social service, then proceeds to discuss possible ways of governance with relevance for social service, including reasons for having a public sector and thereby also to a large degree public intervention with regard to social services. It will then present and argue for the choice of methodology and the four countries used for the case studies in Chapters 8 to 11.

Social Services: A Definition

Two central questions are explained below:

1. What is social service?
2. How can one understand the role of social services?

One way to understand this is to connect risk and the need for services, although it could also be interpreted in a broader context. Social services can thus relate to statutory and other social security schemes covering central issues related to risk as well as 'those services provided directly to the person and playing a preventive and socially cohesive role such as social assistance service, employment and training services, social housing, childcare and long-term care services' (European Commission 2010: 7).

These social services are often paid for by public finance, albeit sometimes by obligatory social insurance. Social services thus cover an important part of welfare state activities, such as care for children, the elderly and the unemployed.

Another way to approach and understand social services could be to relate them to the criteria for their existence:

- Personal rather than related to the production or distribution of services.
- Fulfilling personal or social rather than physical or intellectual needs.
- Focused on social roles.
- Performed in direct social contact (Bahle 2003).

Social services can further be defined as a specific field of services of general interest (European Commission 2006, European Commission 2007a). Services of general interest cover a broad range of activities from large network industries such as energy, telecommunications, transport, audiovisual broadcasting and postal services, to education, water supply, waste management, health and social services. All these services are perceived as essential for societal development, although their delivery can be public or private (either for-profit or non-profit), provided that the correction of possible market failure might be coped with by other types of steering than direct public sector delivery. In this book the central focus on services relates to care for children, care for the elderly and employment service.

Social services can be of an economic or non-economic nature, depending on the activity and the area of the service. The EU Commission has provided definitions of the two main categories of social services:

1. Statutory and complementary social security schemes, organised in various ways (mutual or occupational organisations), covering the main risks of life, such as those linked to health, ageing, occupational accidents, unemployment, retirement and disability.
2. Other essential services provided directly to people. They comprise services such as what type of support in daily life; services which complement the role of family in caring like long-term care and child care; employment, training and social housing.

Although there are various definitions for the term 'social services' (Huber et al. 2008), this analysis starts with a 'narrow' definition of social services. In relation to the first category, social services include only provisions in kind, like health and care of children and the elderly, but not social security benefits (except those designed to be used for the purchase of the services mentioned under point two above). The second category is basically provided in kind (although user fees may be charged) and fits into what will be understood as a social service. Recent years have seen certain kinds of cash benefits, in the form of, for example, vouchers that can only be used to buy a particular kind of service, thereby blurring the boundary between provision in-kind and in-cash.

Looking further into the types of areas that relate to the welfare state, then according to the Commission of the European Union, social services that play and can have a crucial role in improving the quality of life and providing social protection include:

1. Social security in kind (like health care).
2. Employment and training services.
3. Social housing.
4. Child care.
5. Long-term care.
6. Social assistance services, including services for people with disabilities (European Commission 2010).

Another way to approach a workable definition is to look into specific personal social services. These social services can include:

1. Long-term care, care for the elderly, care for disabled persons.
2. Social integration and re-integration with a focus on migrants and users of illegal drugs.
3. Labour market services including those focusing on disadvantaged and disabled people.
4. Childcare with a focus on services offered to families for children before they enter kindergarten and for afternoon care of school-age children.
5. Social housing (Hubert et al. 2010: 28).

Some authors use a broader definition of social services (Wollmann and Marcou 2010: such as 'services for people and families' which include '…child care, long-term care for the elderly and frail, and health services; and they include basic education, basic cultural amenities (for example public libraries) and sports facilities (for example swimming pools).'

This analysis uses the definition made by the Commission of the European Union since the other categories of 'services' like education, cultural amenities and sport facilities fulfil broader societal functions beyond those corresponding to 'social risks' or 'social needs', thereby blurring the boundaries between social and mainly economic services. Furthermore, focus is especially on personal social services as defined by Huber et al., mentioned above. The definition is selected due to delimitations of the analysis and to be in line with the understanding of what welfare and welfare states are (Greve 2013).

The advantage of the chosen definition and focus is also that it is then possible to distinguish the activities (although in broad categories) through the available comparative statistics on employment and financing within the EU.

Social services may be financed both from public resources of various types and through different channels, or by the service users/consumers themselves (compare Chapter 4). As they can be provided both by public and private entities, employment in social services may thus be public or private. When analysing employment in social services, beyond the above-mentioned categories of social services, the analysis will also pay attention to the category of government employment (public administration), since most public servants create conditions for the provision of social services, or directly provide these services at the local and regional levels, as well as at the national level through the ministries and other bodies (compare Chapter 3).

Governance of Social Services

The growing role of social services has been associated with the current socio-economic changes. This includes the ongoing change in some countries from industrial to service economies. European societies are still characterised by dynamic labour markets, new employment structures, an ageing society and changing family structures. All these changes bring new and growing demands on social services and pressures on the sustainability in the longer term perspective of the welfare states. The most profound change is the rapidly growing demand for health care and long-term care for the elderly. In a broader perspective, the changing structures of the 'risks' covered by welfare state arrangements are described as 'new social risks' (Esping-Andersen 1999, Hemerijck 2002, Taylor-Gooby 2004a). These new risks can be classified as the following: reconciling work and family life, single parenthood, having a frail relative, possessing low or obsolete skills and insufficient social security coverage due to atypical career patterns (Bonoli 2006). These risks represent an economic challenge for health, childcare, elderly care and employment services in order to ensure citizens access and coverage related to changing societal risk compared to the old risk covered by welfare states. Furthermore, the processes of globalisation and population ageing might also bring long-term pressures on public budgets both in terms of revenue and expenditure, implying a need for innovative solutions – different ways to manage and steer the welfare state, including new types of governance.

The above challenges have also had profound consequences for welfare state adjustments in terms of what might be labelled welfare state retrenchment, recalibration or recasting (Pierson 2005), or welfare state restructuring (Giddens 1998, Taylor-Gooby 2008). More generally, the reforms in welfare states include several aspects: they have changed the 'generosity' limits of public expenditure and in some instances have implied changes led by an 'activation paradigm'. The EU countries have explicitly adopted employment targets and guidelines that emphasise the role of employment services, labour market policies, and caring services as expressed in the European Employment Strategy, or recently in Europe 2020. Similarly, the Commission (European Commission 2010: 6) emphasises the fundamental role of social services in meeting 'a growing, increasingly complex demand due to structural changes in our societies, such as population ageing, changing gender roles and more flexible labour markets.'

According to the Commission, social services play a major role in European societies by 'contributing to social protection and social inclusion and enhance the capacity of individuals to enjoy their fundamental rights and to participate fully in the social, economic and political life. They are an important source of job generation and a key tool for poverty reduction and strengthening social cohesion' (ibid.).

Understanding the concept in this way also helps to explain why social expenditure informs the role of social services. Historical development in social spending shows that social expenditure grew between 1960–1998 (and even between 1980–1998) in 21 OECD countries and the share of expenditure on state services (for the elderly and family) increased in 21 OECD countries from 4.4 per cent to 6.5 per cent on average between 1980–1998. At the same time, the share of expenditure on poverty alleviation and health care dropped from 43.5 per cent to 41.6 per cent on average (Castles 2004). Differences between countries were also highlighted; for example, the share of state services was 20.9 per cent in 1998 in Denmark, while only 1.4 per cent in Belgium.

The use of OECD social expenditure data has made it possible to explain that the relative weight of social services and social transfers shapes the profile of welfare states significantly (Jensen 2008). The cluster of three Scandinavian countries had expenditure on social transfers at 14.5 per cent of GDP, on average, and 12.4 per cent on social services (the highest compared to the other clusters of countries). In the cluster of continental countries like Austria, Belgium, France, Germany and Italy, the expenditures on social transfers were high (18.2 per cent), while expenditures on social services were considerably lower (8.2 per cent). Lastly, there is the cluster of mainly Anglo-Saxon countries along with Finland, the Netherlands, Spain and Japan where the expenditures on social transfers were considerably lower on average (11.4 per cent) and expenditures on social services were slightly lower than in the second cluster, but still much lower than in the first cluster (7.2 per cent). The differences in expenditure on social services are mainly explained by the differences in social care services (the dimension of de-familialisation matters the most) and only marginally by the differences in expenditures on health care. The difference in spending will be addressed in Chapter 4, with regard to its more specific composition, its development over time and possible convergence.

Recently, the European Commission (2010) illustrated that on average the EU-27 member states spend 8.7 per cent of GDP on in-kind social security provisions (including health care) and 16.5 per cent on cash benefits (data for 2007 by ESPROSS). Countries like Belgium, Austria, Italy and Germany spend more on cash benefits and less on in-kind benefits than the average, while Sweden, Denmark and the Netherlands spend less on cash benefits and more on in-kind social protection. Some countries like Latvia, Estonia, Romania, Lithuania and Bulgaria spend less on both types of social protection than the average. The welfare state has however also continued to grow in many countries. However, one problem with making comparisons is that there are differences with regard to the taxation of social spending, making the net-expenditure between the countries less different (Adema et al. 2011, Greve 2008), also showing that expenditures could have been expected to grow during the recent financial crisis.

The welfare state crisis (for example in the wake of the oil-price crisis in the seventies, the recession in the eighties and the recent financial crisis in 2008) has often been related to the ability to finance the welfare state, especially social services, now and in the future.[1] The welfare state in crisis was already mentioned in the 1980s – at the OECD seminar on the Welfare State in Crisis (OECD 1981), in books by Mishra (1984) and even earlier by O'Connor (1973). At the same time, the inbuilt automatic stabilisers in the public sector budgets have had an impact on the level of the public sector deficit. This is due to lower revenue from fall in income and higher level of spending to unemployment benefits.

An analysis of a change in governance of welfare, which combines the economic and social policy roles of the welfare states, thus is not in itself a new approach. However, the need to be aware of the combination of changes in the economic conditions and the management of the welfare state is a reminder of how this will influence the welfare state and the provision of social services. Thus it seems that although capitalism cannot easily coexist with the welfare state, it cannot exist without it either. The Keynesian welfare state thus supplements market forces in securing the 'conditions for economic growth and social cohesion' (Jessop 1999: 350). Although nation states might have a reduced role due to Europeanisation and globalisation (compare Chapter 7), it may seem that the impact of the traditional welfare state 'is giving way to a new post-national mixed economy in which networks and partnerships have become more important' (Jessop 1999: 356).

It has been argued that the recent crisis has shown unsustainable fiscal imbalances as well as a possibly negative impact on long-term growth (OECD 2011a). The fiscal crisis might thus be more profound given the large public sector deficit in many EU countries, as well as in those outside the EU. The consequences and decisions taken in the wake of these deficits, especially with impact on spending on welfare state issues (including social services and to a lesser degree an increase in the level of taxation), might involve profound changes in the welfare states of Europe (see Taylor-Gooby 2012). Rising public sector spending (to cope with the crisis in the financial sector), increased unemployment and reduced public sector income have thereby brought great pressure on the welfare states in Europe. This has also prompted a discussion about short-term financial possibilities, longer-term deficits and debt reductions (compare Chapter 4).

Crisis in the fiscal and welfare systems 'affect especially deeply the institutional orders, just as the stagflation crisis of the 1970s did'; the changes demanded in the 1970s for new forms of governance implied more centralised planning, which

---

1   For an overview and discussion of the recent impact of the latest crisis, compare Special Issue of *Social Policy & Administration*, 45 (4) 2011: The times they are changing? Crisis and the welfare state.

involved a combination of deregulation and re-regulation. The re-regulation for correcting the market was done in order to ensure the 'promotion of human, social and environmental rights' (Veggeland 2011: 4 and 8).

The ongoing demographic changes in most European countries (that is the increasing number of elderly people compared to those of working age) create further pressure on the financial viability of the welfare state, which has engendered a need to restructure public sector spending and change the pension systems in many European countries. This is especially due to the fact that the demographic changes will presumably imply a growing need for social service. The need to include the impact of ageing also means that the actual level of debt and deficit is not the only pressure on the welfare states (compare Chapter 4). It has therefore been argued that there is a need for a 'sustainable commitments rule which would place a ceiling on the flow of future debt interest and other pre-committed payments rather than on the stock of accumulated public sector debt' (Brewer, Emmerson and Miller 2011). These pre-committed payments could, for example, relate to the expected increase in the level of social service.

For this reason, the financing of the welfare state does not only relate to the ability to find the right balance of tax and duty, but also the level of expenditure in the welfare state and especially on social services. In principle, one problem in financing could be solved both through changes in the expenditure and income sides of the equation. Therefore, the analysis need not only deal with the rationale or reasons for public sector financing, but also with public sector expenditure focused on social services. This includes the division of tasks and the borderline between public and private expenditure on welfare issues.

In order to understand the impact on social services, one needs to look into whether there are changes in the structure of expenditure. This includes determining whether there are changing or alternative forms of financing and delivery. Changing forms include issues such as user fees and whether the welfare state will reduce its role (for example by issuing vouchers that the individual will have to top up to obtain the necessary service). Changes in delivery towards outsourcing might shift the number of persons directly employed by the public sector, but not necessarily the level of public sector spending or the number of people in the labour force working in the area. In recent years, several countries have deployed a strategy of involving more private providers to cope with the increasing demand for care. This did not reduce demand for employment in social service, but changed the balance between public and private employment in the area. This raises issues of quality and quality management (Hoffman and Leichsenring 2011), and of equity in access.

In the following section, some theoretical assumptions and considerations regarding social service are presented; the more empirical parts are in Chapter 3 on employment and Chapter 4 on financing.

What is Included in Social Services?

Before embarking upon an analysis of employment and financing of social services (compare Chapters 3 and 4), an understanding of what is included in social service is important. This understanding is also important in order to look into factors having an impact on current and future employment (compare Chapter 6).

A way to understand the need for social services is to characterise them in relation to elements often involved in studying market failures such as:

* Externalities.
* Information asymmetries, including difficulties for some to exhibit choices.
* Distributional concerns.

These three elements run parallel to the main arguments and reasons for having a public sector (Greve 2002, Barr 2012), although without prescribing the exact nature of intervention. In many social service areas it can be argued that these three attributes occur in tandem (Blank 2000) and have implications for what will and can be delivered by the public sector, and what will and can be delivered by the family, voluntary sector or the labour market. As mentioned, this also revolves around reasons for having a public sector and public sector delivery (without, however, answering the question of the scope and size of social services) and implying that a level of service can be delivered by the private sector, not only by the public sector. Furthermore, given that government failure might exist, this may explain the continuing change in roles between state, market and civil society.

The last 20 to 30 years (and even longer in the Nordic welfare states) have seen a changed role in several countries – away from family towards state-related provision of welfare services, especially in terms of care for children and the elderly (for example welfare states have taken over the delivery of social services from civil society). Combined with the general economic development and the financial crisis this has increased the pressure on the welfare state, but at the same time has moved the welfare state away from mainly being the provider of income guarantee and income security in the case of a social event taking place (such as the old risk of unemployment, sickness, industrial injury and old age).

Given that the aim is to understand and know how to finance social services and also how this is related to the level of employment, it is important to grasp why over the years of welfare state development there has been growth in social services.

There are in general three main theoretical explanations for the growth of employment in the service sector and social services (Schettkat and Yocarini 2003):

* Demand-side explanation.
* Supply-side interpretation.
* Inter-industry division of labour (for example structural changes).

These explanations will be discussed as they indicate how possible development in the area of services could be in the future.

The demand-side explanation focuses on issues such as the shift in the hierarchy of needs and the 'luxury goods' argument (for example service has an income elasticity above 1). Therefore, with increasing societal wealth there will be a higher level of demand for social services, although this (as with the reason for public sector intervention) does not inform us about whether delivery should be public or private. The shift from a demand of more traditional goods to social services thus becomes related to changes in the composition of overall demand in a society. A growth-oriented development strategy thus implies that social services will increasingly come into focus and, depending on the innovative and technological process, will also thus implicitly increase the need for more people employed in the sector.

The supply-side interpretation especially refers to the by now rather old debate regarding Baumol's disease, which relates to expected lower productivity growth in the service sector compared to other sectors in society (Baumol 1967). According to this, the public sector (for example social services) will be ever-expanding given that the increase in productivity is not sufficiently high compared to other sectors of societal development. Baumol's disease has been criticised in that gains in productivity in the public sector, and especially in social services, are difficult to measure, and that the measurements only focus on the cost of labour rather than the outcome of the use of the labour in the provision of social services.

However, the overall impact of social services on sustainable development also relates to the interpretation of social service function in welfare states. Looking at social services from an investment approach would, for example, imply that the calculated result would have a higher positive impact on societal productivity than if only direct impact was measured. This is the case with care for children, given that this implies a better option for increasing the labour force in most EU countries. Employment service can also improve efficiency if its use ensures a better match on the labour market. Finally, from a financing perspective, care for the elderly can be more efficient if done by the welfare state (compare also Chapter 4).

The inter-industry division of labour suggests that outsourcing, at least of certain functions, implies a statistical shift in the measurement of services; this is due to differences in the location of services, thereby making statistical interpretation difficult. The ongoing restructuring of services further implies that clear information on input (except for financing) and output might be less transparent. The implication is that the main way to measure and analyse the development might have to revolve around a combination of available economic resources for the welfare state with the output being given by the number of persons receiving various types of care.

Another critical issue relates to the difficulty in measuring productivity in the public sector. In the national accounts, focus is based upon the number of people employed by the public sector; therefore public sector productivity measurements are not very precise. For this reason, there is a need to be more precise concerning the overall impact of social services. This also includes the quality of the services delivered.

The European Commission has seven overall principles for social service provision, dealing with whether they are available, accessible, affordable, person-centred, comprehensive, continuous and outcome-oriented (European Commission 2010: 95).

Furthermore, it is difficult to obtain sufficient information given that information on tax expenditures (Adema and Ladaigue 2005, Sinfield 2007, Greve 2004) and occupational welfare (Farnsworth 2004, Greve 2007a) is often sparse. Thus the statistical risk is that the available information only presents a part of the picture such as the public sector spending and those directly employed in the public sector, but not those provided by the private sector or by employers. Nevertheless, it seems that in most European welfare states the public sector is the central provider, therefore data dealing with public sector provision, although neglecting the market and civil society, will provide important information regarding the size and composition of social services.

The development of the welfare state as a social investment state delivering, for example, care for children has been that welfare provision and services relate to deindustrialisation and the need for increased female labour force participation and increasing public attention to these. This implies that the provision of welfare services is less related to ideological factors (Jensen 2009), although more related to ensuring a sufficient level of labour supply and equality in access to the labour market. In recent years with high levels of unemployment, the need for a greater labour supply has been difficult to see; however, the demographic transition still points to the risk of a lack of manpower in social services in the future in many EU countries.

Fiscal constraints affect all EU member states due to global competition. These more global constraints have increased due to the fiscal crisis and deepening public budget deficits with dire consequences for public sector performance, employment and the ability to finance the welfare state. Nevertheless, since the need and demand for social services are generated not only by the size of the public sector, but are also dependent on private financing being in place, individual and private collectives, including companies, will be influenced by a change in the ability to finance the welfare state. The impact on services has been and presumably will continue in years to come to be associated with broader factors like the ageing of the population, dynamic labour markets and skill bias, the employment of women and the reconciliation of work and family.

The use of a market type mechanism within the public sector has meant that in several aspects the distinction between the public and private sectors has become even more blurred. Thus the core issues are not only who is financing and making decisions about who has access to social services, but more importantly, the criteria used to determine access.

It is not possible to just make a distinction between public service and market provision, because it does not include non-profit service; support for this can represent a way between state and market provision. Furthermore, as a constantly recurring issue, in line with the Baumol argument above, it is difficult to measure productivity in services. For this reason, there is a need to measure quality and outcome, which are difficult to measure, rather than just quantity and outputs (Graefe 2004).

As indicated above, in recent years there has been a movement towards more individualised service, which also has a tendency towards making a service more like a classical market type of delivery. Trends in the provision of social services, with a focus on activation services, can be seen as individualisation services that are a part of public governance and social policy reforms (Borghi and Berkel 2007).

The more detailed country case analysis (compare Chapter 8–11) will therefore also focus on how countries in the enlarged EU are coping with fiscal constraints on their public sectors/social services and convergence/divergence tendencies in the 'patterns' of fiscal policies, governance of social services, public/private mix and employment in social services, and innovation in terms of financing, governance, production and service delivery. This analysis will mainly be of an empirical nature.

There is a need to be clear about the use of services in cash and in-kind given that they might be substitutes. Therefore a direct comparison between countries, without taking different pathways into consideration, can be difficult and data can thus also be biased due to differences in the way different welfare states are organised. As such, the aim and outcome might be very similar, even though the roads towards them can be very different. Although the focus is mainly on the delivery of service, when appropriate a look into certain kinds of income transfer can be useful to ensure a full picture.

Methodological Considerations and Choice of Countries

This book uses a variety of methodological approaches combining existing knowledge, public documents and quantitative data to ensure a systematic approach to answer how welfare states especially in the field of social services are changing and to try to find patterns with regard to new jobs in Europe as well as how this is steered and managed. In order to make a deeper analysis, four countries have been chosen as case studies.

These country case studies have been chosen in the classical way by looking at welfare regime typologies and using this as a heuristic device. Following this form, there is a country portraying the liberal regime (UK), the corporatist (Germany), Northern (Denmark) and a newcomer from Eastern Europe (Czech Republic); the four countries thus represent a variety of welfare system countries. The case analysis in combination with the quantitative analysis makes it possible to present and analyse the change in relation to social services with regard to financing, employment and governance. Analysing EU member states also implies that Eurostat data will be used as much as possible, as they to a large degree are harmonised in the way they are produced.

Furthermore, the methodology enables a cross-national comparison, thereby also being of relevance in connecting the development at the supranational level and showing how this interacts and can be combined with overall development.

The methodological choice of time period (that is predominantly since 2000) has been selected as this includes times of rapid economic development and a downturn after the financial crisis. Some overarching data are used in the first chapters, whereas more detailed data are used in the country chapters.

Conclusion

The selection and definition of social services (as of an economic or non-economic nature) form the background for the analysis in this book. The choice of definition implies that OECD data, especially Eurostat are used. Therefore, the focus will mainly be on service in kind related to children and the elderly, although discussion on and reference to the borderlines regarding the use of in-cash benefits as a substitute will also be included. Changes in employment and the financing of social services are thus central for the analysis, including a focus on how provision and financing can be implemented in a sustainable way.

The choice of countries ensures that the analysis, although not directly applicable for providing information on changes in welfare models, can describe trends and changes in such a way that a clear picture of development can be painted.

Chapter 3

Employment in the Health and Social Services: Evidence and Problems

Ondřej Hora and Tomáš Sirovátka

Introduction

In this chapter, the situation and development in employment in the sector of social services over the ten years between 2000 and 2010 are discussed. The aim is to gather information about employment in health and social services from internationally comparable data sources and studies. The chapter is also focused on issues and problems which are key aspects of employment in social services. Previous coherent analyses about employment patterns and characteristics in social services are relatively rare. In their aims, some analyses discuss social services more generally (for example European Commission 2008a, 2010). Other studies are more general, from the sector perspective, and focus more on specific topics such as part-time work, education and specific aspects of job quality (for example some Eurofound studies). The third group of literature is focused on specific sub-sectors such as elderly care or childcare (for example Plantenga and Remery 2009, Simonazzi 2010). Good quality, internationally comparable data about employment in social services are rare. Most data presented in this chapter generally relate to the Health and Social Work (HSW) sector. This sector includes two at least partially different fields of human activity: health and social services. Unfortunately, in most cases the data are not available separately for health and social services.

Three kinds of social services are highlighted: Early Childhood Education and Care services (ECEC), Long-Term Care services (LTC) and employment services. When such data are available, they are presented separately for several reasons: a) As most data used in this chapter are for whole HSW sector, it is useful to compare these data with the data for specific social services, b) ECEC, LTC and employment services are often seen as services of paramount importance, c) In many countries, these services constitute the prevailing part of employment in social services, d) These are the only social services for which we were able to track some, at least partially, internationally comparable data. Detailed data about employment in the health sector are beyond the scope of this chapter.

Data and Methodological Issues

The sources, formats and methodological issues of the data used will be discussed. Most information presented is based on Labour Force Survey data (LFS).[1] Data, provided by Eurostat, is considered to be the best long-term, reliable and internationally comparable source of social services employment data. Individual data are used for some analyses about topics not normally presented by Eurostat (for example education levels of workers in social services). Other data used in this chapter include the European Working Conditions Survey 2000, 2005, 2010 (EWCS), the Establishment Survey on Working Time and Work-Life Balance 2004–2005 (ESWT), the European Company Survey 2009 (ECS) and the Structure of Earnings Survey 2010 (SES).

For this analysis, the most important aim is to distinguish the sector of Health and Social Work from the rest of the economy. For this purpose, the 'statistical classification of economic activities in the European Community' (that is NACE classification) is used. There were changes in NACE classification between NACE rev. 1, which was used until 2008, and NACE rev. 2, used from 2008 (see Annex 3.1 for details). For the purpose here the most interesting are the data about employment in sector Q: Human health and social work activities (this was sector N in NACE 1.1 classification).[2]

There are several problems with the data on employment in social services:

- Eurostat usually does not publish data about the employment characteristics of employment in the health and social work sector separately (probably because of the small survey samples in many EU member countries).
- Because of various methodology (count in, count out) issues, there are usually substantial differences between internationally comparable data and the data from national statistical sources.
- The distinction between home and institutional care is often blurry, especially in countries which provide cash care allowances.

---

1   In LFS employed persons are those aged 15 and over who performed work, even for just one hour per week, for pay, profit or family gain during the reference week, or were not at work but had a job or business from which they were temporarily absent because of, for instance, illness, holidays, industrial dispute, or education or training (Eurostat metadata). The definition for EWCS is very similar (see survey description).

2   Of the 23 countries for which data about employment in the HSW sector are available for both NACE rev. 1.1 and NACE rev. 2 classification (2008), there was a difference of over 2 per cent in employment when comparing both classifications in only three cases (Cyprus, Latvia and Romania). In nine cases it was less than 1 per cent and in 11 cases it was between 1 and 2 per cent. This difference probably results from the fact that in NACE rev. 1.1, a small category of veterinary services (about 1.3 per cent of employment in 2001) was included in sector N (Health and Social Work) (Huber et al. 2006), while NACE rev. 2 includes only Human Health Activities in sector Q. Thus, for the purpose of our analysis, the data based on NACE rev. 1.1 tend to over-estimate employment by 1 to 2 per cent.

- It is often hard to get data about informal arrangements; nevertheless, in our interpretation we must keep in mind that informal care options may be available (Plantenga and Remery 2009). In the LTC sector there might be more informal than formal workers (see Fujisawa and Colombo 2009). Part of the care is in the form of private hidden informal contracts provided by cash paid workers (for example immigrants) and such care is 'invisible' in the statistics.
- It is usually difficult to adequately distinguish public and private employment in social services. For example OECD data for the UK are collected only for staff working for social services authorities; data for the private and voluntary sector are not collected (Fujisawa and Colombo 2009). LFS contain data about all social services employment, but it is impossible to distinguish between private and public employment. EWCS enable us to present only aggregate results for EU-27.[3]
- The demarcation between healthcare (medical component) and social care (the non-medical component) is often blurred, especially in LTC services (Huber et al. 2006, European Commission 2008a). There is a similar problem in the blurry distinction between ECEC for pre-school as well as school-age children (Plantenga and Remery 2009). In some countries ECEC services are not a part of the NACE HSW sector, but are included in the education sector.
- The available data on earnings (SES) and working time (ESWT) are limited to organisations with 10 or more employees.
- Since several kinds of social services are also regulated, financed or provided through staff in public administration (national level and more often municipal level), we must also pay attention to employment in public administration, social security and the defence sector (the L and O sectors in the NACE classification). This information is rather supplementary (see table 3.1); nevertheless, it may help us understand the trends of employment in the public sector and social and community services.

The Development of Scope of Employment in the Health and Social Services (HSW) Sector

The growth of social services in Europe began slowly after the Second World War in connection to three other important developments: more female labour market participation, the ageing of the population and growth of the public sector. After the year 2000, employment in the HSW sector in many EU countries grew much

3   According to EWCS the share of public employment in HSW (NACE rev. 1) decreased from 55.1 per cent to 46.6 per cent in EU-27 between 2005 and 2010. Private employment increased from 30.4 per cent to 36.9 per cent and NGO employment increased from 4 per cent to 7.6 per cent.

faster than in other sectors of the economy with a 4.2 million net increase of employment between 2000 and 2009 (European Commission 2010). The HSW sector was the third fastest growing sector in the EU economy between 2000 and 2007 (Holman and McClelland 2011). Employment in the HSW is less cyclical than employment in the rest of the economy, as it is largely financed by public funds (European Commission 2008b). This is confirmed by our data – the recent economic crisis did not have much impact on employment in the HSW sector until 2010.

Although the growth of the HSW sector in EU member states is substantial, it is uneven. Three groups of countries can be distinguished in the LFS data regarding the employment change between 2000 and 2010.

The first group consists of a majority of countries with substantial growth (between 74.6 per cent and 19.7 per cent) of employment in the HSW sector both between 2000 and 2005 and between 2005 and 2010 – in descending order: Ireland, Spain, Cyprus, Luxembourg, France, Portugal, Austria, Italy, Germany (28.9 per cent), Greece, Malta, Netherlands, Romania, United Kingdom (25.8 per cent), Belgium and Slovenia. In most of these countries, employment in the HSW sector also grew as a share of the total economy.

The second, a small group of countries, faced uneven development with stagnation, small growth or substantial growth: substantial growth in the first period and small growth in the second period – Finland and Czech Republic (18.7 per cent); stagnation in the first period and substantial growth in the second period – Denmark (8 per cent); and small growth in both periods: Slovakia.

The third group of countries experienced one period of growth and one period of decline: Estonia, Latvia, Lithuania, Hungary and Poland. Employment in the HSW sector decreased in both periods in two countries: Bulgaria and Sweden. Huber et al. (2006) shows that the development of employment in these countries was influenced by reforms of the economy, including public sector and budgetary constraints. Nevertheless, some other post-Soviet bloc countries like the Czech Republic, Slovakia, Slovenia and Estonia had relatively high growth of HSW sector employment between 2000 and 2010.

The drivers of high employment growth in most countries included population ageing, an expansion of services in order to meet better quality requirements and a rising demand following a lag in investments during a lengthier period of restriction on budget growth (European Commission 2010). The growth of employment was particularly strong for women (82.5 per cent of new jobs) and older workers (European Commission 2008b). In most countries employment in social work activities grew faster than employment in the health sector (Huber et al. 2006).

A potential problem with employment data is that a large part of the employment growth is due to redistribution from full-time to part-time work. LFS data were used to compare the change in full-time and part-time employment between 2000 and 2010. In some countries, both full-time and part-time jobs increased and the number of part-time jobs increased more than the number of full-time jobs:

Netherlands, Austria, Luxembourg, Denmark, Germany and Belgium. In the second group of countries, both full-time and part-time employment increased and part-time employment increased less than full-time employment: Finland, Ireland, France, Spain, Hungary, United Kingdom, Slovenia, Czech Republic, Portugal, Greece and Cyprus. In Italy both types of jobs increased approximately simultaneously. In Latvia the decrease in full-time jobs was compensated by the creation of more part-time jobs; in Poland most of decreased full-time jobs were replaced by part-time jobs; in Sweden only a third of a decrease in full-time jobs was compensated by the creation of part-time jobs. Lithuania is the only country where both types of jobs decreased.

So while in some countries (for example in Germany) the growth of employment was more due to a growth of part-time jobs, in other countries (for example United Kingdom), the growth was driven more by the growth of full-time employment.

There is only limited information available about the development of employment in the ECEC and LTC sector. Reports of the European Commission and Eurofound usually state that the number of jobs in the ECEC sector has increased very markedly in recent years. The possibilities of assessing employment changes in the LTC sector are similarly complicated. Nevertheless, there is evidence that the number of formal and informal LTC workers has steadily grown over recent years in most OECD countries. The growth of employment was faster than the growth of people aged 65 and over (Fujisawa and Colombo 2009). This is confirmed by the IAQ (2007) analysis of growth of employment in health – personal care. As the growth of women's employment was similar or even faster, we assume that mainly women benefit from the growth of this sector.

Nowadays, the importance of the HSW sector varies among EU member states. There were 21.4 million jobs in the HSW sector in the EU in 2009, of which 89 per cent was in the EU-15 member states (European Commission 2010). According to Eurostat LFS data for 2010, there are four distinctive groups of countries when comparing by the share of employment in the HSW sector as a percentage of employment in the total economy (see Table 3.1).

First, the group of countries with less than 6 per cent of HSW employment in total employment includes: Cyprus, Romania, Latvia, Bulgaria, Greece, Estonia, Poland and Slovenia. The second group, with 6–10 per cent of employment, includes: Lithuania, Hungary, Slovakia, Czech Republic (6.9 per cent), Italy, Portugal, Spain, Malta, Luxemburg and Austria. The third group, with more than 10 per cent, but less than 15 per cent of employment share, includes: Germany (12.1 per cent), Ireland, France, United Kingdom (13.2 per cent) and Belgium. The fourth group, with the highest share of HSW employment, includes: Sweden, Finland the Netherlands and Denmark (19.1 per cent).[4]

The share of employment in public administration and compulsory social security on total employment was between 4.8–11.6 per cent in European countries

---

4   EWCS 2010 data showed similar results: Sweden 16 per cent, the Netherlands 18 per cent and Denmark 20 per cent (Eurofound 2012).

in 2010 (see Table 3.1). Increases of employment there were not as sharp as in the HSW sector; in some cases we see evidence of stagnation or slight decreases.

The share of sub-sectors in the HSW sector is compared to total employment in the national economies in Appendix 3.2. The share of the health sector on total employment is the highest (that is more than 7 per cent) in Finland, Germany (7.2 per cent), Netherlands, United Kingdom (7.2 per cent) and Denmark (7.1 per cent), and the lowest (that is less than 4 per cent) in Bulgaria, Romania, Latvia and Cyprus. The share of residential care activities ranges from less than 1 per cent – in Greece, Bulgaria, Romania, Cyprus, Poland, Latvia and Lithuania – to more than 4 per cent – in Denmark (4.6 per cent), Netherlands and Sweden. A similar situation is evidenced in the case of social work activities (without accommodation) with the highest share in Denmark (7.5 per cent), Finland, the Netherlands and France. Jobs in employment services in most countries constitute less than 1 per cent of employment with a lower share in countries like Spain, Italy and Hungary and the highest share in the Netherlands and Sweden.

The share of social work activities in the HSW sector is less than 30 per cent in Greece, Romania, Cyprus, Poland, Latvia, Italy, Czech Republic (27.1 per cent), Slovenia and Bulgaria. The second group of countries, with a share of social work activities ranging from 30–50 per cent, consists of Austria, Slovakia, Spain, Ireland, Hungary, Germany (40.6 per cent), Portugal, the United Kingdom (45.1 per cent), France, Belgium and Luxembourg. The last group, with a prevalence of social work activities, includes Finland, Sweden, the Netherlands and Denmark (63 per cent). The countries with the greatest share of the HSW sector in the total economy also tend to have the biggest share of social work activities in the HSW sector (for example Denmark). Meanwhile, countries with the lowest share of the HSW sector in the economy also have the lowest share of social work activities in the HSW sector (for example Greece); see Table Annex 3.2.

Colombo et al. (2011) show that the share of LTC workers in the total working age (15–65) population varied in 2008 from 0.3 per cent in the Czech Republic and Slovak Republic to 2.9 per cent in Denmark and Norway and 3.6 per cent in Sweden. The share of home working formal workers is 25 per cent in Denmark, 26 per cent in the Czech Republic and 30 per cent in Germany (Colombo et al. 2011).[5] In most countries institutional care employment is substantially higher than the employment of home caring workers. Some institutional care must be maintained for people with severe disabilities and conditions for whom home care is not the most appropriate alternative (European Commission 2008b).

---

5   The numbers of older dependent people who receive institutional care varies from less than 2 per cent in Italy and Ireland to more than 7 per cent in Sweden and 8 per cent in Hungary (European Commission 2008b).

Table 3.1 Share of employment in NACE sectors Public administration and defence; Compulsory social security (ADM) and Health and social work (HSW) as a per cent of total employment in the economy (2000–2010)

TIME	2000				2005				2010			
	Females		Total		Females		Total		Females		Total	
GEO	ADM	HSW	ADM	HSW	ADM	HSW	ADM	HSW	ADM	HSW	ADM	HSW
Belgium	4.2	9.1	10.1	11.9	4.4	9.4	10	12.2	4.4	10.7	9.1	13.6
Bulgaria	2.5	4.5	6.9	5.8	2.8	4.2	7.2	5.4	3.3	4.2	7.5	5.2
Czech Republic	3.1	5	6.6	6.1	3.3	5.5	7	6.9	3.2	5.6	6.8	6.9
Denmark	2.9	14.9	5.9	17.5	3.1	14.5	6	17.4	3.2	15.7	6	19.1
Germany	3.6	7.7	8.3	10	3.5	8.7	7.8	11.2	3.4	9.3	7.3	12.1
Estonia	3.1	4.3	5.5	4.9	3.3	4.9	6.2	5.7	4.2	5	7.2	5.8
Ireland	2	6.4	4.8	8	2.6	8.1	5.1	9.7	2.8	10.5	5.8	12.8
Greece	2.4	3	7.5	4.7	2.6	3.3	8.1	5.1	3.2	3.8	8.6	5.6
Spain	2.4	3.7	6.3	5.3	2.4	4.4	6.3	6	3.2	5.7	7.6	7.4
France	4.4	8	9.3	10.5	4.7	9.6	9.7	12.2	5.3	10.3	10.1	13.1
Italy	3.1	3.6	8.9	6.1	2.1	4.6	6.4	6.9	2.1	5	6.2	7.3
Cyprus	2.9	2.7	9	3.8	2.5	3.2	7.8	4.3	2.8	3	7.7	4.3
Latvia	3.3	4.3	7.8	5	3.4	4.7	7.6	5.4	3.4	4.2	6.7	4.9
Lithuania	2.3	5.7	5.3	6.6	2.5	5.5	5.6	6.7	3.2	5.8	6.2	6.8
Luxembourg	3.7	5.9	11	8.1	4.4	7.1	12.2	9.7	4.5	7.1	11.6	9.4
Hungary	3.3	4.9	6.9	6.5	3.7	5.3	7.3	6.7	4.2	5.4	8.1	6.8
Malta	2	3.2	7.9	7.3	1.9	4.3	8.6	7.7	2.8	4.8	8.6	8.3

Table 3.1   *Concluded*

TIME	2000				2005				2010			
	Females		Total		Females		Total		Females		Total	
GEO	ADM	HSW	ADM	HSW	ADM	HSW	ADM	HSW	ADM	HSW	ADM	HSW
Netherlands	2.2	10.8	6.8	13.5	2.7	12.5	7	15.4	2.6	13.6	6.5	16.4
Austria	2.5	6	6.2	8	2.7	6.9	6.3	9.2	3.1	7.6	6.9	9.7
Poland	2.5	5.4	5.4	6.6	3.2	4.7	6.4	5.8	3.3	4.8	6.6	5.8
Portugal	2.4	4.3	6.8	5.4	2.7	5.5	7.1	6.7	2.4	6.1	6.7	7.3
Romania	1.4	2.6	4.4	3.2	2	3.1	5.6	4.1	2.1	3.6	5.3	4.6
Slovenia	3	4.2	6	5.3	3.1	4.5	6.2	5.5	3.1	4.7	6.3	5.9
Slovakia	3.9	5.8	7.7	7	3.5	5.5	7	6.7	4	5.7	8.1	6.8
Finland	2.5	12.4	4.9	13.9	2.4	13.5	4.6	15.3	2.7	13.8	4.8	15.6
Sweden	2.6	16.3	5.3	18.7	3	13.8	5.6	16.6	3.3	12.7	6	15.4
United Kingdom	2.9	9	6.2	11	3.6	9.7	7.1	12.3	3.2	10.4	6.7	13.2

Source: Eurostat – LFS (own calculations)

Employees in the Health and Social Services (HSW) Sector

In this section the socio-demographic characteristics of workers in the HSW sector are presented with a special focus on childcare and elderly care.

From a historical perspective, in the 1960s and 1970s governments deliberately encouraged women to enter the labour market and work in the public sector (Heinemann 2008). In many countries, women employed in the HSW sector, are public sector employees, contributing to the overall dominance of women in the public sector (see for example Andersen et al. 2008). According to European Commission (2010), 78.2 per cent of employees in the HSW sector were women in 2009 (it was 77.2 per cent in 2000). The women's employment rate in the HSW sector is growing mainly in countries with a previously lower women's employment rate, while in countries with a previously higher women's employment rate, it decreased slightly. A total of 81 per cent of new jobs in the sector were occupied by women (European Commission 2010). Eurostat LFS data from 2010 confirm this conclusion for all the sub-sectors in focus, with the exception of employment services. In most countries, more than 80 per cent of workers in residential care facilities and social work without accommodation are women.[6]

Employees in HSW sector are expected to gradually have a higher average age. There is already some evidence that the workforce in the HSW is ageing (see European Commission 2010). The share of people aged over 50 years working in the HSW sector increased from approximately 20 per cent to 28 per cent in the EU between 2000 and 2009 (European Commission 2010). This trend is also supported by the fact that the growth of employment in HSW was particularly strong for older workers (European Commission 2008b).

The LFS data about sector employment are presented by Eurostat in three age brackets: 15–24, 25–49 and over 50. In 2000, usually less than 10 per cent of workers in the HSW sector were younger than 25 years, 60–80 per cent were in the age category 25–49 and 10–30 per cent were over 50. There were substantial differences among EU member countries with only 11.3 per cent of workers over 50 in Belgium, and more than 26 per cent in Sweden, UK, Finland, Lithuania and the Czech Republic. Women working in HSW are in most countries slightly younger than men; however, the difference is rather small. Between 2000 and 2010

---

6   Female domination is most typical for the caring services. According to EWCS 2010 data, more than 80 per cent of workers in personal care are women (Eurofound 2012). The share of women workers in childcare facilities is very high: in the Czech Republic, Ireland, Portugal, Belgium and Italy it is close to 100 per cent; in France and Austria 97 per cent; in Germany and Finland 96 per cent; and in Sweden 95 per cent (OECD 2006). Simonazzi (2010) states for elderly care that the share of females never falls below 75 per cent; in the majority of countries it is over 90 per cent. Fujisawa and Colombo (2009) show that in Italy, the Netherlands, Spain and England, the vast majority (over 85 per cent) of formal LTC workers are women. Colombo et al. (2011) present similar data for Germany, Slovak Republic and Denmark.

employees in the HSW sector grew older (for example in the UK from 26.9 per cent to 31.9 per cent of workers aged over 50).

According to studies quoted in Fujisawa and Colombo (2009), the situation in the LTC sector might be similar to that of the HSW sector: in Denmark, France, the Netherlands, Spain, Sweden and the United Kingdom, about one-third of workers were over 45 in the early 2000s. Colombo et al. (2011) quote three studies which show that in some cases workers start to work in LTC in older age, or after a period of economic inactivity, which may also contribute to the ageing of the LTC workforce. The age profile of the LTC workforce may become a problem because of the mass retirement of qualified care workers in the near future (leading to a lack of caregivers). To conclude, the ageing of the HSW sector workforce is perceived as a problem because in the future when they are going to retire en mass, there will be a danger of the emergence of a care gap.

Professions and Qualification Levels of Employees in the Health and Social Services (HSW) Sector

Most workers engaged in the HSW sector are classified in three categories using the ISCO88[7] classification – professionals, technicians and associate professionals, service workers and shop and market sales workers. The important difference between professionals and associate professionals is in their education level. Professionals usually have a university degree or equivalent while associate professionals generally have tertiary education without a university degree (see Elias 1997).

In many countries most workers (30–50 per cent) in the HSW sector are represented by the associate professional category. Countries with more than 30 per cent of HSW workers in the professional category are Poland, Cyprus, Belgium, Ireland, Estonia, Spain and Greece (usually countries with smaller social services sectors). The most important differences among countries are evidenced in the category of service workers. This occupation category is the most prevalent in Sweden, Denmark and Finland; however, it is also important in Portugal, Malta, France and Spain. Two important factors are relevant here: the scope of social services and the level of their professionalisation.

The overall qualification level in the HSW sector is medium to high (European Commission 2010).[8] In the years 2007 and 2008, 40 per cent of employees working in the HSW sector had a higher education, which is considerably above

---

7   The International Standard Classification of Occupations is developed by the International Labour Office (ILO). In this text we use both ISCO88 (for data presented in the next paragraph) and ISCO08 classifications (for Table Annex 3.3), because data are presented this way by Eurostat.

8   ISCED (The International Standard Classification of Education) developed by UNESCO is used here. A high level of education includes ISCED levels 5 and 6; a medium level of education includes ISCED levels 3 and 4. Nevertheless, one has to be cautious

the average in total employment (27 per cent) (CEDEFOP 2010); however, the qualification of social service workers might be lower. The European Commission (2010) presents Eurostat data about education levels in some occupations in the HSW sector. While among healthcare professionals, 97 per cent of workers in the EU-27 have a high level of education, among personal care workers and other social services workers, only 10 per cent and 7 per cent, respectively, have a high level of education. Our analysis for EU-27 on EWCS 2010 data showed lesser differences: in human health activities 49.2 per cent of workers were highly educated, whereas in residential care activities 30.5 per cent of workers were highly educated; in social work without accommodation, 33.1 per cent of workers were highly educated. HSW is one of the sectors with the highest proportion of employees undertaking employer-paid training (52 per cent), or training on the job (49 per cent) (Eurofound 2012). About 28 per cent of workers in the HSW sector feel they possess skills to fulfil more demanding duties, while about 20 per cent feel that they need further training to cope well with their duties (Eurofound 2012).

An analysis of LFS data (Table 3.2) shows that the overall level of education in the HSW sector is high; in many countries most workers belong to the highest education group (ISCED 5 or 6). A distinction can be drawn between countries where healthcare prevails (for example Bulgaria) and those countries where the share of social work is more substantial (like Denmark). In the former group, the educational level of HSW sector workers is higher reflecting the lower level of formal education of some of the workers in social services, whose share is low in the HSW sector within this group of countries.

Concerning the profile of workers with a higher level of education (ISCED 5 or 6), in most EU member states, between 70 per cent and 90 per cent of cases have obtained their education in 'Health and Welfare' (LFS data). There are only a few countries with less than 65 per cent of highly educated workers who are educated in Health and Welfare (Netherlands, Poland and the United Kingdom). Workers who have attained a medium level of education have much more various fields of the highest education. Usually between 20 per cent and 60 per cent of HSW workers with a medium level of education have an education in Health and Welfare. In some countries (for example in Bulgaria and Estonia), a high proportion of medium educated workers have a general education. In other countries, the highest proportion of medium educated workers obtained their education in social sciences (for example in France and Denmark). Many workers with a medium level of education have training in industrial fields (for example in engineering, manufacturing or construction). This is typical for central and eastern European countries (for example Czech Republic, and Hungary). It is likely that they have been re-qualified for the HSW sector by attending a short occupation training course.

---

about these comparisons because of differences in various education systems in the EU member states.

Table 3.2   Education levels of workers in the HSW sector by gender and age (2010)

GEO/ AGE / GENDER / Educational level	Education	High	Medium	Low	Education	High	Medium	Low
Belgium	Male	62.6	22.9	14.5	15–29	50.5	38.7	10.8
	Female	48	37.3	14.7	30–49	51.6	35.5	12.9
	Total	51.2	34.2	14.6	50+	50.6	27.6	21.8
Bulgaria	Male	51.5	39.4	:	15–29	80	:	:
	Female	66.2	28.5	5.4	30–49	63.3	32.2	(4.4)
	Total	63.2	30.7	6.1	50+	60.3	28.6	11.1
Czech Republic	Male	47.8	49.3	2.9	15–29	34.8	63	2.2
	Female	20.3	74.2	5.5	30–49	25.1	71.7	3.2
	Total	25.9	69.1	5	50+	23.6	67	9.4
Denmark	Male	44.4	35.6	20	15–29	26.1	51.1	22.8
	Female	42.4	36.1	21.5	30–49	50.4	34.7	14.9
	Total	42.8	36	21.2	50+	40.1	29.9	29.9
Germany	Male	46.2	39.6	14.1	15–29	20.3	56.1	23.6
	Female	30.4	56.9	12.7	30–49	37.3	53.7	9
	Total	34.2	52.8	13	50+	39.1	49.1	11.8

Table 3.2 *Continued*

GEO/AGE/GENDER / Educational level	Education	High	Medium	Low	Education	High	Medium	Low
Estonia	Male	:	:	:	15–29	:	:	:
	Female	53.3	40	(6.7)	30–49	:	:	:
	Total	55.9	38.2	(5.9)	50+	:	:	:
Ireland	Male	59.5	23.8	16.7	15–29	63.2	31.6	:
	Female	58.5	26.6	14.9	30–49	63.4	25.2	11.4
	Total	58.7	26.1	15.2	50+	49.3	23.2	27.5
Greece	Male	66.3	22.5	11.3	15–29	58.8	35.3	:
	Female	51.2	34.8	14	30–49	58.3	31.8	9.9
	Total	56.1	30.7	13.1	50+	50	26.7	23.3
Spain	Male	65.6	19.1	15.3	15–29	70.7	22.1	7.2
	Female	57	26.5	16.6	30–49	60.3	25.7	14
	Total	59	24.8	16.3	50+	51	24.2	24.9
France	Male	45.9	34.3	19.8	15–29	39.2	48	12.8
	Female	35.4	43.5	21.1	30–49	38.1	43.3	18.6
	Total	37.7	41.5	20.8	50+	36.2	34.3	29.6

Table 3.2 *Continued*

GEO/AGE/GENDER / Educational level	Education	High	Medium	Low	Education	High	Medium	Low
Italy	Male	56.8	29	14.3	15–29	51.9	39	9.1
	Female	37.8	42	20.1	30–49	41.9	41.5	16.6
	Total	43.8	37.9	18.3	50+	44.8	31	24.2
Cyprus	Male	:	:	:	15–29	:	:	:
	Female	58.3	25	16.7	30–49	:	:	:
	Total	64.7	23.5	11.8	50+	:	:	:
Malta	Male	:	:	:	15–29	:	:	:
	Female	:	:	:	30–49	:	:	:
	Total	35.7	21.4	42.9	50+	:	:	:
Netherlands	Male	58.3	31.5	10.2	15–29	32.6	51.5	15.8
	Female	32.8	49.8	17.4	30–49	38.9	48	13.1
	Total	37.2	46.6	16.2	50+	37.8	40.8	21.4
Austria	Male	43.7	48.3	8	15–29	17.3	66.7	16
	Female	20.1	65.9	14	30–49	25.3	64.2	10.5
	Total	25.3	62	12.7	50+	32.1	53.6	14.3

Table 3.2   *Continued*

GEO / AGE / GENDER / Educational level	Education	High	Medium	Low	Education	High	Medium	Low
Poland	Male	50.9	46.2	(2.9)	15–29	63.8	34.8	(1.4)
	Female	37.4	59.5	3.1	30–49	38.8	59	(2.1)
	Total	39.9	57.1	3.1	50+	29.8	64.5	5.7
Portugal	Male	49.2	18.6	32.2	15–29	54.9	25.4	19.7
	Female	33.1	18.6	48.3	30–49	31.9	21.4	46.7
	Total	35.8	18.6	45.6	50+	28.4	8.4	63.2
Romania	Male	39.8	57.8	:	15–29	38.3	58.3	:
	Female	24.4	66.6	9.1	30–49	26	68	6
	Total	27.5	64.8	7.7	50+	25.5	59.6	14.9
Slovenia	Male	45.5	54.5	:	15–29	:	:	:
	Female	35.6	57.8	(6.7)	30–49	37.5	56.3	(6.3)
	Total	37.5	57.1	(5.4)	50+	46.2	46.2	(7.7)

Table 3.2   *Concluded*

GEO/AGE/GENDER / Educational level	Education	High	Medium	Low	Education	High	Medium	Low
Slovakia	Male	45.8	54.2	:	15–29	40.9	59.1	:
	Female	26.5	69.7	3.8	30–49	29.1	68.6	(2.3)
	Total	29.5	67.3	3.2	50+	24.5	67.3	8.2
Finland	Male	50	39.1	10.9	15–29	35.6	50.8	13.6
	Female	46.3	46.3	7.3	30–49	54.9	41.8	3.3
	Total	46.8	45.5	7.8	50+	41.5	47.6	10.9
Sweden	Male	51.2	36	12.8	15–29	29.1	55.6	15.4
	Female	40.1	43.3	16.6	30–49	46.7	44	9.3
	Total	42.1	42	15.9	50+	42	33.5	24.5
United Kingdom	Male	57.3	30.3	12.4	15–29	43.1	46.1	10.8
	Female	46.4	39.4	14.2	30–49	52.8	36	11.1
	Total	48.7	37.4	13.8	50+	45.5	34.7	19.8

Source: Labour Force Survey (own calculations)

Comparing educational levels by gender (Table 3.2) the main difference between the sexes is in the percentage of HSW sector workers with a high level of education. The percentage of highly educated workers is 10–20 per cent, higher for men in most counties (in Netherlands and Austria it is more than 20 per cent). In Ireland, Denmark and Finland the difference is less than 5 per cent in advantage of men. Bulgaria is the only country with a higher percentage of highly educated women.

Educational levels were compared in three different age groups: 15 to 29, 30 to 49 and over 50 (Table 3.2). Differences are rather small for low educated workers (except for Austria, Netherlands and Portugal). In most countries the percentage of low educated workers is lower in the younger age groups. Higher education profile is confirmed in the younger age groups in Slovakia, Romania, Portugal, Poland, Spain, Czech Republic, Bulgaria, France and Greece. In other countries, the younger workers less often have a high level of education than their older cohorts (Germany, Netherlands, Austria, Denmark, Finland, Sweden, United Kingdom). Note that in countries like Denmark, Sweden and the United Kingdom, it is the middle age group that has the highest share of highly educated workers, while the youngest workers have the lowest share of highly educated workers.[9]

The educational level of workers in HSW and especially in social services in the EU member states is influenced by several factors:

- prevailing education levels of the workforce in the country; the younger generations tend to have higher education profiles (IAQ 2007)
- the general up-skilling of the occupations associated with increases in the educational level is required (IAQ 2007); on the contrary, Fujisawa and Colombo (2009) expect that rising education levels are likely to reduce the supply of workers for less skilled jobs – such as providers of care for the elderly and disabled people
- over-qualification, which is typical during states of high unemployment (with workers forced to accept jobs below their qualification level) (IAQ 2007), or for migrant workers (whose education credentials are often not accepted in their new country)
- a high staff turnover of workers who do not have enough time to acquire the necessary qualifications (see IAQ 2007).

In some countries HSW sector workers can still complete their university education when they are over 30. In other cases, social services are seen as a good option for older workers (especially women) to restart their career.

The ECEC workforce is not highly trained: people caring for children below school age usually completed secondary vocational schooling, but do not normally

---

9   This may be partly a consequence of the rapid growth in the number of simple service jobs like cleaning for the elderly, as well as an indication of de-professionalisation connected to the marketisation of services.

have an academic education (Huber et al. 2006, European Commission 2008b). Plantenga and Remery (2009) state that the required qualification levels differ among EU member states from personal skills to education degrees. The qualification demands and real qualification levels are lower in some countries such as Belgium, Germany, the Netherlands and United Kingdom (Plantenga and Remery 2009).[10] There is a substantial difference in education levels between state-owned facilities (higher qualification) and private childminders (lower qualification) (Plantenga and Remery 2009). Another important difference in some countries is between people caring for children aged 0–2 (lower qualification) and 3 to school age (higher qualification), as well as between leading pedagogically qualified staff (higher qualification) and their less qualified assistants (OECD 2006). Education requirements are rising (OECD 2006) and younger pre-school educators have become more educated, increasingly with university degrees (Huber et al. 2006).

Overall, in LTC there are substantial differences among countries in the educational requirements and real educational levels of the workforce. An IAQ (2007) analysis on LFS 2005 data shows that the proportion of low skilled (ISCED 1,2 and 3c) among caring workers is 1.8 per cent in the Czech Republic, 8.3 per cent in Germany, 26 per cent in the United Kingdom and 16.7 per cent in the EU-15. According to Simonazzi (2010), training levels and credentials are the lowest in the Mediterranean countries, France and the UK, where employers offer short-term (from 2-day to 2-week) training programmes. Higher qualification levels are required in countries like Austria and Germany, where workers have to possess a variety of credentials in order to practice their professions. LTC workers in Germany usually have courses requiring three years and the highest education levels are in the Scandinavian countries (Simonazzi 2010). Colombo et al. (2011) distinguish between the qualification levels of qualified nurses (usually at least three years of targeted education) and the usually lower qualification levels of other care workers. In many countries, there is a split between the more formal, more qualified and more trained workforce and the more informal, less qualified workers (including completely unrelated qualifications).

Jobs Characteristics and Quality in Health and Social Services (HSW)

Most EU member states recognise the provision of social services as being of general interest and finance them from public budgets (European Commission 2010). Since the second half of the twentieth century, three main changes have been discussed in regards to social services and public sector employment. One of them is the transition from the logic of civic service to the logic of the labour

---

10   For childcare occupation qualification requirements and profiles see OECD (2006), Huber at al. (2006), IAQ (2007) and Plantenga and Remedy (2009, Box 4).

contract (Derlien 2008).[11] Some examples of the more extreme consequences of such transitions are agency work and quasi self-employed workers (see Colombo et al. 2011).

Another change is connected to the 'flexibilisation' of employment in social service. This is mainly based on the assumption that work in the services in the twenty-first century is generally less standardised and less protected than the industrial work typical for the twentieth century. Firms and workers are forced to flexibly respond to the rising or fluctuating demand for services through numerical and time flexibility (for example temporary labour contracts, night and shift work, or part-time contracts). In some professions, these working conditions are also embedded in the legislative regulations and in the character of the service provided.

A third transformation is connected to the privatisation of service provision in some countries. There are substantial differences among countries in their share of public and private providers – while public providers are dominant in the Czech Republic and Sweden (with shares of 80 per cent and 70 per cent of the supply, respectively), they account for only 10 per cent in the United Kingdom and 5 per cent in Germany (see European Commission 2008b: 38).

One of most discussed issues connected to job quality is temporary (fixed-term) employment. The scope of temporary employment can be influenced by several factors including the state of the economy, type of labour contract, age and gender profile of the workforce and staff turnover. According to European Commission (2010), the share of temporary employment in the health and social services sector in the EU (12.7 per cent) is slightly higher than that of the total economy (11.3 per cent). Only in several countries was there a difference of more than 3 per cent in the share of temporary employment between the HSW sector and the total economy in 2010 (see European Commission 2010).

In most EU countries, the share of employees with temporary employment contracts in the HSW sector increased between 2000 and 2010 (except for Belgium, Czech Republic, Denmark, Finland and the United Kingdom). The highest shares of temporary employment are observed in the Mediterranean countries: Spain and Portugal; they are followed by Finland, Sweden and Germany (16.7 per cent). The lowest shares of temporary employment occurred in some central and eastern European countries such as Slovakia, Bulgaria, Hungary, as well as in the United Kingdom (5.3 per cent). However, temporary employment can have very different causes in EU member states. In some countries firms use temporary employment to avoid risks and reduce payments typical for permanent contracts (Aust and Bönker 2004). Other authors argue that fixed-term contracts are most common in the (female-dominated) fields of education, health-care and social work (Timonen 2004). In some countries, temporary employment can also be connected with transitions from economic inactivity.

---

11   Civic (public) service status is understood as a specific law defined as 'work for the state' with certain privileges but also duties (see Christensen and Pallesen 2008, Sirovátka et al. 2011).

The growing share of part-time employment in the public sector since the 1960s and 1970s is strongly associated with the growth of women's employment in Germany, UK, Denmark and other EU countries (see Derlien 2008, Hogwood 2008, Andersen et al. 2008).[12] In the 1990s, Sweden and Denmark were exceptions to this rule with a substantial decrease of women's part-time work in the public sector (Pierre 2008). In some countries part-time employment (reduction of the hours of the work week) has been used as a deliberate political strategy aimed at increasing the number of jobs, saving money in the public sector (Rouban 2008), or down-sizing in a humane way (Derlien 2008).

An analysis by the European Commission (2010) shows that part-time employment in HSW (31.6 per cent) in the EU-27 is much higher than in the whole economy (18 per cent) and it is growing; however, there are substantial differences among countries (see also EWCS 2010 data in Eurofound 2012). Eurofound (2010) research shows that more than 80 per cent of organisations in the HSW sector employ at least one employee part-time and about 50 per cent of companies employ more than 20 per cent of employees part-time. Of the organisations in the HSW sector with some part-time workers, 31 per cent employ at least one employee in a 'mini job' (fewer than 15 hours a week) (Eurofound 2010). Part-time work is rather rare for skilled or management positions (Eurofound 2010). Usually a vast majority (70–90 per cent) of part-time workers in the public sector in EU countries are women (Derlien 2008, Hogwood 2008, Rouban 2008).

According to LFS data in several EU member states the share of part-time work is higher than 40 per cent in the HSW sector: Netherlands, Sweden, Belgium, Austria, Denmark (42.5 per cent) and Germany (40.1 per cent). Conversely, part-time employees constitute less than 10 per cent of employees in Greece, Slovakia, Portugal, Lithuania, Hungary, Cyprus, Slovenia, Czech Republic (9.2 per cent) and Poland. This constitutes very important difference between the central-south-eastern group of countries and the north-western group of countries. In almost all the EU member states the share of part-time work was growing or stagnating between 2000 and 2010. Similar to the HSW sector, in public administration and compulsory social security, women are employed more often than men in part-time positions. However, the part-time employment of women is slightly lower there compared to the HSW sector.

The share of part-time work in the childcare sector was 4 per cent in the Czech Republic, 40.1 per cent in Germany, 56.2 per cent in the United Kingdom and 44.6

---

12 Part-time work is sometimes seen as a preferred women's employment strategy, especially in the period of motherhood during the time when children are relatively young (Rouban 2008). In some countries part-time status is legally recognised permitted or even supported in the public sector (Heinemann 2008); however, others argue that part-time work can have negative consequences such as lower pay, overwork, fewer bonuses or career possibilities, and lower social protection than full-time employment (see for example UNIFEM 2006, IAQ 2007). Part-time work is seen as problematic especially if it is involuntary, as is the case of more than a quarter of all German women (IAQ 2007).

per cent in the EU-15 in 2005 (IAQ 2007). In some countries such as Germany, the part-time character of childcare jobs is connected to the provision of pre-school and out-of-school provision on a half-day basis (Huber et al. 2006).

Excessive overtime or long working hours are often considered to be an indication of low job quality, because they are associated with lower physical and psychological well-being (Holman and McClelland 2011). The working time of workers in the HSW sector is not significantly different from the rest of the economy and it did not change between 2000 and 2009 (European Commission 2010). EWCS 2010 data shows that more than 20 per cent of workers in the HSW sector reported an increase in their work time last year (Eurofound 2012).

Workers in the HSW sector work fewer hours than the average value for the total economy. This difference can be explained by the high share of women in the HSW sector and by the high prevalence of part-time work. Nevertheless, the differences between the HSW sector and the total economy are only a few hours in most countries. The general trend has been a reduction or stagnation of working time in the HSW sector between 2000 and 2010. This trend is also confirmed for LTC workers (see Colombo et al. 2011).

On the other hand, the HSW sector was ranked second out of 13 sectors as to the share of unusual working hours (required from at least 20 per cent of company employees) for night, Saturday or Sunday work (Eurofound 2007a). There was a total of 53 per cent of organisations that declared regular Saturday work by their employees; 48 per cent declared regular Sunday work; 38 per cent regular work at changing hours; and 28 per cent regular night work (Eurofound 2007a). Using the same ESWT data, Eurofound (2007b) showed that HSW is a sector with a comparatively high and company-oriented level of flexibility, especially in its atypical work hours. In a later Eurofound (2010) ECS-based study, more than 60 per cent of organisations in the HSW sector regularly employed workers for shifts and Saturdays; more than 55 per cent employed workers for Sundays; and almost 50 per cent for night shifts.

Wage Levels of Workers in the Health and Social Services (HSW) Sector

The wages of workers in HSW are usually compared to the average wage, minimum wage, other low qualification jobs, or primary school teacher salaries (in childcare services). Wages in the HSW sector grew more slowly than in other parts of the economy and are in most EU member states below the average wage in the economy (European Commission 2008b). 'Although skill levels are relatively high and working conditions are often demanding (for instance, night and shift work), wage levels in the health and social services sectors tend to be lower than in other sectors of the economy' (European Commission 2010). The differences in earnings between men and women working in the HSW sector in the EU are higher than in the total economy with substantial differences among member states (see European Commission 2010). Performance related pay elements and profit sharing are not widely used in the HSW sector – only about 23 per cent of establishments declare the use of individual or group performance payments, which is the lowest of all the economic sectors (Eurofound 2010). More than 70 per cent of employees in the HSW sector are covered by collective pay agreements (Eurofound 2010).

The data in Table 3.3[13] show that the wages of females are lower than the average wages by a range of 1.4 per cent (in Luxembourg) to 13.5 per cent (in Cyprus). The age structure of the workers implies even greater differences. In most countries, the under 30 age groups have much lower wages than the average wages: the difference is highest in Cyprus, Germany (-31.1 per cent), Netherlands and the United Kingdom (-25.9 per cent). In other age groups, the wages are usually also higher for older workers.

The average wages in the HSW sector are also compared to two other sectors: manufacturing and professional, scientific and technical (PST) activities (Table 3.3). In most cases, workers in PST activities have much higher wages than workers in the HSW sector. Wages in manufacturing are more comparable, although there are considerable differences among countries. In the first group of countries (France, Finland, Denmark, Germany, Hungary, Sweden and Belgium), the wages of workers in the HSW sector are more than 10 per cent higher than wages in manufacturing. By contrast, in Cyprus, Luxembourg, Portugal and Slovenia the wages in the HSW sector are lower than in manufacturing by more than 20 per cent. In other countries the differences are less than 10 per cent. To sum up, despite the relatively high education level in the HSW sector, wages are much closer to wages in manufacturing than to wages in PST activities.

Wages in the HSW sector are highly differentiated according to professions by ISCO08 classification. Management wages are usually more than 40 per cent above average. The wages of professionals are 12–60 per cent above average (for example in Denmark and Germany). Nevertheless, the wages in the category of service and sales workers, which includes many social service professions with a lower level of qualification, are usually 20–40 per cent below the average wages in the HSW sector and thus they are relatively low paid.

In the following the focus is on wages in ECEC and LTC. OECD (2006) argues that remuneration for unqualified childcare workers is very low (at minimum wage levels) in many countries. Wages of workers in childcare services are usually similar to that of primary education teachers or lower by 15–25 per cent (OECD 2006). In some countries it is typical to have great differences between the starting wages of young workers and the higher wages of the older more experienced workers (Eurofound 2006). The starting wages of childcare workers are about 50–75 per cent

---

13   The first column in the table shows the average yearly wages in the HSW sector in Euros. In the other columns the wages of females and age groups are compared to average wages. This comparison is presented in the percentage of the difference between the average yearly wage and the wage of the sub-group, which can be positive (when wages in the sub-group are higher), or negative (when wages in the sub-group are lower).

Table 3.3 Mean annual earnings (in Euros) and the wage structure of workers (difference from total in per cent) in the HSW sector in companies with 10 or more employees (2010)

GEO	Total (Euros)	Females	Age structure Less than 30	30–39	40–49	50–59	Over 60	Manufacturing	Professional, scient. technical activities
Belgium	39 557	−1.8	−18.3	−6	2.9	13.2	18.9	12.8	47.9
CZ Republic	12 154	−7.2	−13.6	−1.4	1.5	2.4	17.6	−7.1	41.8
Denmark	47 342	−4.4	−17.9	−7.5	0.5	5.8	9.8	22.5	45.1
Germany	35 819	−7.5	−31.1	2.5	7.4	6.7	10	19	37.3
Estonia	10 684	−7.7	−12.9	4	9.6	−1.1	−7.1	−9.5	37
Spain	29 328	−7.6	−24.3	−7.6	−0.8	13.4	20.9	−3.2	4.1
France	28 515	−5.2	−27.3	−7	0.7	9.2	49.2	27.2	59.3
Cyprus	28 109	−13.5	−31.4	−6.4	−1.2	12.7	10.7	−27.1	6.2
Latvia	8 115	−2.5	−10.7	7	5.9	−6.1	−1.7	−8.7	50.2
Lithuania	7 439	−7.4	23.5	−5.8	−3.8	−0.3	8.5	−8.7	39.4
Luxembourg	56 088	−1.4	(c) :	−1.5	7.4	12.5	(c) :	−18.8	16
Hungary	8 108	−5.1	−17.9	−8.1	−2.4	6.1	55.3	18	99
Netherlands	37 957	−11.3	−29.1	1.7	10.2	14.2	10.4	5.1	5.9
Austria	35 487	−5	−20.7	−2.1	3	10.1	45.8	16.1	45.1
Poland	9 712	−4.4	−22.8	−2.2	1.2	5.5	44.7	−5	51.3
Portugal	17 386	−10.2	−12.4	−7	−2	18.3	11.5	−20.5	40.1
Romania	5 689	−2.1	−21.4	−3	−2.6	7	36.9	−11.8	74.5
Slovenia	23 394	−6.1	−22.5	−7.5	−0.2	12.3	107.2	−20.1	18.6
Slovakia	9 908	−8.1	−12.5	5.9	−0.8	−3.2	24.6	−1.8	39.9
Finland	34 373	−4.3	−13	−1.9	1.2	3.1	4.3	24.9	34.4
Sweden	33 151	−3.8	−2.9	−6.2	−0.8	2.8	6.9	13.3	37.6
UK	33 071	−11.3	−25.9	0.2	8.9	8.7	−4.7	5.5	44.2

Source: Eurostat – SES (own calculations); note: some data for Luxembourg (marked c) are confidential.

lower than the starting wages of teachers (OECD 2006). IAQ (2007) shows, for example, that the wages of childminders in Germany are very low. In the Czech Republic qualified nurses and pre-primary teachers earn only about 80 per cent of the average wage (IAQ 2007). In the UK workers are paid low salaries, with many employees receiving the national minimum wage (Eurofound 2006). The wages of pre-school teachers are also low in Sweden (see Eurofound 2006).

According to Fujisawa and Colombo (2009), LTC workers typically earn lower wages than the average wage in the economy, even though their wage levels are often higher than the average wage of many low-skilled professions. Data presented in IAQ (2007) confirm this conclusion in the case of the UK. In the Czech Republic personal care workers earn about 70 per cent of the average wage. For the wages of nursing professions in many EU member states see Colombo et al. (2011:170–171). It is probable that because of the low (especially starting) wages in childcare and elderly care, the sector will face recruitment problems in the future.

Job Quality in the Health and Social Services (HSW) Sector

HSW is perceived in many studies as a sector with (above) average job quality (see for example Tangian 2007). We conducted our analysis on job quality on EWCS data 2000 (EU-15), 2005 (EU-27) and 2010 (EU-27) in order to assess the dynamics. Our aim was to compare job quality in HSW to other sectors of the economy.[14] First, we discuss work process and professional/individual development aspects (see Table 3.4). In most of these issues, HSW workers presented the most positive assessment of all the compared sectors: most of them receive or provide formal training and they declare in most cases good career prospects. Their work is the least monotonous, with the highest work discretion in methods of work: it is most often formally assessed and simultaneously done with the least direct supervision. Between 2005 and 2010, the share increased of those workers in HSW to whom training was provided. On the other hand, the supervision and monotonous tasks also increased a little between 2000 and 2005.[15]

---

14   We compare HSW to industry (NACE rev. 1.1 sectors C to F) and services (NACE rev. 1.1 sectors G to K).

15   According to a Eurofound (2007c) study, compared to other sectors, the HSW sector scores relatively well on the cognitive demands of the job (like job complexity, learning new things, monotony of the job). HSW sector is also sector with second most widespread use (34 per cent) of autonomous teamwork (see Eurofound 2010). On the other hand, the level of autonomy at work, measured by the composite index, was below average at a value of 2.79 (the maximum value being six for six positive answers); this placed HSW sector on the seventh position out of the 13 compared sectors of the economy (Eurofound 2007c). Eurofound (2008) shows that HSW is a sector of the economy with the second lowest share of workers with above average job insecurity.

Table 3.4   **Work process and development aspects of job quality in HSW sector (answers yes, in per cent) (2000–2010)**

	Formal assessment			Training provided			Career prospects		
	2000	2005	2010	2000	2005	2010	2000	2005	2010
Industry		37.1	36.4	24.4	22.1	28.7		29.6	28.7
Services	n. d.	40.9	40.9	28.1	23.9	31	n. d.	33	31.1
HSW		46.1	45.6	45.4	40.4	51.5		33	34.1
Total		39.3	41	30.5	26.1	33.7		30.5	30
	Monotonous tasks			Change methods			Supervision		
	2000	2005	2010	2000	2005	2010	2000	2005	2010
Industry	43	48.2	48.7	64	59	60.5	40.6	44.3	43.2
Services	39.1	41.3	46.6	69.5	65.2	65	28.9	34.3	33.1
HSW	33.1	36.1	37.4	73.7	67.6	68.1	24.4	29	29.9
Total	38.8	42.5	44.4	70.4	66.4	66.9	31.4	35.2	33.9

Source: EWCS 2000 (EU-15), 2005 and 2010 (EU-27) (own calculations)

The second discussed aspect of work is connected with working time, work schedule and health risk factors (see Table 3.5). Work schedule in HSW is in some aspects more demanding than in other sectors. Most workers in HSW work shifts, work at night and in often changing work schedules. Nevertheless, the amount of shift work decreased between 2000 and 2010, while night work and changing work schedules remained at the same level.

This is typical for healthcare as well as for LTC. Working conditions in LTC are difficult for workers in institutions (night shifts, heavy workloads, difficult care cases), as well as for home care workers (travelling often, working in the client's home, having conflicts with the family). Working conditions for immigrant workers seem to be more difficult than for native-born workers (Colombo et al. 2011). The difficult working conditions lead to a high turnover in the LTC sector resulting in many vacant LTC positions in some countries (Fujisawa and Colombo 2009, Colombo et al. 2011).

Health risk factors typical for the HSW sector are presented in the second half of Table 3.5. Overall, the proportion of people who think that their health is at risk because of their work is above average in the HSW sector and is even similar to workers in industry. Most workers identify risks connected to their work in lifting or moving people (can lead to spinal disorders) and handling infectious materials. Not much improvement is seen in 2000–2010. This corresponds to results of other studies (see Eurofound 2007c, Eurofound 2012).

Another important aspect of job quality involves the level of psychological and physical health risk. The pace of the work in HSW is mostly determined by

Table 3.5   **Time schedule and health risks in HSW sector (in per cent) (2000–2010)**

	Night work			Work shifts			Changing work schedule		
	2000	2005	2010	2000	2005	2010	2000	2005	2010
Industry	14.1	16.5	14.5	20.9	19.7	17.7	26.4	29.2	30.4
Services	15.8	17.2	16.2	16	16.6	17.4	31	33,6	36.4
HSW	27.7	31.2	27	40	35	32.8	40.5	41	43.4
Total	15.6	17.4	15.9	18.5	17.2	17	29.3	32	34.1
	Infectious materials			Lifting/moving people			Perceived health risks		
	2000	2005	2010	2000	2005	2010	2000	2005	2010
Industry		7.6	9		3.9	2.6	32.6	34.1	31.4
Services	n. d.	3.8	4.6	n. d.	2.9	2.7	21.5	22	19.2
HSW		45.3	45.8		43.3	44.2	32.7	33.8	29.1
Total		9.2	11.3		8.1	8.8	26.8	28.1	24.3

Source: EWCS 2000 (EU-15), 2005 and 2010 (EU-27) (own calculations)

the direct demands of the people (patients or clients) as was reported by 83 per cent of workers (Eurofound 2012). Work in the HSW sector is also connected with a feeling of some psychological risk factors such as having to hide one's own feelings at work, or being subjected to adverse social behaviour (Eurofound 2012). When comparing to the other sectors, in all cases more HSW workers declare negative health consequences like stress, overall fatigue, sleeping difficulties, depression or, anxiety or even cases of physical violence (Table 3.6).

Although the professional development and career prospects are better for HSW workers than in other sectors, they perceive their work as demanding (in time aspects) and as connected to some rather specific physical as well as psychological risks; this has been without much improvement since 2000. Despite this, a total of 69 per cent of men and 61 per cent of women working in HSW stated that they would be able to do their job at the age of 60 (Eurofound 2012).

Conclusion

This chapter discussed the employment in HSW, the social demographic characteristics of workers in the sector, their professions, qualifications and working conditions.

For ten years (between 2000 and 2010) there has been a substantial growth of employment in the HSW sector in most European countries (with the exception of

Table 3.6 **Possible health consequences in HSW sector, in per cent (2010)**

Sector	Stress	Overall fatigue	Insomnia or general sleep difficulties	Depression or anxiety	Physical violence
Industry	65.1	35	16.3	6.8	0.4
Services	69.1	34.8	17.1	9.1	1.4
HSW	73.3	38.1	22.3	10.1	7
Total	66.3	35.9	18.2	8.7	1.9

Source: EWCS 2010 (EU-27) (own calculations)

some eastern European countries). With some exceptions, this trend persisted even in times of economic crisis. However, there are substantial differences between countries with higher social service employment (North European countries and the Netherlands) and those countries with small social service sub-sectors (usually in South-Eastern and Central Europe). It can be concluded that mainly women benefited from social service sector expansion, because they constitute an overwhelming majority of social service employees. Part-time employment comprised an important part of employment growth, although with substantial differences among countries.

The HSW sector workforce is very diverse. The most notable development trend is the rapid ageing of the workforce. The overall education level of workers in the HSW sector is high or medium, but with substantial differences not only among professions but also within them. What is especially interesting is that while highly educated employees usually have education corresponding to their fields (in Health and welfare or Education), workers with a medium level of education have very diverse backgrounds with education often not relating to their field. Surprisingly, the share of workers with a high level of education is in many Western and Northern EU countries substantially lower for the younger generation than for the older one. Three findings indicate future problems for social services: the fact that the labour force in the HSW sector is rapidly ageing,[16] that the younger generations less often have a high level of education (this luckily is not true for the low level of education) and that workers with a medium level of education are usually not educated in health and welfare. This situation is due to three overlapping processes: the ageing of the workforce, the de-skilling of the workforce and the uneven impact of these processes in the HSW sector (dualisation).

---

16   This trend is clearly not influenced only by the demographic structure of the population, but also by economic factors. The calculation of Eurostat data shows that the development of an absolute number of young (15–24 years) HSW workers is very uneven in EU countries. It was substantially growing (by 30–50 per cent between 2000 and 2010) in France, Spain, Netherlands, Finland, United Kingdom and Austria. On the other hand, in Hungary, Romania, Slovakia and Czech Republic, it decreased by more than 50 per cent in the same period.

Many authors refer to the strong and growing demand for social services and the risk of an insufficient supply of workers in the social services sector, especially in long-term care. This risk is deepened by the ageing of workers in the HSW sector. Although some aspects of working conditions in the HSW sector, according to available data, are definitely better than in many blue collar professions (for example manufacturing), they are definitely demanding, especially concerning working schedule, stress and health risks. Although data are limited, it is possible to conclude that working conditions are probably very diverse within the HSW sector. Some reports show low job quality, especially in the sector of long-term care, resulting in high staff turnover in this sub-sector. Job quality in public social services was negatively affected in some EU countries by the recent economic crisis (European Commission 2010).[17]

There may be two worlds of social services emerging: on the one hand, the world of formal, more standardised, high quality services which are provided by a relatively highly qualified workforce; on the other hand, the world of private (hidden), semi-formal, unknown quality services provided by less qualified people who are often neighbours or immigrant workers.[18] In this process a potential risk can be recognised: labour market dualisation which may lead to future problems of low service quality and affordability for certain kinds of social services. Many EU member states have set service quality frameworks including qualification standards; however, there may potentially be a problem in meeting them if job quality in the social services, including pay, is not perceived as acceptable.

> On the one hand, high quality standards are laid down, thereby strengthening trends towards a more professional service provision. On the other hand, however, the absolute priority given to keeping costs level or reducing them in the social policy sphere generates massive cost pressures, which frequently confront the actors on the ground with irresolvable dilemmas and tend ultimately to pave the way towards lower standards. (IAQ 2007:37)

Thus social services offer much space for future innovations leading to attracting younger as well as older workers for employment in social services and their systematic education, while also addressing the standards of quality and sustainability of social services. Working conditions and wages are crucially important in this process. Those forming policy in the regulation, financing and delivery of social services face many choices in how to solve the various (potentially) problematic issues related to employment in the social services.

---

17   The LTC sector in Germany is an example of deteriorating working conditions (see Simonazzi 2010, Colombo et al. 2011).

18   Some countries are trying to provide various incentives for officially declared employment or provide support only if employment is declared (Fujisawa and Colombo 2009).

Appendix

Annex 3.1   NACE classification

NACE (rev. 1.1): Statistical classification of economic activities in the European Community (1999–2008)	NACE (rev. 2): Statistical classification of economic activities in the European Community (2009–now)
A Agriculture, hunting and forestry	A Agriculture, forestry and fishing
B Fishing	
C Mining and quarrying	B Mining and quarrying
D Manufacturing	C Manufacturing
	D Electricity, gas, steam and air conditioning supply
E Electricity, gas and water supply	E Water supply; sewerage, waste management and remediation activities
F Construction	F Construction
G Wholesale and retail trade; repair of motor vehicles, motorcycles and personal and household goods	G Wholesale and retail trade; repair of motor vehicles and motorcycles
H Hotels and restaurants	I Accommodation and food service activities
I Transport, storage and communication	H Transportation and storage
	J Information and communication
J Financial intermediation	K Financial and insurance activities
K Real estate, renting and business activities	L Real estate activities
	M Professional, scientific and technical activities
	N Administrative and support service activities
L Public administration and defence; compulsory social security	O Public administration and defence; compulsory social security
M Education	P Education
N Health and social work	Q Human health and social work activities
O Other community, social and personal service activities	R Arts, entertainment and recreation
	S Other service activities
P Activities of households	T Activities of households as employers; undifferentiated goods and services producing activities of households for own use
Q Extra-territorial organisations and bodies	U Activities of extra-territorial organisations and bodies

Source: Eurostat

Annex 3.2 Total Employment in HSW sectors and employment services, share of females (per cent) and share of employment in total economy (per cent) (2010)

NACE rev. 2	Human health activities (Q86)			Residential care activities (Q87)			Social work without accommodation (Q88)			Employment services (N78)		
GEO	TOT	% FEM	% ETE	TOT	% FEM	% ETE	TOT	% FEM	% ETE	TOT	% FEM	% ETE
Belgium	307.6	73.8	6.9	142.4	84.6	3.2	154.1	82.4	3.5	34.2	69.9	0.8
Bulgaria	111.1	80	3.7	16.3	81.6	0.5	28.7	84.7	1	:	:	:
Czech Republic	243.2	77.9	5.1	58.9	86.2	1.2	31.5	85.4	0.7	(3.4)	(64.7)	(0.1)
Denmark	189.8	81.5	7.1	122.3	82.5	4.6	200.4	81.2	7.5	17.8	61.2	0.7
Germany	2 743.5	78.2	7.2	1 016.5	75.9	2.7	860	74.7	2.3	353.1	34.8	0.9
Estonia	26	84.6	4.7	:	:	:	:	:	:	:	:	:
Ireland	150.3	78.3	8.4	22.1	86	1.2	57.6	89.9	3.2	5.9	66.1	0.3
Greece	204.9	63.5	4.8	13.5	85.2	0.3	23.2	94.4	0.5	:	:	:
Spain	892.8	73.2	4.9	250.8	86.2	1.4	206.8	85.9	1.1	29.2	66.4	0.2
France	1 749.6	74.1	6.9	567.9	78.9	2.2	1 025.4	86.1	4	127.8	49.8	0.5
Italy	1 194	62.9	5.3	237.6	83.8	1.1	203.8	86.7	0.9	54.4	64.7	0.2
Cyprus	12.5	66.4	3.4	1.9	84.2	0.5	1.6	(75)	0.4	:	:	:
Latvia	33.2	86.7	3.6	6.2	(87.1)	0.7	(5.3)	(88.7)	(0.6)	:	:	:
Lithuania	75.4	85	5.7	9.4	89.4	0.7	:	:	:	:	:	:
Luxembourg	10.4	72.1	4.8	4.2	78.6	1.9	5.9	79.7	2.7	:	:	:
Hungary	161.4	75.5	4.3	56.7	86.2	1.5	35.1	87.7	0.9	6.5	(63.1)	0.2
Malta	8.7	52.9	5.4	3.7	(64.9)	2.3	:	:	:	:	:	:

	TOT	% FEM	% ETE	TOT	% FEM	% ETE	TOT	% FEM	% ETE	TOT	% FEM	% ETE
Netherlands	595.6	75.3	7.2	393.1	85.7	4.8	361.4	91.8	4.4	83.3	45.5	1
Austria	264	76.9	6.6	64.9	83.5	1.6	61.3	78.3	1.5	14.9	(32.9)	0.4
Poland	699.7	80.7	4.5	99.6	81.7	0.6	119	90.6	0.8	(14)	(79.3)	(0.1)
Portugal	198	78.5	4.2	78	90.1	1.7	64.9	92.1	1.4	:	:	:
Romania	321	77.9	3.6	37.6	82.4	0.4	43.6	88.8	0.5	:	:	:
Slovenia	39.3	77.9	4.2	12	89.2	1.3	(3.9)	(82.1)	(0.4)	:	:	:
Slovakia	104.1	81.3	4.5	27.6	88.4	1.2	24.3	92.2	1.1	(3.6)	:	(0.2)
Finland	176.9	85.9	7.3	78.4	88	3.3	120.5	92.7	5	7.5	62.7	0.3
Sweden	307.9	79.8	6.9	215.4	86.9	4.9	161.6	81.1	3.6	61.3	48.5	1.4
UK	2 029.7	77.9	7.2	708.5	78.4	2.5	960.2	81.3	3.4	213.6	55.8	0.8

Note: TOT = total employment in sub-sectors (thousands), % FEM = per cent of female workers in sub-sector, % ETE = workers in sub-sector as percentage of employment in the total economy.
Source: Eurostat – LFS (own calculations).

Annex 3.3   **Mean annual earnings of workers in the HSW sector (in Euros) and wage structure of workers with use of ISCO08 (diff. from average in per cent) in the HSW sector in companies with 10 or more employees (2010)**

GEO / ISCO08	Total (Euros)	Managers	Professionals	Technicians and associate professionals	Clerical support workers	Service and sales workers	Skilled agricultural, forestry and fishery workers	Manual workers
Belgium	39 557	88.1	31.7	12.6	−6.3	−9	:	−29.8
CZ| Republic	12 154	87.8	41.2	−2.4	−21.5	−33.4	−35.2	−40.3
Denmark	47 342	48.3	12.4	−0.9	−10.2	−15.4	−0.1	−22.5
Germany	35 819	71.6	59.9	−7	−17.2	−26.8	−25.1	−33.2
Estonia	10 684	100.7	67.8	−12.4	−40.8	−47	:	:
Spain	29 328	59.7	42.3	−16.8	−25.3	−34	−39.2	−38.7
France	28 515	71.9	54.5	3.6	−21.2	−19.6	:	:
Cyprus	28 109	211.1	41.9	−4.9	−30.6	−32.6	−28.5	−35.4
Latvia	8 115	72.5	32.9	−6.2	−21.7	−39.8	−30.6	−39.4
Lithuania	7 439	67.9	19.2	−19	−37.3	−40.8	:	−40.9
Luxembourg	56 088	84	44.9	21.2	−10.4	−23.8	:	:
Hungary	8 108	102.7	52.5	−5.2	−24.4	−22	−35.8	−33.9
Netherlands	37 957	60.6	34.5	7.2	−9.9	−32.4	−26.4	−18.3
Austria	35 487	75.7	51	3.4	−15.1	−18.4	:	−34.1
Poland	9 712	79	17.3	−19.8	−24.5	−36.3	:	:
Portugal	17 386	106	71.2	−7.3	−26.2	−45.4	:	:
Romania	5 689	126.4	33.9	−2.5	−25.8	−40.1	:	−34.3
Slovenia	23 394	89.1	55.4	−11.8	−31.3	:	−37.6	:
Slovakia	9 908	117.4	61.9	−6.6	−30.2	−39.1	−47	−38.6
Finland	34 373	48.4	48.6	−0.8	−16	−14.9	−20.1	−23.2
Sweden	33 151	43.5	12.2	−7.5	−18	−9.8	−12.7	−20.8
UK	33 071	35.1	40	−9.8	−33	−37.5	−46	−39

Source: Eurostat − SES (own calculations); note: some data is missing due to their confidentiality and/or because the number of cases for the particular category is too small.

Annex 3.4   EWCS questions for indicators in Tables 3.4, 3.5 and 3.6

Formal assessment	Over the past 12 months, have you … ? – Been subject to formal assessment of your work performance?	Yes
Training provided	Over the past 12 months, have you undergone any of the following types of training to improve your skills or not? – Training paid for or provided by your employer or by yourself if self-employed	Yes
Prospects for career	How much do you agree or disagree with the following statements describing some aspects of your job? – My job offers good prospects for career advancement	Strongly agree, agree.
Monotonous tasks	Generally, does your main paid job involve … ? – monotonous tasks	Yes
Change methods	Are you able to choose or change … ? – your methods of work	Yes
Boss control	On the whole, is your pace of work dependent, or not, on the direct control of your boss?	Yes
Night work	Normally, how many times a month do you work at night, for at least 2 hours between 10.00 pm and 05.00 am?	more than once
Work shifts	Do you work … shifts?	Yes
Changes in work schedule	Do changes to your work schedule occur regularly?	Yes
Infectious materials	Please tell me, using the following scale, are you exposed at work to … ? – Handling or being in direct contact with materials which can be infectious, such as waste, bodily fluids, laboratory materials, and so on.	at least one quarter of time
Lifting-moving people	Please tell me, using the same scale, does your main paid job involve … ? – Lifting or moving people	at least one quarter of time
Perceived health risks	Do you think your health or safety is at risk because of your work?	Yes
Stress	For each of the following statements, please select the response which best describes your work situation. – You experience stress in your work	Always, most of the time, sometimes
Overall fatigue	Over the last 12 months, did you suffer from any of the following health problems? – overall fatigue	Yes
Insomnia or general sleeping difficulties	Over the last 12 months, did you suffer from any of the following health problems? – insomnia or general sleep difficulties	Yes
Depression or anxiety	Over the last 12 months, did you suffer from any of the following health problems? – depression or anxiety	Yes
Physical violence	And over the past 12 months, during the course of your work have you been subjected to physical violence?	Yes

Source: Eurofound, EWCS questionnaire

Chapter 4

Financing the Welfare States – Changes and Challenges

Bent Greve

Introduction

In this chapter, the central questions relate to what the trends are in financing the welfare state under the fiscal pressures emerging from globalisation and financial crises (short-term shocks on public finance), as well as the long-term sustainability of public sector financing. The focus is on financing although change in expenditure or efficiency in the public sector could also play a role: Whether it is the financial crisis or the legitimacy crisis which is used as a scapegoat for changes in the welfare state is less important here (Greve 2011). The issue of whether the impact of the financial crisis on the welfare state would be different if there was high electoral support for the welfare state is not the subject of discussion here (Vis et al. 2011).

In recent years, economic development has moved taxation from being on specific goods more towards elements such as wage income, sales, profits and added value. Tax and social spending seem to be related to national income per inhabitant (Gough and Shar 2011).

Given the financial crisis and expected future fiscal pressures on the welfare states, the core issue is how to proceed towards and develop long-term sustainability in the financing of the welfare states, including the creation of new jobs (compare also Chapter 3 and 6). Fiscal pressure due to globalisation and changes in demography is one issue; another is the expected outcome of the fiscal crisis leading to fiscal policy that is even more prudent than before. Thus there is also the central policy issue of how to deal with this development. First, this chapter will briefly present positions on how to finance the welfare state. This will be followed by an empirical analysis at the aggregate EU level of development since 2000, including as a central issue whether convergence in ways of financing has taken place. Then the chapter will proceed to a discussion on how to sustainably cope with the fiscal pressure on the welfare state.

This chapter will therefore present data on the development of spending and financing of the welfare state in the EU, establishing a context for a discussion on how to cope with fiscal and other pressures on the welfare states now and in the future. The focus in this chapter is thus a combination of theoretical understanding of how to finance welfare states and an analysis of empirical data on the development and methods of financing the welfare states in the EU. This will also include some data on public sector spending, deficits and debts, given that these issues are necessary in regards to the financing of the welfare state and relevant in the wake of the financial crisis. A short depiction of the possible demographic pressure on welfare state spending is also included.

The ability to have a sustainable level of financing does not only depend on the level of public sector spending, but also on the level of public sector income, as well as the size of the hidden welfare state (Howard 1997, Greve 2007b). Reductions in subsidies through the tax system and the broadening of the tax base could thus also serve as instruments to pursue in order to achieve sustainability. This is in line with the development in the last 30 years (OECD 2011b). Given the limits of available data, the focus will be placed especially on those issues related to the tax and duty systems, having an implication for sustainable financing. The choice has been to mainly use data from 2000 and onwards, given that this covers different economic business cycles; using this time span also indicates that possible structural changes in societies are included in the analysis.

In this way the analysis will mainly deal with public welfare in a Titmuss framework of understanding. Nevertheless, a reduction in the level of fiscal welfare could increase the likelihood of more sustainable financing; a change in tax rates (that is if this is connected with changes in the tax base) might imply that the total tax income remains the same despite a change in the tax rate. The broadening of tax bases has also been part of the historical fiscal process in several countries, as this also makes the tax system more coherent, simple and sustainable.

Theoretical Approaches to Financing the Welfare State

There are many varied ways of financing the welfare state. Box 4.1 below shows the advantages and disadvantages of the different approaches to financing the welfare states.[1] The aim here is mainly to present an overview more than give a detailed prescription of how different combinations and structures of financing work with regard to revenue and other types of impact. Nevertheless, the table is an indication of how the different varieties of taxes and duties all have different kinds of benefits and drawbacks. Therefore, it will often be the combination of taxes and duties that needs to be analysed – how they influence different goals for a society, including sustainable financing, environmental issues, impact on the labour market, impact on equality and simplicity of administering. Furthermore, different kinds of taxes and duties can have a different impact on allocation, distribution and stabilisation, as was historically argued by Musgrave and Musgrave (1976); this is important as the structure will often have to change depending on the desired goal and the overall development in the economic system and its structure. Finally, it is

---

1   For a more elaborated discussion of pros and cons and the various ways to finance, cf. Sirovátka et al. (2011).

Box 4.1   Main instruments of financing welfare states including possible advantages and disadvantages

Main tax instruments	Advantages	Disadvantages	Used in – and in reference to a main welfare regime
Income tax	Can ensure a high level of revenue and can be made progressive. Can be applied to both wage-earners and companies	Risk of changing balance between work and leisure, especially with high marginal tax rates	All European countries, especially Nordic universal welfare regimes
Value-Added Tax	Relatively simple, and can vary between types of goods (for example low or zero on foods); will also be paid by tourists and those not paying income tax	Might have a negative impact on distribution as persons with lower income tend to have a higher propensity to consume	All European countries, especially Southern and Eastern welfare regime countries
Duty	Can be targeted to luxury goods thereby having a positive impact on distribution. Can also help to enhance the environment; might be more stable and less prone to international tax-competition	Complex administration and, if not targeted, an upside-down effect	To a varying degree in all EU-countries, but Southern and Eastern to a higher degree
Social security contributions	Simple and effective; ensure financing of welfare activities	Risk of no coverage for those outside the labour market	Especially in the central continental and liberal welfare models in Europe
User-fees	Increase information on consumer preferences and paid by those receiving the services	Risk of low income earners not obtaining the service or obtaining it later	Especially used in the health care area, but also transport, day-care for children in many EU-countries; liberal model countries to a high degree
Others	Can be a way to tax inheritance, wealth, housing	Mainly administrative, but also possible negative side-effects in relation to mobility	Only more limited; with a very varied structure
Tax expenditures	Simple and can be targeted to areas deemed by the political system to be important; less visible in the political process	Up-side down effect; make the priorities unclear; therefore, also labelled hidden welfare state	In most countries, but size not clear, and no clear relation to model; high in Nordic countries

Source: Based on Greve (2010)
Note: The examples given above are only indicative and serve as a way to interpret the goals; they are not always the precise outcome of the uses of the various instruments available.

important how sustainable those taxes and duties are. Sustainability (understood here as being able to ensure stable revenue within the decided tax-structure and to finance social services given changes in the global economy over the business cycle) is the factor that ensures a balance within public sector finances.

One need to be aware that decisions about the structure of the tax and duty system is not only influenced by the composition of the national economy, but also by European integration and the decisions in neighbouring countries. Therefore, decisions related to tax and duty are taken within an existing national and international economic framework. Given the increasing globalisation and interconnectedness of trade and financial systems, as evident from the last financial crisis, this also raises the issue of how and to what degree individual countries can pursue their own tax policy. Coordination and limits (for example already existing in the EU directive on value-added taxes) might thus be needed to ensure stability in the European economic system. This issue will be discussed and analysed by examining the changes over the last ten years of the financing of the welfare state, including a look at whether the systems on the overall level have converged.

Finally, the issue of whether taxes and duty are to be imposed on movable or non-movable sources of income and wealth. Generally, in order to ensure sustainability and stability in the level of state income, it is best to tax non-movable goods and services such as housing, use of water, electricity and heating (compare also OECD 2011b). This is because movable sources of income and wealth can to a greater extent be moved to countries with lower tax-rates, thereby allowing a reduction or even avoidance of tax payment. This can especially be seen in the case of companies where taxable income can easily move from country to country, therefore making it a less sustainable way of financing welfare states. Areas with possible tax-competition among countries are thus less reliable as sustainable sources, unless there is either international co-operation or common economic development making the differences between countries less prominent. Consumption taxes might also become more important for reasons of growth and stability in public sector income; however, there is a risk of a reduced level of equality (OECD 2007).

Spending on Social Protection

This section will give a short overview of spending related to the social area, as this is part of the need to finance welfare states, or at least to also reduce deficits in the future. As a general rule, development measured in per cent of GDP has been used despite the fact that this measurement can be criticised for not fully reflecting several factors:

- the real change in the level of spending
- spending per user of the system

Table 4.1   Trend towards convergence in spending on social protection in the long run – EU-12 and EU-27 – measured by the coefficient of variation

	1980	1993	2000	2009
EU-12	0.3	0.21	0.20	0.10
EU-27	..	0.24 (1996)	0.25	0.21

Source: Greve, B. (1996) and calculations based upon Eurostat data for spending on social protection as a per cent of GDP

- new needs arising or old needs declining in their need for coverage (for example a need for better coverage for the elderly, or fewer children in need of day-care due to demographic changes)
- possible change due to shifts in GDP – both in upward and downward directions.

Given that the ambition here is to present an overview and discussion of the overall development in expenditures related to the welfare state, this has been seen as a reasonable methodological choice. Spending on social protection is seen as a relevant concept when looking into the area of social service and welfare state development.

There has been a historical trend towards convergence on spending in the EU, as indicated in Table 4.1. These tendencies towards convergence will be further elaborated in different sub-elements of financing as a way of probing into how there might have been a development in the same direction.

Among the 12 old member states,[2] where data is also available for a longer time span, the tendency for convergences in spending can be clearly witnessed. Although there is also a tendency for increased convergence for all 27 member states, the starting level for differences in spending is less than it was among the 12 old member states. This indicates that convergences take place at the overall level and an important question thus further relates to whether this also has implications on the financing of the welfare states: for example, whether financing both on the aggregate level and the use of different instruments will converge (compare the discussion in Chapter 7 on Europeanisation). Table 4.2 shows figures for all the years since 2000 on the average spending of the EU-27 countries calculated as simple arithmetic averages, the standard deviations and coefficients of variation. Annex 4.1 presents for all EU-27 member states the development in spending on social protection as percentages of GDP. The annex thus shows the variation ranging from 16.7 per cent in Bulgaria to 32.5 per cent of GDP in Denmark.

---

2 France, Belgium, Netherlands, Italy, Germany, Luxembourg, Denmark, Eire, UK, Portugal, Italy and Greece.

Table 4.2   **Average spending on social protection as percentages of GDP for**
                  EU-27, standard deviation and coefficient of variation (2000–2010)

	2000	2001	2002	2003	2004	2005	2006	2007	2008	2009	2010
Arithmetic average	20.9	21.1	21.5	21.9	21.7	21.4	21.2	20.8	21.7	24.5	24.4
Standard deviation	5.2	5.4	5.4	5.7	5.7	5.8	5.7	5.5	5.2	5.2	5.2
Coefficient of var.	0.25	0.26	0.25	0.26	0.26	0.27	0.27	0.26	0.24	0.21	0.21

Source: Eurostat, compare Appendix 1, and calculations based hereupon

The above table shows that since 2000, there has been an increase on average of around 3.5 per cent in spending on social protection. Furthermore, among all the member states, there has been a tendency to more similarity, given the decline in the coefficient of variation. Although variation still exists (that is from 17.4 per cent in Romania to 32.4 per cent in Denmark), the tendency to move towards the same level of spending is an even more relevant aspect in the need for looking into sustainability of financing in the European context, as this will be a prerequisite for sustainability in the welfare states. The movement in the same direction is also an indication of the fact that there has been a move towards the same level of spending, despite the differences in the levels of income among countries.

The tendency towards convergence is even higher when looking at only cash-benefits, as shown in Table 4.3, although this is not the case for benefits in kind, where the deviation among the countries is still rather large. Especially from 2008 to 2009, there is clear convergence in relation to cash-benefits. The implication is that the main differences related to spending on social protection have been reduced due to less diverse approaches with regard to the level of income transfers among the countries in the EU. On the contrary, the spending on in-kind benefits is still different, presumably also implying a diverse picture in relation to the delivery of service.

Spending on social protection can be seen as the best proxy for public sector impact on the level of social services. However, the increasing level of unemployment has also had an impact. Furthermore, social protection expenditure has mainly been developing in line with general growth in the economies, albeit with an increase on average for all EU-27, in relative terms (especially due to the increase in 2009, which was one of the first indications of the impact of the financial crisis).

The growth in average spending in 2009/10 can partly be explained by the fact that many countries were witnessing a decline in the level of GDP. As such, a constant level of spending implies a relatively higher percentage of GDP. This was further exacerbated by the pressure on social spending in the wake of the increase

Table 4.3 **Social protection cash benefits and in kind benefits in per cent of GDP in EU-27 and changes towards convergence (2000–2010)**

	2000	2001	2002	2003	2004	2005	2006	2007	2008	2009	2010
Cash benefits							·				
Arithmetic average	14.2	14.3	14.5	14.7	14.6	14.3	14.1	13.7	14.3	16.3	16.2
Standard deviation	3.5	3.6	3.6	3.8	3.7	3.7	3.6	3.4	3.1	2.7	2.8
Coefficient of variation	0.24	0.25	0.25	0.26	0.26	0.26	0.26	0.25	0.22	0.17	0,17
Benefits in kind											
Arithmetic average	6,7	6,8	7,0	7,2	7,1	7,1	7,1	7,0	7,4	8,2	8,2
Standard deviation	2,3	2,3	2,4	2,5	2,5	2,6	2,6	2,6	2,6	3,0	3,0
Coefficient of variation	0,34	0,34	0,35	0,35	0,36	0,36	0,37	0,36	0,35	0,36	0,36

Source: Eurostat, compare Appendix 1, and calculations based hereupon

in the levels of unemployment. Pressure on a welfare state that was due to rapid and marked changes in the international economy can thus be witnessed; in the future, this may also be an issue, therefore welfare states need to be aware of that sudden shocks can have a strong negative impact on the overall economy.

While financial shocks are difficult to predict, this is not the case with the expected pressure arising from demographic changes. These further increase the likely pressure on welfare state spending and the need to ensure a structural surplus in the public sector budget. This is in addition to the changes needed in the wake of the financial crisis. Given that pressure on public sector expenditure is also related to the level of unemployment, the need for an effective active labour market policy increases: economic policy can ensure a higher level of employment, which could reduce the pressure on public sector spending. This is a further reason for changing the methods of financing the welfare states in Europe, especially with a focus on sustainability.

Revenues to Finance Welfare States

This section will study revenues for financing the welfare states by looking into the changes that have taken place mainly since the year 2000, and by determining

Table 4.4 **Development in average total receipts from taxes and social contributions in percentages of GDP, standard deviation and coefficient of variation in EU-27 (2000–2011)**

	2000	2001	2002	2003	2004	2005
Average EU-27	37.0	36.4	36.1	36.1	36.1	36.6
Standard deviation	6.7	6.5	6.3	6.2	6.2	6.2
coef. var.	0.18	0.18	0.17	0.17	0.17	0.17
	2006	**2007**	**2008**	**2009**	**2010**	**2011**
Average EU-27	36.7	37.1	36.7	36.0	35.6	35.8
Standard deviation	5.9	5.6	5.7	6.3	6.2	6.2
coef. var.	0.16	0.15	0.16	0.17	0.17	0.17

Source: Calculations based upon Eurostat data

whether convergence has taken place. This is not intended to be analysed for the detailed structure of the tax systems, but in the ways that revenues for public sector activities have been developing. Table 4.4 shows the trend with regards to total financing. This is supplemented in Annex 4.2 with data for all EU-27 member states on their total income from 2000 to 2011. It shows that the highest level is in Denmark (with 47.7 per cent of GDP) and the lowest in Bulgaria (with 27.2 per cent of GDP).

Table 4.4 shows a slight decline in the relative size of total revenue since 2000. It also indicates that in the wake of the fiscal crisis, revenue decreased, although a decline in revenue is more limited when looking at all the EU countries (although Germany from 2005 to 2011 was an exception in that it had a slight increase in the overall level of taxes and duties). The overall decline was sharper from 2008 to 2009, where it also declined in absolute figures. In 2011 the level of tax revenue in the EU member states was highest in Denmark (48.6 per cent) and lowest in Latvia (26.4 per cent); the average for all 27 member states was 40 per cent. Germany had 40 per cent, UK 37.8 per cent and Czech Republic 34.5 per cent (Eurostat 2012a). As a consequence of the financial crisis, development in recent years has resulted in a lower level of taxes and duty as percentages of GDP. However, there is a relatively stable level of convergence at a relatively high level, although since 2007 a slight increase towards a lower degree of convergence has taken place. Nevertheless, the changes are rather limited.

The following section will look into whether there is a very diverse or common structure of tax and duty systems and a movement towards using different or same kinds of taxes and duties. A variation in the tax structure might show different options for having a sustainable method of financing in the future. The direct consequences need to be analysed with caution, as different routes to achieve the same result can be used. For example, all countries have some user charges which especially prevail in the health care sector, child care and in some circumstances, elderly care.

Table 4.5   **Taxes on labour as per cent of GDP in EU-27, standard deviation and coefficient of variation (2000–2010)**

	2000	2001	2002	2003	2004	2005	2006	2007	2008	2009	2010
Average EU-27	17.7	17.7	17.5	17.4	17.2	17.1	17.0	17.0	17.3	17.5	17.1
Standard deviation	5.5	5.5	5.5	5.5	5.4	5.3	5.2	5.1	5.3	5.4	5.1
coef. var.	0.31	0.31	0.31	0.32	0.31	0.31	0.31	0.30	0.30	0.31	0.30

Source: Calculations based upon Eurostat

One area of great interest has been tax on labour, as this has been argued to have an impact on the level of employment and economic competitiveness both for the individual countries and the EU.

With an average of 17.1 per cent in 2010, tax on labour is still one of the most central elements regarding the financing of the welfare state. Table 4.5 also reveals that in the area of tax on labour, no real changes have taken places in the last ten years, nor has there been any tendency towards convergence. Thus there is still a considerable difference between countries with low levels (Malta and Bulgaria below 10 per cent) and those with high levels (Denmark and Sweden above 27 per cent).

Thus tax on labour does not seem to have been used as a parameter for tax-competition, although some Eastern European countries have experienced a low flat-rate tax in contrast to more traditional progressive income taxes. The picture is slightly different when looking at taxes on capital; see Table 4.6.

There has been a slight decline in the overall level of taxes on capital as percentages of GDP and it is now at 6.7 per cent. At the same time, the dispersion has remained the same, despite some variation over time. Given the free movement of capital and goods, the expectation could be that this would be an area where

Table 4.6   **Taxes on capital and development for EU-27 as per cent of GDP, standard deviation and coefficient of variation (2000–2010)**

	2000	2001	2002	2003	2004	2005	2006	2007	2008	2009	2010
Average EU-27	7.3	7.1	6.9	6.8	6.9	7.2	7.5	8.0	7.5	6.6	6.6
Standard deviation	2.9	2.7	2.6	2.5	2.4	2.6	2.6	2.7	2.6	2.4	2.5
coef. var.	0.39	0.39	0.38	0.37	0.34	0.36	0.35	0.34	0.35	0.36	0.38

Source: Calculations based upon Eurostat data

Table 4.7   **Taxes on consumption as per cent of GDP in EU-27, standard
               deviation and coefficient of variation (2000–2010)**

	2000	2001	2002	2003	2004	2005	2006	2007	2008	2009	2010
Average EU-27	12.0	11.8	11.8	12.0	12.1	12.4	12.3	12.2	12.0	11.7	11.9
Standard deviation	1.4	1.4	1.4	1.5	1.7	1.7	1.8	1.9	2.0	2.0	1.7
coef. var.	0.12	0.12	0.12	0.13	0.14	0.14	0.15	0.15	0.17	0.17	0.14

Source: Calculations based upon Eurostat data

member states would gradually move towards convergence (unless the conditions are already very similar), although taking into consideration the geographical proximities to other countries. Unless the levels are not too varied, the taxes on capital might be at the risk of downward competition, thereby less able to serve as sustainable elements in long-term tax strategies.

On the other hand, tax on consumption, which is common practice in the nation state, is a more obvious possible element for developing a sustainable tax structure; however, cross-border and internet trade reduce the options for having exceedingly varied structures for certain goods and services. Table 4.7 shows the development and degree of convergence with regard to taxes on consumption. Depending on what type of consumption is taxed, the distributional impact can be different. For example, VAT is typically expected to have a regressive impact due to the fact that low income earners spend a relatively higher proportion of their income on consumption than high income earners.

The table shows that, on average, tax on consumption has remained a stable element in the financing of welfare states in the EU, remaining at around 12 per cent of GDP. It is somewhat surprising that the systems seem to have moved away from a less coherent structure and towards more divergence among the EU member states, although more coherent in 2010. As a part of financial packages to deal with public sector deficits in recent years, changes in VAT in several countries might again reduce these differences. Increased divergence has also taken place in relation to green-taxes (compare Table 4.8).

Historically, in the way the tax system provides incentives and motivates people towards specific action, it has also been an argument for implementing green taxes, although the revenue issue has been central. Furthermore, in the wake of the discussion on the options for green (renewable resource) taxes, there appear to be possibilities for both ensuring revenue and reducing the use of resources. However, the overall use of green taxes may only play a partial role (compare Table 4.8) in the financing of the welfare state in the EU. This is further mainly related to duties on fuel and gasoline.

Table 4.8   Revenue from green taxes as per cent of GDP in the EU-27, average, standard deviation and coefficient of variation (2000–2008)

	2000	2002	2004	2006	2008
Arithmetic average	2.8	2.7	2.9	2.7	2.6
Standard deviation	0.7	0.7	0.7	0.9	0.8
Coefficient of variation.	0.25	0.25	0.25	0.31	0.32

Source: Calculations based upon European Commission (2011a), Table II-5.1

There has not been an increase in the use of these taxes and duties since the mid-1990s. For all the EU-27 there has even been a slight reduction in this century in the use of this type of tax and duty. In some countries there has been an environmental tax reform, such as in Germany in 1999 (Koske 2010). It seems even to have been reduced indicating that a constant focus is needed to ensure the continuation of the use of financing as a way also to promote environmental sustainability.

Environmental taxes and duty are said to include a double dividend by making it possible to increase taxes at the same time as reducing pollution and lowering taxes on labour. However, the picture is blurred by the fact that if the policies work (for example if consumers and producers change their behaviour as a consequence of the new duty), it would have a negative impact on the size of revenue; a tax base of this kind would therefore be less stable (Koske 2010). Thus, the amount of revenue cannot be the only indicator of public sector impact or the influence of sustainable environmental development.

The overall picture of development in the last ten years in the EU countries shows that there have been only limited changes in the overall composition of the way the welfare states have been financed. Furthermore, there has not been any significant development towards a higher level of convergence (for example similarities among the tax systems), understood as the importance of the different levels of revenue from different taxes and duties. On the contrary, they have, in fact, become even more divergent regarding taxes on consumption and taxation related to sustainability in the area of environmental sustainability. Seen from this perspective, the tax system has not become more sustainable in the last ten years, nor has it become connected with increased pressure on spending or higher levels of debts and deficits (compare next section, which implies, all other things being equal, a higher level of pressure on the financing of the welfare states in the coming years).

Another problem with the above analysis is that this might hide some of the structural changes in the financing of the welfare states. In the last ten years, some important structural changes have taken place. From 1994 to 2010, the top personal income tax rates have declined in the OECD area from an average of 49.3

Table 4.9　　　**Public sector deficit as per cent of GDP in the EU-27, average, standard deviation and coefficient of variation (2000–2011)**

	2000	2001	2002	2003	2004	2005
Arithmetic average	-1.0	-1.6	-2.5	-2.7	-2.0	-1.5
Standard deviation	4.0	3.2	2.9	2.9	2.7	2.9
Coefficient of variation	-4,08	-2,00	-1,19	-1,11	-1,32	-1,95
	2006	**2007**	**2008**	**2009**	**2010**	**2011**
Arithmetic average	-0.9	-0.3	-2.1	-6.5	-6.3	-4.0
Standard deviation	3.2	2.9	3.3	3.8	5.8	3.6
Coefficient of variation	-3,45	-11,32	-1,60	-0,59	-0,91	-0.92

Source: Calculations based upon Eurostat (2012b) data

per cent to 41.5 per cent. The corporate income tax rate has dropped from 32.6 per cent to 25.4 per cent, on average, between 2000 and 2010. At the same time, the average VAT has remained stable, except for a slight increase from 17.8 per cent to 18.0 per cent in 2010 (Brys et al. 2011). Despite the fact that the overall structure has only slightly changed and that the revenue has been relatively stable as a percentage of GDP, the change in the system has tended to broaden the tax-base and lower the tax on movable income (for example corporate income). At the same time, there has been an inclination to lower the top tax rate as well as to place a greater focus on using the tax system in order to make work pay, compared to be on income transfer, even more than before.

If the distributional impact is also a part of what can be understood as a sustainable tax system, then it is important to analyse the impact of the chosen tax-and-duty structure on the degree of inequality.

Deficit and Debts as an Issue

The level of public sector deficit and debts will be discussed, as this also implies a pressure on the sustainability of public sector finances. A high level of debt can imply a higher level of interest on the debt, thus the deficit would require higher income and/or other taxes and duties, or an increase in economic growth. In recent years, the high deficit in the wake of the financial crisis can be expected to further influence the ambition to have a more prudent approach to public sector financing, including the building of a buffer to prevent the repetition of the present situation.

Tables 4.9 and 4.10 show the development of public sector deficit and debt.

Table 4.10   Public sector debt as per cent of GDP in the EU-27, average, standard deviation and coefficient of variation (2000–2011)

	2000	2001	2002	2003	2004	2005
Arithmetic average	49,5	49,3	48,7	48,9	48,5	47,4
Standard deviation	27,5	26,9	26,1	25,8	26,2	27,3
coef. of var.	0,56	0,55	0,54	0,53	0,54	0,58
	2006	2007	2008	2009	2010	2011
Arithmetic average	45,8	43,9	47,1	55,9	61,4	65,3
Standard deviation	28,0	27,9	28,5	29,9	32,2	35,8
coef. of var.	0,61	0,64	0,60	0,53	0,52	0,55

Source: Compare Table 4.9

Table 4.9 is a clear indication of increased diversity in the situation of the public sector in the EU, especially in the years after the financial crisis started. This is further depicted in Table 4.10, which shows the development of public sector debt as percentages of GDP since 2000.

The table indicates that although the overall average level of public sector debt has risen substantially since 2008, there has at the same time been a limited convergence (still this as compared to other indicators at a very high level). Thus the table indicates that the financial crisis had a strong negative impact on the public finances of all EU member states.

The overall picture gleaned from the above information is that the financial crisis has had a profound effect on the public sector deficit and the level of debt in most countries, thereby increasing the pressure on the welfare state. Naturally, a deficit due to rapid change in economic activity only is less a problem, from a sustainability point of view, than more structural deficits in the public sector. This also explains why the crisis and the measures taken have been so diverse in various countries. Increased pressure from an external economic shock is more problematic for a country which already has a high structural deficit and high public sector debt than for a country which is more stable and has low debt levels. This shows that countries might need to use different kinds of intervention strategies, depending on the overall level of public sector debt.

Impact of Change in Demography

Not only historical issues related to the structure of the tax system and the levels of debt and deficit have an impact on the sustainability of public finances. This is also the case with regard to how possible changes in demographic composition can influence the expected development in public sector spending on social security.

**Table 4.11   Changes in ageing and related public sector spending in OECD area
on average in per cent of GDP (2010–2025)**

	Health care	Long-term care	Pensions	Total
OECD Average	1.3	0.6	1.0	2.9

Source: OECD (2011b)

This is especially relevant given the expected increase in the number of elderly needing care. More specifically, in relation to care for the elderly (which is highly labour-intensive and where expenditures are expected to grow due to the demographic transition), countries have a variety of options in the organising and financing of long-term care.[3] In this respect, governments have the option of providing support either in cash, through services, or a mix of both. Most EU and OECD countries have collectively financed schemes for personal and nursing care costs. Naturally, having a universal system, as is the trend, does not in itself guarantee the size, depth or breadth of the services delivered. All the countries still face the real issue of balance between the roles of the private carer (mainly family) and that of the state. If the family's role is reduced (that is to the extent that the employment rate increases, especially for women), there may be pressure on public sector spending through the demand for more publicly provided service, especially care for children. In the longer-term, there may also be problems in finding the necessary labour supply, given the change in demographic composition. Table 4.11 shows the expected developments in ageing and related spending on average for OECD countries from 2010 to 2025.

It is evident that a scenario based on stylised calculations (that is not taking any future policy initiatives into consideration) and the assumption of a 1 per cent rise in healthcare spending over income per year is a challenge; nevertheless, it would be less so than is often assumed. If national governments are able to keep the level of growth in public sector spending in line with increases in national income spending and the population becomes healthier, the pressure from demographic transitions could be less than is often predicted.

Sustainable Financing Methods

Increased focus on using environmental taxes and duty to reach the 'double dividend' (that is less pollution and greater employment, resulting from the

---

3   For an overview of long-term care in Europe, including how it is organised and financed, cf. 'Special issue on Long-Term care in Europe', *Social Policy & Administration*, Vol. 4, 2010.

reduction of distortionary taxes on labour, for example) (Beuermann and Santarius 2006) can be seen as important for most EU countries (compare data on green taxation in Table 4.8). At the same time, a shift towards the use of green taxes could also increase growth by about 0.25 per cent in the short-term per 1 per cent of GDP change in taxation (Johansson et al. 2008). However, the development towards a higher use of these kinds of taxes and duty as instruments (as shown in Table 4.8) has not taken place. From 1995 to 2001, the share of tax stemming from green taxes declined slightly. However, over a longer period, it increased slightly as percentages of GDP from 2.2 per cent in 1980 to 2.8 per cent in 2001 (Albrecht 2006). A part of the reason is that changes in the composition of the tax system often relate to the need for more revenue, or a wish to lower taxation. Increases in environmentally-friendly taxation are often used to justify lower taxes on labour. This also helps explain why energy taxes are the most central.

Environment-related taxes and duties can be based on quantity used, time scale and access. In principle, environmental taxes should at least ensure that the marginal social cost of pollution is paid for by the polluter. One criticism is that the possibility of buying rights for emissions implies that the rich could continue to pollute, whereas low-income groups would implicitly have to sacrifice a relatively larger proportion of their income to pay green taxes. Another criticism is that if only one country introduced this kind of taxation, but the free movement of goods and services continued, the products would simply be produced in another country. Furthermore, tax reforms of this kind have met with opposition: there has been a lack of trust in that governments would recycle the revenue to lower taxes on wages (Dresner et al. 2006, Beuerman and Santarius 2006, Klok et al. 2006). A fair outcome of the increased use of environmental taxes and duties might be achieved by reducing taxes for very low income groups, or increasing income tax thresholds or the direct transfer of benefits (Clinch et al. 2006).

The UK serves as an example in the area of green taxation. They have implemented reforms to increase environmental incentives, including vehicle excise duty linked to emissions. However, the revenue has been declining slightly as a percentage of GDP, because the government stopped the annual above-inflation increase on fuel duty. They did this due to the risk of fuel poverty, that is, that especially poor families were highly influenced by change in these duties (Choe et al. 2007). The risk of having to trade between efficiency, reaching different revenue targets and the equality issue is therefore also at stake in relation to sustainability.

Further balance can be attained between environmental changes and the other elements of the tax and duty system. Another issue has been the fact that using environmental taxes and duties can be quite an administrative burden. The overall effect can be difficult to measure (for example the exact impact on the nature of different types of activities), whether pollution can be reduced by specific types of taxes such as those on CO_2, NO_x and SO_2. Therefore, it has been suggested that the focus should be on product differentiation, whereby sustainable products are not taxed, while non-sustainable ones are taxed (Albrecht 2006). However strong this argument might be in theory, it might be rather difficult to implement. The reason is the lack of precise data, including difficulties in establishing a specific borderline between different goods where substitution is possible. A good example is the taxation on transport: cars can move at different velocities (that is distances per kilometre); however, the time used for travel also relates to societal welfare. Consequently, even if it were environmentally more efficient for everyone to use public transport, it could reduce the overall level of production. Furthermore, if taxes on cars did not differentiate in the extent of pollution, there would not be any incentive to reduce pollution. Thus the low level of duty on gasoline in several countries might help explain why the incentive to make more energy-efficient cars has been very limited. This can also explain the lack of trust in such reforms: the argument for the idea that a 'simple tax shift contributes to the solution' (Beuermann and Santarius 2006: 923) is difficult to substantiate, because in principle unemployment and the environment are two very different and complex problems. If environmental tax reforms have been oversold, as is argued in several countries (Klok et al. 2006, Beuerman and Santarius 2006), this might also help explain why it has been less emphasised on the agenda in recent years in relation to reforms of the tax and duty system.

Furthermore, analyses indicate that there might be possibilities for at least some reduction in energy consumption based on imposing environmental taxes and duty (Agnolucci 2009); this also refers to a study based on 140 simulations showing that 'reductions in carbon emissions can be significant' (Agnolucci 2009: 3044). These reductions can be achieved without a negative impact on employment. The possible negative impact on employment relates to the issue of whether a country is to change the tax system alone, thereby risking lower competitiveness vis-à-vis other countries. This also points to the fact that using duty in order to reduce environmental problems might best be done through concerted actions.

Even if there is the option of reducing the negative impact on the environment from production and consumption, another question arises as to whether this reduction would be sufficient in the case of an increase in the average income and the expectation that those with a lower consumption level expect to attain a higher one in the future (that is there would be an increase in the overall level of production, thereby creating a greater impact on the environment).[4] This illustrates the risk that classical Keynesian demand management for increasing employment might actually 'be environmentally destructive' (Forstater 2006). Nevertheless, the analyses indicate that development in taxes and duties has not shown a clear trend or focus on this type of financing.

There is still, however, a need for a more detailed understanding of what sustainable financing is. The Economic and Monetary Union of the EU has set targets of a maximum of 3 per cent public sector deficits and a maximum of 60 per cent public sector debt. Thus the question is whether these are sufficient criteria

---

4   This discussion is not only European, but relates to a more global framework. This is, however, not within the scope of this chapter.

when related to other types of sustainability (that is environmental, demographic and equity issues). Furthermore, it is important to see how different ways of using the financial system might have an impact on the growth of the economy.

At least the debate on sound public finance is not new. The balanced budget multiplicator in several economic textbooks shows this, but Lerner (1943) also points out that financing should not be judged based upon overall effects or only on sound finance, as the impact of changes on the public sector economy and the level of activities also depend on the overall economic situation in a country (compare below on economic growth).

The demographic impact on the welfare states has been discussed, analysed and debated for years now. The challenge is that the number of elderly compared to the young will increase due to the fact that the average life expectancy has increased and the fertility rate has been below the reproduction level. However, there are a number of problems related to taking merely demographic data into consideration (Greve 2006). The implication is that if issues such as living a healthier life and the use of new welfare technology are included, the pressure from demographic changes in many welfare states may not be profound.

In relation to ensuring economic growth, there is the challenge of choosing appropriate financial instruments, given that economic growth will have a positive impact on sustainability; this typically has an impact on both the overall level of public sector spending and income.[5] An OECD study has thus pointed to the general rule that the growth of taxes on immovable property has the least impact and that taxes on corporations have the highest impact (Johansson et al. 2008). However, as indicated in the presentation of how the tax and duty systems work and the types of impact and goals they have, this has to be considered against the impact of the overall efficiency of the system, as well as the impact on distribution, allocation and stabilisation.

The nation state might be defined by and related to its taxation powers: 'The diversity of the tax base is a telling indicator of the ability of the state to engage with different sectors and regions, and is indicative of the degree to which state authority permeates society' (Di John 2011: 270). The study also points to the clear issue, as indicated above, that the state has to balance equity and growth.

This then again refers to the welfare state as an investment state (for example in establishing care for children to enable both the mother and father to be a part of the labour market), as has been seen in most EU countries, and also in corporatist and liberal welfare regimes, which have previously been seen as rather service-lean states (Fleckenstein 2010). Whether one focuses on sustainable social development over sustainable development (that is more focus on investment and social issues than merely the financial sector) is a more normative question, as some suggest (Tangian 2010). However, social policies can be seen as having an impact on

---

5 This is not the place to discuss issues concerning how to measure economic growth, whether GDP is a good measure for this, or the impact of economic growth on environmental sustainability and happiness.

reducing risk in modern societies and influencing economic development through the provision of a more extensive welfare state.

This also points to the fact that the fiscal sustainability of a welfare state is not only narrowly related to the national economic development, but also to external shocks such as the financial crisis that started in 2008. Given that this was not clearly foreseen, it highlights another issue: that long-term forecasting is a very difficult issue, as individuals have the tendency to extend their actual knowledge and understanding, but not take into account what happens over time with different types of unexpected shocks in the economy (for a longer discussion of outliers and Black Swans see Taleb 2010). Nevertheless, the public sector has had the ability to dampen the impact of the fiscal cycle, although unemployment insurance itself seems not to have always had a clear and consistent cyclical pattern (Lefresne 2010).

Earlier automatic stabilisers have generally been fully used during economic crises in most countries. However, automatic stabilisers can only be used for a limited period of time (that is if the crisis is very long and deep, the level of debt will become too high despite the fact that the deficit might return to a lower level).

It can thus be argued that the way to ensure sustainable finance is through several different channels, including more efficient use of public sector spending; furthermore, 'given the magnitude of fiscal consolidation required, the spending cuts will most likely have to be accompanied by revenue raising measures' (Koske 2010: 18). Phasing out tax concessions and changes towards a better structure for the tax base as well as increasing environmental taxes and duties could also be elements of fiscal consolidation. This implies a greater focus on taxes on consumption and property, as they have less impact on growth. For use on houses and land, it is also argued that 'the tax base is relatively stable' (Koske 2010: 20). Tax expenditures thus 'cause inefficiencies, reduce revenue, and undermine fairness' (Hagemann 2012: 2).

The ability to ensure compliance within the tax system is also an important aspect of a sustainable tax system. Even with what in principle are the same tax rates, the lack of compliance implies an overall lower level of public sector income. Especially in relation to multinational companies and small open economies, both national and international collaboration can be seen as an important part of a possible strategy to be used in order to ensure sustainability in the financing of the welfare state (compare also Matthews 2011, OECD 2011b).

Conclusion

This chapter has shown that no further convergence in the way that revenues are generated within the EU countries has taken place over the last ten years. The level of revenue has remained relatively stable as a proportion of the overall economy, making the financial situation less stable given the increase in spending as well as the effects of the financial crisis. At the same time, there have been trends towards a broader tax-base, but also lower tax rates, especially for corporate income tax and taxes on the highest income earners. This will also be a challenge for welfare states in the future.

For this reason, it seems that a variety of measures is needed to ensure fiscal sustainability with regard to creating long-term stability in public finances while taking environmental issues into consideration. However, there is still a gap in knowledge in that the long-term impact of tax reforms is difficult to disentangle from other changes in public sector spending/income and societal development.

There is a further need to be more precise about what sustainable financing is and what it can be. This includes measures on the level of deficits and debts (as the type within the EU finance pact), as well as determining what types of instruments can best ensure sustainability in the financing of the welfare states. This also involves taking initiative in ensuring compliance with the rules and paying the taxes and duties as prescribed in the legislation.

Given the continued pressure on the welfare states and the stability of development in employment, it can be important to have automatic stabilisers in place to reduce changes in the level of unemployment. Thus in the future, employment in social services can be an important part of reducing the yearly change in the level of unemployment (compare Chapter 6).

There is also a need to continuously be aware of how and to what extent the welfare states are influenced by the on-going and presumably frequent and different types of external shocks. How to finance the welfare states in the most efficient way thus also raises questions about the composition of taxes and duties, given the different purposes and ambitions of the tax systems.

Those measures already implemented show that there could be a rule enacted even for the structural deficit. A limit to the structural deficit should in principle not be a hindrance to active fiscal stimulus in times of crisis; however, unless there has been a focus on ensuring a surplus in prosperous times, there might be a stronger focus on public sector spending, despite the fact that deficits in public sector finance can be changed both by variation in expenditures and income.

A continuous focus on the tax-base and its broadening through the reduction of loopholes and tax concessions also seem to be ways of ensuring sustainable revenue for the public sector; this has been in line with the trends of recent years. This also emphasises that looking merely at tax-rates – whether for persons or companies – does not necessarily provide the information needed for a comparative analysis. Moving towards a higher reliance on non-movable assets (that is property) can also contribute to more stable development.

Furthermore, compliance with the rules seems to be even more important given the constraints on various types of taxes and duties of increasingly open economies. International cooperation to ensure compliance and agreement on part of the tax-structure, to avoid competition on the level and composition of the tax-system, can be important in the future.

The sustainable financing of the welfare state could further enhance the option for sustainability in the provision of social service, as this would imply a lower risk of the possibility that cuts and reductions in services are needed in order to ensure balanced public sector finances.

Appendix

Annex 4.1   **Social protection benefits in percentages of GDP (2000–2010)**

GEO/TIME	2001	2002	2003	2004	2005	2006	2007	2008	2009	2010
EU-27	:	:	:	:	26.0	25.7	25.0	25.7	28.5	28.2
Belgium	24.7	25.4	26.1	26.1	26.0	25.7	25.5	26.5	28.9	28.4
Bulgaria	:	:	:	:	14.6	13.8	13.7	15.0	16.7	17.6
Czech Republic	18.1	18.8	18.8	18.0	17.8	17.4	17.5	17.5	19.7	19.5
Denmark	28.4	28.8	30.0	29.8	29.4	28.5	28.0	28.6	32.3	32.4
Germany	28.7	29.3	29.7	29.1	29.0	27.9	26.8	27.0	30.2	29.4
Estonia	12.8	12.5	12.4	12.8	12.4	12.0	12.0	14.8	19.1	17.9
Ireland	14.1	15.9	16.5	16.7	16.7	17.0	17.6	21.0	26.0	28.3
Greece	23.6	23.4	22.7	22.9	24.2	24.1	24.1	25.4	27.4	28.2
Spain	19.2	19.5	19.8	19.8	20.1	20.0	20.2	21.6	24.7	25.2
France	27.8	28.6	29.2	29.5	29.6	29.6	29.3	29.7	31.9	32.0
Italy	23.8	24.3	24.8	25.0	25.3	25.5	25.4	26.4	28.5	28.6
Cyprus	14.7	16.0	18.0	17.8	18.0	18.2	17.8	18.6	20.8	21.3
Latvia	14.4	13.8	13.3	12.6	12.3	12.4	11.0	12.5	16.7	17.6
Lithuania	14.3	13.6	13.1	13.0	12.8	12.9	14.0	15.6	20.6	18.3
Luxembourg	20.5	21.2	21.7	21.9	21.3	20.0	19.0	21.0	23.6	22.3
Hungary	19.1	20.0	20.9	20.4	21.5	22.0	22.3	22.5	23.0	22.5
Malta	17.2	17.3	17.7	18.4	18.2	18.1	17.8	18.2	19.7	19.6
Netherlands	24.8	25.8	26.5	26.4	26.0	27.0	26.7	26.9	29.7	30.2
Austria	27.7	28.1	28.5	28.2	27.8	27.4	26.9	27.6	29.7	29.5
Poland	20.5	20.7	20.7	19.7	19.2	19.0	17.8	18.2	18.8	18.6
Portugal	19.2	20.9	21.6	22.3	22.9	23.0	22.6	23.2	25.6	25.5
Romania	12.5	13.3	12.8	12.5	13.2	12.4	13.2	14.1	16.9	17.4
Slovenia	23.8	23.8	23.1	22.8	22.5	22.2	20.7	20.9	23.6	24.3
Slovakia	18.4	18.5	17.8	16.6	15.9	15.7	15.4	15.5	18.2	18.0
Finland	24.2	24.9	25.7	25.8	25.9	25.6	24.6	25.4	29.5	29.7
Sweden	29.7	30.5	31.6	31.0	30.5	29.8	28.6	28.9	31.4	29.9
United Kingdom	25.9	25.1	25.3	25.5	25.6	25.5	24.0	25.2	28.1	27.1

Source: Eurostat (2012b)

Annex 4.2   Total receipts from taxes and social contribution in percentages of GDP (2000–2011)

GEO/TIME	2000	2001	2002	2003	2004	2005	2006	2007	2008	2009	2010	2011
EU-27	40.6	39.7	39.1	39.1	38.9	39.2	39.7	39.7	39.5	38.6	38.6	39.0
Belgium	45.1	45.1	45.2	44.7	44.8	44.8	44.4	43.9	44.2	43.4	43.8	44.1
Bulgaria	31.5	30.8	28.5	31.0	32.5	31.3	30.7	33.3	32.3	29.0	27.5	27.2
Czech Republic	33.8	33.8	34.6	35.5	35.9	35.7	35.3	35.9	34.5	33.4	33.5	34.5
Denmark	49.4	48.5	47.9	48.1	49.1	50.9	49.7	48.9	47.8	47.8	47.5	47.7
Germany	41.7	39.8	39.3	39.5	38.6	38.6	38.9	39.0	39.1	39.7	38.2	38.9
Estonia	31.0	30.2	31.0	30.8	30.6	30.6	30.7	31.4	31.9	35.9	34.1	32.8
Ireland	31.3	29.6	28.4	28.8	30.0	30.6	32.1	31.6	29.8	28.3	28.3	28.9
Greece	34.6	33.2	33.7	32.1	31.3	32.2	31.7	32.5	32.1	30.5	31.7	32.4
Spain	34.1	33.7	34.2	33.9	34.7	35.9	36.8	37.1	33.0	30.7	32.1	31.4
France	44.2	43.8	43.3	43.1	43.3	43.8	44.1	43.4	43.2	42.1	42.5	43.9
Italy	41.5	41.2	40.5	41.0	40.4	40.1	41.7	42.8	42.7	43.0	42.5	42.5
Cyprus	30.0	30.7	30.9	32.2	33.0	35.0	35.8	40.1	38.6	35.3	35.6	35.2
Latvia	29.7	28.9	28.6	28.6	28.6	29.2	30.6	30.6	29.2	26.6	27.2	27.6
Lithuania	30.0	28.6	28.3	28.0	28.1	28.4	29.3	29.5	30.1	29.2	27.0	26.1
Luxembourg	39.2	39.8	39.3	38.2	37.4	37.6	35.9	35.7	37.5	39.3	37.6	37.3
Hungary	39.8	38.7	38.0	38.0	37.7	37.4	37.3	40.5	40.4	40.1	37.9	37.0
Malta	27.9	29.7	30.6	31.1	32.2	33.7	33.9	34.6	33.6	34.0	33.0	33.7
Netherlands	39.9	38.3	37.7	37.4	37.5	37.6	39.0	38.7	39.2	38.2	38.8	38.4

Annex 4.2   Continued

GEO/TIME	2000	2001	2002	2003	2004	2005	2006	2007	2008	2009	2010	2011
Austria	43.1	45.0	43.7	43.5	43.1	42.2	41.6	41.8	42.8	42.5	42.0	42.2
Poland	32.6	32.2	32.7	32.2	31.5	32.8	33.8	34.8	34.3	31.8	31.8	32.4
Portugal	31.1	30.9	31.4	31.7	30.5	31.4	32.2	32.8	32.8	31.0	31.5	33.2
Romania	30.2	28.6	28.1	27.7	27.3	27.9	28.6	29.1	28.1	27.0	26.9	27.3
Slovenia	37.3	37.5	37.8	38.0	38.1	38.6	38.3	37.7	37.3	37.3	37.8	37.2
Slovakia	34.1	33.1	33.0	32.9	31.5	31.4	29.3	29.3	29.3	28.9	28.1	28.6
Finland	47.4	44.9	44.8	44.3	43.6	44.1	43.9	43.1	43.0	43.0	42.6	43.6
Sweden	51.9	49.6	47.7	48.0	48.3	49.1	48.5	47.6	46.7	46.9	45.7	44.6
United Kingdom	37.4	37.2	35.9	35.7	36.2	36.8	37.6	37.1	38.7	35.8	36.5	37.2

Source: Eurostat (2012b)

Chapter 5

Social Innovation in Social Services

Tomáš Sirovátka and Bent Greve

Introduction

Innovation and social innovation have become a topic of discussion in social sciences. Throughout welfare states there has been an expansion of innovative approaches and practices that aim to address social needs and challenges better and more efficiently than the traditional solutions thanks to the actors which are close to the service users. Mobilisation of the social capital of the actors, 'community social capital' as well as empowering of the users contributes both to tailored and effective service and cost efficiency of the service. This experience implied that 'social innovation' has become a part of the Europe 2020 strategy. In the conditions of crisis and pressures on the public budgets the policy goal to implement such innovative approaches and practices gain much support both on national and European level.

Basically, there are four streams in the discussion on innovation issue in social service. The first stream of the discussion is concerned with the role of innovation in the knowledge economy. It focuses on innovation in technologies (typically ICTs) and also on organisational forms like in business and public management as well as to the uses of their synergy (for example Room et al. 2005).

The second stream of discussion is focusing on innovation in the public sector (for example Bloch 2010). This stream looks into two types of innovation in the public sector: the first is the support to private businesses in innovations and their dissemination. The second is the innovation in effective and efficient provision of the public services of various kinds.

The third stream of discussion more explicitly aiming at social innovation is dealing with the governance reforms in various kinds of social services – although these governance reforms are not often strictly labelled as innovations. Nevertheless, many authors understand them as specific types of innovation (for example Bode 2006, Jensen 2009) while others rather understand them simply as governance reforms like marketisation, decentralisation, new public management or networking, expected to increase effectiveness and efficiency in service delivery (Dingeldey and Rothgang 2009, Wollman and Marcou 2010, van Berkel et al. 2011, and others).

The fourth stream of discussion is concerned with social innovations as grass roots initiatives by the civil society and hence it pays much attention to the strategies of empowerment and new solutions suited to the needs of the most marginalised groups in society enabling their social inclusion (for example Klein and Harrison 2007).

The above-mentioned streams of discussion are closely interlinked.

The role of innovation in social services and public sector is associated with five general processes in post-industrial society:

1. The overall shift towards the knowledge economy;
2. The societal challenges emerging from 'new social risks': outdated skills in the labour market, needs of combination of work and family, ageing of society, social exclusion due to insufficient access to social services (see Bonoli 2006, Taylor-Gooby 2004a);
3. The increasing financial pressures on the public budgets and on adequate financing of social services (see Gough 2011);
4. The changing forms of governance – from the one hand public-private mix has become an important form of service delivery since participation of private bodies and NGOs implies more room for innovation processes (see Room et al. 2005); from the other hand post-new public management practices are leading to the substantial innovations in governance of public services;[1]
5. The manifold technological innovation, information and communication technologies (ICT) and other which bring new possibilities in ensuring demanding health and social care services (see OECD 2012a).

The need for social innovation is increasing with the pressures on public budgets due to crisis and secondly, with an effort to improve the quality and scope of the services to respond the abovementioned social problems. On the other hand '...the crisis is likely to have a paradoxical effect: while it may prompt civil society social actors to device, out of necessity, more innovations and more solutions to difficult situations, it will also cause them to suffer badly due to the public expenditure cuts made in its wake' (Hubert et al. 2010).

The governance reforms in the welfare states are aiming to solve the above dilemma. Reforms like decentralisation, marketisation and competition, new public management and interagency cooperation are motivated by a set of expectations on their ability to increase efficiency in the public sector. For example decentralisation is typically associated with the possibility of policy flexibility, the adaptability and responsiveness to local needs and circumstances and the capacities of the local partners to develop a more integrated provision of services suited to the individual problems. New public management is supposed to deliver the mechanisms by

---

1   A new wave of public-sector reforms emerged during the 1990's ('post-NPM', Christensen and Lægreid 2010) as reaction to the failures of NPM. Instead of quasi-markets and incentivising the actors with help of the methods of corporate governance these new reforms rather rely on the long-term, trust-based, collaborative relations/networks between individuals/organisations while enhancing central control and accountability.

which public policies can be designed more in terms of steering by targets and of accountability in results. This may also entail the stimulation of interagency cooperation, which by itself is deemed to be more effective by combating silo management and by enhancing a greater choice and voice for the clients (van Berkel et al. 2012).

In recent years, many reforms and changes in governance and substance of social services provided in different countries have been observed. These changes have brought a lot of innovative solutions of service regulation, financing and delivery. In this chapter the notion of innovation and social innovation, and different forms of social innovation will first be presented. The links between social innovation and governance of social services will then be shown.

Understanding Social Innovation

The OECD and Eurostat (OECD 2005a) define innovation as 'the implementation of a new or significantly improved product (good or service), or process, a new marketing method, or a new organisational method in business practices, workplace organisation or external relations.' Here an innovation is defined as being one of four types of innovations – product, process, marketing or organisational: the overall definition is dependent on the individual types of innovations.

Bloch (2010) refers to Koch and Hauknes (2005) who proposed the following definition of innovation: 'Innovation is a social entity´s implementation and performance of a new specific form or repertoire of social action that is implemented deliberately by the entity in the context of the objectives and functionalities of the entity´s activities.' Innovations are thus new, implemented, and intentional, and can refer to broad range of changes in the organisation. The Audit Commission (2007) conducted an innovation survey of local government authorities in the UK which defined innovation as: 'practices undertaken by organisations in order to improve the product or service they provide, characterised by: Change – step-change and impact; Novelty – new to the organisation in question; Action – completed, not just an idea.'

Bloch (ibid.) then suggests the new definition:

> An innovation is the implementation of a significant change in the way organisation operates or in the products it provides. Innovations comprise new or significant changes to services and goods, operational processes, organisational methods, or the way organisation communicates with users. Innovations must be new to organisation, although they can have been developed by others. They can either be the result of decisions within organisation or in response to new regulations or policy measures.

Innovation in the profit sector is typically defined as a process for better aligning products and services to the requirements of the client, and three main types of non-technological innovations are recognised: new services conceptions, new interfaces with clients and new systems of service delivery (UNECE 2011: 7).

From the discussion on the innovation the distinction of four types of innovation emerges:

1. A product innovation, which is the introduction of a service or good that is new or significantly improved compared to existing services or goods in the organisation. This includes significant improvements in the service or good's characteristics, in customer access or in how it is used.
2. A process innovation, which is the implementation of a method for the production and provision of services and goods that is new or significantly improved compared to existing processes in the organisation. This may involve significant improvements in for example, equipment and/or skills. This also includes significant improvements in support functions such as IT, accounting and purchasing.
3. An organisational innovation, which is the implementation of a new method for organising or managing work that differs significantly from existing methods in the organisation. This includes new or significant improvements to management systems or workplace organisation.
4. A communication innovation, which is the implementation of a new method of promoting the organisation or its services and goods, or new methods to influence the behaviour of individuals or others. These methods must differ significantly from existing communication methods in organisation (see Bloch 2010).

The above distinction of types of innovation may be applied in social services. Coming from the general definition, innovation in social services thus may be understood as a change and novelty leading to the improvement of product, process, method or organisation, and communication. The other stream of innovations is only partly overlapping with point 4 above; rather, the recently emerging new welfare technologies in health and social services represent a specific category of innovation. The new technologies are intended to enable people to live in their home without compromising their safety and well-being, to increase appropriateness, quality, timeliness and efficiency of service, and to reduce health and social care expenditure at the same time. There are several technologies distinguished here according to the purpose and type of technology: communication support (including monitoring, social groups, patient information); compensatory and assistive technologies (including safety systems, tracking system, cognitive training); help to everyday practical tasks, disease monitoring and remote treatment (OECD 2012a:5).

Nevertheless, social innovation also includes some other aspects which are related to social well-being, social needs and social potentials. Hubert et al. (2010: 7 and 21) explains that social innovations are 'new responses to pressing social demands, which affect the process of social interactions. It is aimed at improving social well-being'. More specifically these are:

- Innovations that are social both in their ends and their means (like new ideas – products, services and models)
- That simultaneously meet social needs (more effectively than alternatives)
- Create new social relationships or collaborations that are not only good for society but also enhance society's capacity to act.

Similarly, the definition by Phills et al. (2008) is a good reference point in that

> Social innovation is a novel solution to a social problem that is more effective, efficient, sustainable, or just than existing solutions and for which the value created accrues primarily to society as a whole rather than private individuals.

The literature refers strongly to the dimensions of social relationships, social capital, participation, empowerment, trust and social inclusion. Moulaert et al. (2005) state that:

> Social innovation is path-dependent and contextual. It refers to those changes in agendas, agency and institutions that lead to a better inclusion of excluded groups and individuals in various spheres of society at various spatial scales; Social innovation is very strongly a matter of process innovation – that is changes in the dynamics of social relations, including power relations.

Similarly, Hubert et al. (2010) emphasise the social return produced by social innovations, through the creation of new social relationships or partnerships which involve the end users. This all makes policies more effective. BEPA societal brief on Social innovation (October 2009) recognises social innovation as:

> A means to empower citizens to be actively engaged in an innovative and learning society and to recognise the value of social capital.

This dimension is crucial in another respect: to make the actors involved in also being able to see social challenges as opportunities and to mobilise their creativity (for example Hubert et al. 2010).

The recent work on social innovation in social services (Caulier-Grice et al. 2012) defines social innovation as follows:

> Social innovations are new solutions (products, services, models, markets, processes, and so on) that simultaneously meet a social need (more effectively than existing solutions) and lead to new or improved capabilities and relationships and/or better use of assets and resources. In other words, social innovations are both good for society and enhance society's capacity to act.

The abovementioned definitions of social innovation may help to assess the effects and the innovative potential of the changes in governance of social services. The following aspects of social innovation are central in this respect:

Social innovations meet new social needs or better meet the already existing social needs (of specific vulnerable groups, communities or society as a whole);

1. Social innovations find new ways/initiatives in meeting social needs which are more effective and/or efficient and/or sustainable than the alternatives (by which three aspects are included: functionality, quality and economics);
2. Social innovations empower people by giving them a voice, allowing them to participate and increasing their capabilities (in terms of Sen's understanding of the notion);
3. Social innovations turn social challenges to opportunities perceived by creative actors;
4. Social innovations increase social capital, social trust and enhance society's capacity to act at the general level as well as on the local.

When assessing the dynamics of social services and their governance, these aspects should serve as the main reference points/benchmarks.

Thus social innovation is an intentional implementation of a new and improved product, process, organisation, method, or communication/promotion which is leading to the better satisfaction of the societal needs and/or it enhances the potential of the actors involved to act effectively and efficiently and/or it also empowers the service users (they are user-driven). This means that the positive societal objectives and effects (in terms of needs satisfaction) and/or the ability and creativity of the actors to needs satisfaction and participation/empowerment represent the reference points/benchmarks. Of course there might be different indicators of social innovation: the provision of the adequate service, sufficient scope and quality of the service, cost effectiveness, sustainability of the provision of the service and social well-being in general. The assessment of needs satisfaction depends very much on the position of the stakeholders involved, especially the service users and employees in social services.

A distinction is between innovation as such and successful innovation. As some authors claim, the main output of innovations are the innovations themselves – the actual implementation of changes to services or other parts of the organisation's operations. Then:

> ...successful innovation is associated with some form of performance improvement, either in terms of higher quality in the organisation's activities, increased efficiency, or both. In addition, innovation efforts can be associated with greater satisfaction among both employees and users. Social outcomes (social cohesion, equality, reduced crime, poverty reduction, better educated population, improved health, and so on) are also important, as they represent central aims of public services. Moreover, successful innovation can carry other,

intangible benefits, such as improving the image of the organisation and the services it delivers, thus strengthening its legitimacy and trust from users or other stakeholders. (Bloch 2010: 24)

In this understanding of innovation the social outcomes are a central point. The consideration about some improvements in meeting social needs is also possible to specify: more precisely the social innovations should bring any (or more) of the following impacts (Bloch 2010):

- Address social challenges (like health problems, inequalities, others).
- Fulfil new regulations, policies or other politically mandated changes.
- Improve the quality of services or goods.
- Increase efficiency (costs per service/good; reduced administration).
- Improve user satisfaction.
- Improve online services.
- Improve working conditions for employees in social services.

With respect to the above possible impacts of the innovations in social services the notion of 'improvement' may be understood differently in public sector contexts, and depend – as mentioned already – on the perspective of the respective stakeholders. Whereas companies in the private sector operate with a single objective, public organisations count on a multiplicity of objectives, for example increase quality, equity and efficiency (Bloch 2010).

Kelly et al. in Bloch (2010) identify three forms of value creation in the public sector: services, social outcomes and trust. Value creation in services may take place through increased efficiency, improved quality, user satisfaction, increased usage of services, greater equity (fairness) in service provision or greater choice or variety. Social outcomes such as social cohesion, equality, reduced crime, poverty reduction, better educated population or improved health, represent central aims of public services. So, the range of social objectives and outcomes is broad.

For many of social and public services there are no well-functioning markets to provide services for those that need them. In this sense public activities can be seen as compensations for shortcomings in market economies. Trust and legitimacy are also identified as important public objectives, as they will influence user satisfaction with public services and the public sector's ability to achieve broader societal goals. Among the objectives here are improved public perceptions of public service institutions, accountability of public service institutions in meeting public needs, and beliefs that public sector activities are aligned with stated societal objectives (Bloch 2010).

Social innovations, however, do not represent a separate stream: rather, they overlap with the other kinds of innovations and 'absorb' them. 'Social innovation in organisations, policies, rules and regulations as well as in collective norms, values and cognitive frames are needed to complement the more traditional technological and economic innovations, in order to reach systematic synergies, productivity growth, increasing returns and steadily growing incomes' (Hamalainen and Heiskala, in Hubert et al. 2010).

The Forms of Social Innovation

From the general perspective there are two main forms of innovation:

1. Innovation in the substance of the policies/social services which is leading to the better satisfaction of societal needs;
2. Innovation in organisation or in governance of the policies/social services which is expected to create the preconditions for better satisfaction of societal needs and which enhances the potential of the actors to do so.

Such a distinction is in line with the distinction of the formal (substantive) and procedural (organisational) reforms within the welfare state (Carmel and Papadopoulos 2003). The above aspects are closely connected with each other.

From another perspective social innovations may be classified depending on the level where social innovation takes place. Three broad categories according to the level of implementation of social innovation can be distinguished (Phills et al. 2008):

1. Grass roots social innovations that respond to the pressing social needs and demands not addressed by the market and are directed towards vulnerable groups of society.
2. Broader level of social innovations that address societal challenges in which the boundary between social and economic blurs and which are directed towards society as a whole.
3. The systemic type of change that relates to fundamental changes in attitudes and values, strategies and policies, organisational structures and processes, delivery systems and services (often initiated by institutions, play a part in reshaping society as a more participative arena where people are empowered and learning is central).

The central focus here is in examining the third type of social innovation, since the greatest potential for social innovation in social services is expected to be generated in the welfare and governance systems: in regulation, financing and delivery of social services at the central, regional and local levels. The systemic changes in governance structures and procedures are again crucial to the potential of social innovation, since they also empower grass roots capacities and capabilities of individuals and groups. Finally, these innovations can have the greatest impact on the employment in social services.

The following governance levels of social innovation are explained in some detail:

- *Public Policy and Governance Innovation at the General/Central Level or Regional/Local Level*

This level of innovation is overlapping with the general level of the welfare state reforms both in substance and in governance undertaken with the objectives to improve product, process, organisation/method or promotion of social services in general or the performance capacity of the public sector and the other actors providing social services (see Dingeldey and Rothgang 2009, Wollman and Marcou 2010, van Berkel et al. 2011).

- *Local and Regional Development*

Social innovation in relation to territorial/regional development covers innovation in the social economy, that is strategies for satisfaction of human needs; and innovation in the sense of transforming and/or sustaining social relations, especially governance relations at the regional and local level (Klein and Harrison 2007). More recent works focus on the societal role of the economic life in terms of innovations in social practices and social relations at the local and regional levels. Social innovation, therefore, is increasingly seen as a process and a strategy to foster human development through solidarity, cooperation, and cultural diversity (Bloch et al. 2010).

- *Social Economy and Social Entrepreneurship*

The typical form of social innovation is represented by the 'social entrepreneurial ventures' and 'socially innovative entrepreneurs' which are 'blending and integrating prominent social intentions and objectives (that is social change) with innovative and rigorous venture-development strategies' (Perrini 2005: 22). The social economy represents an area where innovative solutions are being developed to increase productivity and where opportunities for innovation are foreseen in, for example, services for older consumers, education, social and health services (Huber et al. 2006).

- *Grass Roots Initiatives*

Societal grass roots or 'bottom up' movements, self-organisation groups, citizen's initiatives, leading to local innovative projects (often run by NGOs), addressing social exclusion of specific vulnerable groups. They typically rely on their own resources, including volunteering and also give empowerment and voice to the target groups.

Focus here is mainly with the first level of social innovation, however, there is a need to assess the mainstream of top-down policy and governance of social services in the close relationship with the other levels since the innovations in the public policies and social services presume the synergy of all the other levels of activities in services and their innovation.

Governance and Social Innovation in Social Services

As we have already explained the innovation in governance systems – in other words – in the process of service organisation and delivery represents the central aspect of social innovations. These innovations are on the two mutually interlinked organisational levels:

1. The first one is the innovation at the level of the organisations which are providing social services, either they are public of private (for-profit, non-profit) organisations:

For this level Room et al. (2005) specified the organisational forms of innovation which include:

   a. Changing structures – that is shift towards less hierarchical design of organisations, decentralisation, and more flexible project-based organisational structures;
   b. Changing processes – intensive interaction and communication (role of ICT), people and knowledge they possess are recognised as key resources;
   c. Changing boundaries – focus on core competences, shift towards small, decentralised units, network economy.

According to (Bloch 2010) there are the following types of changes – innovations of the organisational forms that could be considered for the public sector: new incentive structures, new practices for gathering and disseminating knowledge, changes in organisational structure, new management systems (that is Lean management, Strategic Performance management, Quality management), new programs for developing staff competences or strengthening innovative capability and new external relations. It is argued that on a broad level there are four elements of how the innovation process is organised in public sector organisations: first, the placement of innovation in the organisation's overall strategy; second, the role of management in promoting innovation in the organisation; third, the structuring of innovation processes; and fourth, the competences within the organisation.

2. The second type of innovation is the innovation at the system level which means the organisation of the relationships among the various actors which influence the processes of service regulation, financing and delivery, and the modes and methods to coordinate their activities.

In recent years, social innovations have empowered people and organisations to develop participative solutions to pressing societal issues, having been generated by social entrepreneurs and grass roots organisations (Huber et al. 2006). A recent trend is the role played by the public sector, not only in supporting social innovation, but in implementing new internal participatory processes which change the way in which actors interact (ibid.). Some EU countries are leading the way in building innovation into their governmental structures and economies with new funds and teams, and with open processes like pooling resources to improve accessibility, quality and affordability.

The literature on governance in social services has until now mainly explored the new trends in regulation, financing and delivery of social services like marketisation, decentralisation and re-centralisation, networking and public-private partnership, corporate governance, empowerment and participation. At the same time, some consequences on the size, quality, access and costs of the services were explored (Seeleib-Kaiser 2008, Jensen 2008, 2009, Dingeldey and Rothgang 2009, Wollmann and Marcou 2010, van Berkel et al. 2011). The issue of social innovation was marginally addressed, although this is implicitly present in the new trends in governance. The impact of the trends on employment in social services (level, structure, quality) is the least explored issue.

Nevertheless, there is a trend of general convergence found in Western European countries with the emergence of a new type of government regulation. For example in caring services the new policies include these characteristics: i) they combine monetary transfers to families with the provision of in-kind services; ii) they establish a new social care market based on competition; iii) they empower the users through their increasing purchasing power; iv) they introduce funding measures intended to foster care-giving through family networks. They are associated with the decentralisation of government responsibilities at the local level, by providing incentives to develop private services and competition as well as support for some services like care in the family. Besides expanding care and curbing costs, citizens' choices and autonomy are better served at the same time (Pavolini and Ranci 2008, Jensen 2009). In employment services there is a similar trend of marketisation, decentralisation and recentralisation, new public governance, networking and empowering the clients (Dingeldey and Rothgang 2009, Wollmann and Marcou 2010, van Berkel et al. 2011).

Besides, studies focusing on the shift in public management towards 'new governance' emphasise the involvement of broader society in the process of governing, the role of self-organising networks, and policy communities (Rhodes 1992, Pierre and Peters 2000, Salamon 2002, 2005). Attention is shifted away from public organisation or specific public programs towards methods of fulfilling public intentions; away from hierarchical organisations towards organisational networks; from public versus private services towards public and private services, and so on.

In these more complex processes the distinct loci in the policy-making process – 'the political administrative system', mediating 'institutional relations' and the street-level bureaucracy (Hill and Hupe 2002: 183) – may produce innovative strategies and policies owing to their ability to reconsider the broad policy context, identify needs, redefine and negotiate goals and policies, and mobilise resources at the local level.

Social innovations are born from – and experimented within organisations – the processes of negotiating and implementing policies 'a deep reflection of social innovation requires reflection of collective action, a look at the actor and his/her relationships to the institutional environment he/she is confronted with, but at the same time, to the construction to which he/she contributes, through social compromises and governance regulations' (Klein and Harrison 2007: 6, own translation). Within this institutional context the external variables (social, economic, political) interact with the internal variables in organisations (past decisions which structure current relationships between actors – path dependency) (ibid.: 8). Some institutional and organisational arrangements characterised by the forms of governance which facilitate adoption and diffusion of innovations may create '*milieux innovateurs*' (ibid.: 11).

An effective coordination of different levels of governance requires a sufficient room for social innovations. This means, on the one hand, room for negotiating and establishing legitimate goals and setting/adjusting adequate rules and institutional structures, and providing the actors with adequate discretion and resources to follow the rules and to achieve the goals. Governance must be supportive of the processes of bottom-up policy institutional learning, creation of 'policy communities' ('policy collaborative networks'). 'Experimental implementation' (Matland 1995) sensitive to contextual conditions as well as to the needs of individuals, groups and communities may generate viable and effective 'program mutations' – innovations.

A supportive 'millieu' for innovation is developments of the various interactions of public and private actors. According to Bloch (2010: 17–18) there might be a number of different types or forms of public-private interaction (regardless of whether this involves innovation), including:

- Businesses as suppliers;
- Outsourcing of activities previously done by organisation itself;
- Privatisation of public services previously provided by organisation itself;
- Public-private collaborations in providing a service or completing a task;
- Businesses as users, involved in public sector activities (user groups, and so on);
- PPP – Public Private Partnerships, collaborative projects that involve both development and implementation.

Some authors like Pavolini and Ranci (2008) see the innovative potential for social services at the general level in combining state-market-family resources supported by two key innovations: split between providing and financing functions (that is quasi-market) and greater recognition of the citizen's freedom of choice.

According to the survey by European Commission (2011a) innovations improved the work of public administrations and only rarely had negative effects been reported. The positive effects of innovation included: improved user access to information due to service innovations; improved user satisfaction; more targeted services; a faster delivery of services; simplified administration; improved working conditions or employee satisfaction; and cost reductions resulting from innovations.

Bode (2006: 355) explains that 'the new governance regime in social services leaves greater room for creativity and local innovations, hence for meeting contemporary needs or reinventing routines. In cases where agencies find the right way to save money, manage to generate new synergies or succeed in political campaigning it becomes possible to offer new solutions to acute social problems.' On the other hand some problems might arise. Social welfare provisions become more heterogeneous in principle: this generates loss of resources when some providers achieve poor results. On the top of this local management of resources becomes critical for the quality of service.

Conclusions and Discussion

To summarise, social innovations meet social needs in new ways which are more effective than the alternatives by enhancing the capacity to act and by empowering the broad range actors, involved, including the users of services. The reforms in the governance of social services will be analysed in the four national cases (among other factors) from the perspective of social innovations and their effects which correspond to the above understanding of the notion of social innovation. This approach will have some implications: first it will take into consideration a variety of forms of innovations: they are related to the product (policy outcome), to the process, organisation/method and promotion. Second, it will further look at the relationship between the governance reforms in social services, on the one hand, and social innovations as improvements in the provisions of social services in substance (in the several aspects discussed above), on the other hand.

In other words, the analysis will examine how the reforms in governance – that is, in regulation, financing and service delivery – are associated with social innovation in the sense of the better satisfaction of societal needs, in enhancing the capacity and creativity of the actors to act in the process of providing the services, in providing more power to the users of services and, finally, in improving social capital, social inclusion and trust.

Briefly, social innovation may be understood as successful innovation in the above respects. For this reason, focus in the national studies is on the various aspects of governance like regulation (management, coordination and control, incentive mechanisms), delivery (role of different levels of governance, role of the actors, marketisation, forms of cooperation) and financing (forms and methods), and at the various indications of how the services meet the societal needs or how they enhance the capacity of the actors. These outcomes can be characterised by the quality and accessibility of the services, the scope of the services and coverage, service guarantee and user choice, and employment in social services. Lastly, attention will be on the question of how the governance framework and implementation conditions can contribute to the other factors to create an innovative milieu suitable for the implementation and dissemination of successful innovations in social services.

Chapter 6

Factors Shaping Employment in Social Services

Tomáš Sirovátka

Introduction

The role of social services in contemporary societies is increasing due to the complex of societal, economic and demographic changes and central hereto is the emergence of new social risks (Bonoli 2006, Taylor-Gooby 2004b), the quiet revolution in the role of women (Esping-Andersen 2008), ageing of society and the general trend towards a service economy. In this context, social services can meet the above challenges by providing various kinds of accessible, affordable and quality services. At the same time, they are becoming an important source of job generation, contribute to poverty reduction and strengthen social cohesion (European Commission 2010: 6).

The fast progress of modern social services can be tracked back to at least the end of the nineteenth century (see an example of French pre-school care in Bonoli 2006, or Bönker et al. 2010) but their importance has grown with the above-mentioned demographic, economic and societal processes since the 1970s (see Daguerre 2006). Jensen (2009) refers to studies by Allan and Scruggs (2004), Korpi and Palme (2003) and OECD (2005b) which found that transfer programmes have seen retrenchment, while welfare services have experienced an overall increase. For similar conclusions compare also European Commission (2008a).

The provision of social services varies greatly among European countries depending on the welfare state regime. The increasing emphasis on social services is further seen as a general contemporary trend in welfare state architecture. Taylor-Gooby (2004a: 224) argues that 'the new social risk policies now being developed do not invariably reflect the characteristics of the existing old social regime.'

Since most social services are financed or provided by the public sector, the economic pressures on public finance and the measures of fiscal consolidation adopted in the context of economic crisis make it difficult to meet the above-mentioned expectations towards the provision of social services and employment opportunities. Innovations in the governance of social services, like new combinations of public-private mixes and other new arrangements in service provision, should help both to overcome the financial pressures on public budgets and to provide adequate, flexible and quality services suitable for the needs and tastes of people.

Questions are emerging about the overall sustainable development of social services *per se* – about their capacity to provide the expected volume, quality and accessibility of service and, lastly, about their potential for job creation; the aim is for all of these to be achieved in the context of fiscal consolidation and sustainability.

In this chapter we focus on the last question – the prospects of sustainable employment in social services. However, this aspect cannot be split from the more general questions of the overall development of social services and their capacity to provide services in accord with the expectations of people. Focus here is on employment in social services and this serves as an indicator of their overall development, because the other indicators are not so easy to capture. When measuring the development of social services with the use of expenditure on social services (like in kind social protection expenditure) the difficulty arises that many services are supported through cash benefits used for purchasing a specific service. Similarly, mostly only public expenditure on social services is available for measuring. Lastly, a lot of difficulties emerge when measuring the coverage or volume of the real use of social services.

The assumption is that social services both directly and indirectly contribute to the higher level of employment not only in social services as a specific sector, but in other sectors of the economy as well:

1. Social services provide new jobs in social work, social security and social care, employment services, community services, and so on.
2. The employment services sector is providing additional employment by facilitating job mediation (matching effect), providing counselling and training (employability gains) and by creating subsidised jobs (lower costs of job creation for those who are disadvantaged in the labour market).
3. Caring services such as childcare and elder care help people balance work and family life – this usually leads to a higher level of total employment (the highest gains are evidenced in the employment rates of women).

Central here is the direct link as in point 1, concerned with the impact of the development of social services on employment in the specific sectors of social services. The question of employment in social services includes three highly relevant interconnected aspects: the first is the scope/level of employment in social services (job creation aspect: how many jobs?); the second is the quality of jobs in social services (job quality aspect: what kind of jobs?); and the third is the sustainability of jobs (sustainable employment aspect: are the jobs sustainable). This chapter deals mainly with the first aspect of the level of employment, although also briefly touching on the other two aspects of employment – job quality and sustainability of employment in social services.

The chapter is structured as follows: first a discussion of the general and specific factors which influence the overall development of social services and employment in social services: supply and demand factors; second, analysis of which of these factors are most relevant in the context of the economic crisis and austerity of the public budgets; third, presentation of basic empirical evidence about the scope of employment in social services in the last ten years and an examination of the indications about which factors have been most important for the level of employment in social services. The concluding section will summarise the findings and discuss the future development of social services.

Factors Influencing the Development of Social Services and Employment in Social Services

The range of drivers and factors which stipulate the developments of the provisions in social services is broad. Central is: demand factors and supply factors (see also Chapter 2). From another perspective the general drivers which influence the general trend of the growth of social services also have country-specific impacts – depending on other factors determining different paths of development of social services.

Demand Factors

The most important factors of employment in social services are the 'general drivers' of social service growth. It is assumed that the growth in demand of social services will be translated into growing employment in social services, since social services are a labour-intensive sector.

The changing of women's roles, their growing labour market participation and employment are leading to the increasing demand for social and community services, mainly care services. 'As the women's revolution matures, demand for child and elder care inevitably grows' (Esping-Andersen 2008: 79). Esping-Andersen argues about the strong association between day-care coverage and women's employment rates (1999: 60). Similarly, Bosch and Lehndorf (2001) documented a strong correlation between women's full-time, equivalent employment and the scope of social and community services ($r = 0.78$). In this respect, the defamilisation of care is becoming not only a policy facilitating a combination of work and family, but also a workable family policy which is relevant for investment in children, not to mention the prevention of poverty (for example Esping-Andersen 1999, McDonald 2002, Castles 2003). This is also compatible with the policy drive in many countries aiming to achieve more gender equality – although the aspirations are different in various countries, they are supported by EU recommendations (Barcelona targets, Europe 2020).

The change in women's roles, with multiple societal consequences, is a general trend in most countries, however, at the same time it is a country-specific factor. A number of studies have shown (Esping-Andersen 1999, McDonald 2002, Castles 2003, Esping-Andersen 2008, Jensen 2009) that welfare states differ very much not only in the dimension of de-commodification, which is associated with transfers/benefits in cash, but also in the dimension of defamilialisation, associated with benefits-in-kind/services: Jensen (2009) documents that the difference is due less to healthcare services and more to care services.

The above differences are emerging from different patterns of preference, in other words, from different *gender order* (Pfau-Effinger 2004), patterns of family and gender roles and consequently from the differences in the combinations of familialism and defamilialism in policies (for example Korpi 1999, Leitner 2003), as well as from the corresponding different patterns of female employment.

Thus, demand for social services is usually influenced by traditional as well as emerging preferred family models, culturally rooted shared beliefs and expectations around the roles of men and women in various countries. For example, in Germany the welfare state has been based on a legacy of Social Catholic thinking, the principle of subsidiarity and the traditional understanding of gender roles. The experience of fascism and state socialism increased reservations about public childcare (see Aust and Bönker 2004). In certain respects, a similar situation was traditional in Mediterranean countries (Greece, Italy and Spain), where women tended to prefer family to work (see Moreno 2004). In liberal regimes such as the UK, the dominant assumption is that care is primarily a private matter (Larsen and Taylor Gooby 2004), while in Nordic countries the availability of childcare has enabled labour market participation to become a norm for mothers (Timonen 2004).

Second, a more general trend is in place in the overall employment structure where services dominate over industrial production due to the demand shift towards sectors of services. This is compatible with Engel's Law: as nations become richer, consumption shifts from necessities towards 'luxuries'. In other words, 'the service economy is driven by broadening purchasing power throughout the population' and 'the disappearance of cheap domestic servants and of the housewife' (Esping-Andersen 2008: 4). Similarly, according to Wagner's Law (Wagner 1911), 'economic development creates demand for new types of government services, and that these government services will tend to rise at a faster pace than economic development' (Martínez-Vázquez and Yao 2009). Some empirical studies have found that the growth of the public sector is to a certain point driven by the economic development of the state, but afterwards, public sector employment becomes much more stable (ibid.).

In this respect, the impact of growing overall purchasing power may be different in various countries, depending on the income inequalities. Bosch and Lehndorf (2001: 24) have already denied the hypothesis that income differentials may help to combat the negative consequences of 'cost-disease' for employment in social services by creating demand from higher earners for the services offered by those earning less. They found a negative correlation ($r = - 0.64$) between the volume of work in the service sector and income differentials. Their finding rather supports the Keynesian assumption of the volatility of demand due to increasing income inequalities and provides an argument for the introduction of inbuilt stabilisers like income redistribution, among other things, in order to stimulate demand for services.

Income elasticity implies a stronger demand for social services in countries with a higher degree of income per capita and those where income inequalities are not very wide, like in Scandinavia. Besides overall wealth and income inequalities, the amount of subsidies provided within the country-specific service mix also plays a crucial role. As Esping-Andersen (2008: 105) suggests, 'unless subsidised, commercial social services are priced out of the market for most households below median income and [are] less accessible.' This will also have social repercussions: for example, if parents are unable to afford quality care, sub-standard care may be harmful to children. If women are withdrawn from the labour market, the risk of poverty for families increases.

Third, population ageing is an increasingly important driver of employment in social services due to rising demand for elder care, long-term care and health care (Bosch and Lehndorf 2001, European Commission 2010, Jensen 2008, 2009, Esping-Andersen 2008, Tepe 2009). Not only is there an increase in the volume of services needed with the increase in dependent people, but due to the 'level of dependence and the poly-pathologies of the elderly, long-term care services are increasingly called upon to provide more professional and often more medical services to a broader and more differentiated segment of the population. This trend will also impact on the skills required to provide these services' (European Commission 2008a).

Fourth, the emerging new social risks are increasingly pressing on the provision of various social services in order to meet the challenges of work–family reconciliation, especially for single parents (demand for care services): challenges emerging from the dynamics of the post-industrial labour markets like outdated skills in the labour market (demand for employment services and life-long learning) and challenges of poverty and social exclusion (demand for social assistance services, social housing, social work services and emergency services), see Chapter 2.

Lastly, when social services are easily accessible and of good quality they tend to create additional unsatisfied demand for these services. Lipsky (1980: 35) states that ' ... perceived availability of service pulls demand, not the other way around' and 'The better the program and more responsive it is to the needs of the citizens, the greater will be the demand for the service' (ibid.: 38). To conclude, path dependency is also due to the 'neofunctionalist' assumption that in post-industrial economies, social services play an increasing role due to women's employment and increasing skill demands. This trend is most apparent in those countries which follow a social investment strategy like that of Scandinavian countries; compare for example Esping-Andersen (2008) or Jensen (2009). We may argue that once social services are developed to a certain level, the economic and social systems become 'service dependent'.

In spite of the permanent austerity or financial crisis and pressures on public budgets, many aspects of the quality of life, labour market performance, employment and economy growth are very much dependent on the scope and quality of social services and built into the expectations and preferences of the economic and social actors.

Supply Factors

The most important supply factor is represented by Baumol's Disease (Baumol 1967) and its consequences: the problem is that productivity growth in the service sector is slower when compared to manufacturing. This implies that if wages in services are tightly coupled with wages in manufacturing, private service production will contract Baumol's disease and employment expansion will be slowed down. On the other hand, a *productivity lag* could foster employment growth in the sector if services were produced by government, or consumers were subsidised to purchase the services. As Esping-Andersen (2008: 111–114) explains, there are three possible responses to the cost-disease problem. First, allowing labour costs to adjust (market cleaning) may result in many services disappearing due to low earnings and lack of labour supply. Another possible approach is to adjust earnings in the services to the level of earnings in the overall economy (typical in Nordic and continental countries). Then, due to high labour costs, personal services grow very sluggishly, if at all (resulting in growth in joblessness). The third solution is to subsidise services via government production or subsidies to consumers (through something like special tax benefits).

Second, Jensen (2009) has emphasised another supply factor which consists of the increasing technical complexity of the provision of social services, which has played a role, for example, in health care, independent of the ideological/welfare regime constellation. For this reason, those countries with low spending in social services are expected to expand spending and the provision of services more rapidly. Third, another group of supply factors involve political interests and circumstances. The point of departure is that political elites are interested in electoral results and manoeuvre in order to avoid electoral punishment (in this respect, the theory of political-economic cycles is relevant). Most of the authors emphasise the risks which may emerge from cutbacks in social services. The down-sizing of the public sector can result in a loss of votes, especially if welfare programmes are involved (Tepe 2009). Similarly, Jensen (2009) posits that globalisation leads to an increase in welfare services because of the public's demands, which result from the public's fears of novel economic changes. Nevertheless, in some circumstances (see next paragraph, point ii) down-sizing of the public sector may be a rational strategy. Furthermore, there are some pressure groups in society (typically public sector employees, often engaged in social services, sometimes party members) in whose interest it is to promote employment in the public sector. In the context of fiscal austerity, it is assumed that policy-makers' dominant response toward growing personnel costs is to reduce public administration employment via privatisation. Nevertheless, Tepe (2009) notes that prior studies exploring the effect of fiscal austerity on welfare spending suggest that office-oriented policy-makers have limited willingness to scale down popular welfare services as such attempts involve a high risk of electoral punishment.

Fourth, path dependency is an important factor (Pierson 1994, 2005). In the period of welfare state expansion, social services have been well developed in some countries. As some authors argue (for example Huber and Stephens 2006, Anderson and Meyer 2006), this is because the expansion of social services was easier in the period of welfare state expansion (as took place in the Nordic countries) than in the phase of welfare state retrenchment, whereby new programs are hard to finance (through higher extraction from an existing source base) and rather require an expansion of the resource base and/or a reallocation of resources away from established programs.

In addition, in recent years many countries have followed the strategy of welfare state re-orientation with more emphasis on social services (European Commission 2008a, Jensen 2009). This path can be expected to continue the advancement of social services. The process works through several mechanisms. Jensen (2009) explains that in some countries (Nordic), well-developed policies in social services during the 'golden age' may persist long after the factors that caused them have been exhausted. More specifically, Tepe and Vanhuysse (2013a) following Bonoli (2007) formulate the 'timing hypothesis' claiming that the advancement of policies responding to new social risks (typically it is a substantial part of public/social services like education, ALMPs and childcare) is difficult for those countries which have been confronted with these risks later, in times of challenges emerging from population ageing and economic austerity affecting the welfare programmes.

Furthermore, the left-wing parties have continued to matter after the Golden Age. Due to financial pressures, these left-wing parties may often be better suited to implement retrenchment measures since they are more credible to the electorate than right-wing parties opposed by the public. It is not clear how the left-wing parties will resolve the distributional conflicts between different electorate groups in conditions of financial austerity and what fields of social services would be affected by cuts. For example, Keman et al. (2006) argue that the new risks groups are not overlapping with the established political parties and for this reason the, until now, strong association between the welfare state and political parties of Social Democracy and Christian Democracy which has been underpinned by the majority coalition of the working and middle classes is disappearing. This could have negative impact on the level of social services. Vested interests matter (Pierson 1994): service providers tend to form coalitions with service consumers. Since social services are labour-intensive and partly consist of highly skilled and influential professional groups (like civil servants, doctors and teachers), their interests are very likely to play a role.

Similarly, according to the *social security thesis*, the public sector serves as a buffer against the risk of economic instability. The expectation being that the public sector may be relatively large where other employment possibilities are scarce (see for example Rouban 2008, Pierre 2008), or that public employment grows as a response to growing unemployment (Tepe 2009). Tepe (ibid.) discusses and examines the assumptions on the determinants of public administration employment which are suggested by Cusack et al. (1989):

1. since governments follow anti-cyclical public employment policy in order to reap electoral benefit, growing unemployment should have a positive effect on public employment growth;
2. growing public budget deficits cause a reduction in the growth of public employment, whereas
3. growing GDP per capita should have the opposite effect.

Tepe's empirical analysis confirms the above assumptions. In contrast, the rising cost of public employment might in the future lead to a reduction. Following the theory of political business cycles, Tepe and Vanhuysse (2013b: 5) suggest that if voters evaluate incumbents on their recent performance, politicians can be expected to shift the use of the cycle mechanism towards policy domains that are easier for them to manipulate such as public employment which is more 'street visible'.

The user profile also plays a role: In healthcare and most social services, unlike in social transfer programmes, high- and middle-income individuals are also likely to be the users and these services are thereby likely to gain more electoral support. This is in line with the hypothesis of the Matthew effect: the welfare state will contribute most to the middle class.

The last group of factors emerges as the impact of governance reforms in social services like marketisation, decentralisation, public-private mix and new public management (NPM), which includes standardisation, benchmarking and management by objectives. These reforms are inspired by several challenges: the objective to reduce the costs of the services, on the one hand, and the provision of accessible services that are more tailored to the needs and tastes of the consumer, on the other. Since it is not certain how these objectives may be compatible, emphasis on the specific objective has specific consequences for the regulation and delivery of social services and for employment in social services.

There are diverse segments of welfare services, which have varied sizes in different countries. For example, social services have been decentralised to a great extent in European countries. Many authors (for example Aust and Bönker 2004, Timonen 2004, Larsen and Taylor-Gooby 2004, Daguerre 2006, Bönker et al. 2010) note that the competencies of national governments in the field of social services (like childcare, elder care, employment services) have been limited in some countries (for example in Germany, Finland, Switzerland, UK). Local governments may lack resources for providing social services or caring benefits (Aust and Bönker 2004, Morel 2006). In some cases, the institutional fragmentation works against an expansion of services. The entitlement, scope and quality of services can vary greatly in countries with high decentralisation and fragmentation where clear standards are not set, or various standards are allowed (for the case of Italy see Bönker et al. 2010). For example, it is very important to provide services not only in urban areas, but rural ones as well (CEDEFOP 2010). For this reason, there have been some recent policies of re-centralisation in childcare and/or elder care implemented in Italy and the UK (Bönker et al. 2010).

Marketisation and contracting-out are seen as processes of opening social services to competition (Aust and Bönker 2004) and allowing private providers to enter previously highly regulated or even inaccessible markets (Domberger and Jensen 1997).[1] Privatisation is connected to the abolition or selling of state-provided social services and the expansion of private social services. The marketisation process was most advanced in the UK and also important in Germany (see Bönker et al. 2010). For example, according to Larsen and Taylor-Gooby (2004), in the UK the number of publicly provided long-term care beds fell from 124,000 to 39,000 between 1987 and 2001; the number of private beds rose from 115,000 to 198,000. This example illustrates that reduction of publicly provided services can be at least partially be replaced by the private sector. A similar situation, with a prevalence of private providers, is evidenced in the UK in the case of childcare (Daguerre 2006).

The increasing involvement of private service providers is also documented in employment services (European Commission 2010). Those countries which privatised or never had public social services have to rely on negotiating and stimulating private provisions. Van Berkel et al. (2011) have examined the expectations related to government reforms in employment services and also their real effects. Greater efficiency of policies is expected for several reasons: the local actors are in a good position to deliver tailor-made individualised services thanks to their knowledge of the local contexts and target groups, multi-dimensional and innovative solutions and the use of local actors' potential/resources. On the other hand, it can create inequalities in service provision and individuals' rights, as well as difficulties in coordination. Regarding implementation it requires capabilities and resources at the regional or local level. The expectations related to the marketisation of employment services are numerous: competition should have a positive impact on the efficiency and effectiveness of services, on their quality and flexibility, their responsiveness to local and individual needs (with more choice for users), as well as their price.

In contrast to the expectations, there is a risk with the quality of the services, with 'creaming' and parking within the marketised service delivery sector. Similarly, emphasis in the contracts placed on the quantitative performance targets can also limit the investment of suppliers to specialised training activities and innovative services (Bredgaard and Larsen 2007). Lastly, the administrative burden may be high, although favourable to the competitive nature of a quasi-market; a large number of suppliers and short-term contracts increase the complexity of the negotiations of contracts, their implementation and supervision (Sol and Westerveld 2005, Bredgaard and Larsen 2007). Some of the above discrepancies may be explained by the unfavourable implementation conditions, as well as more general problems

---

1 Publicly owned and private agencies can compete for the contract. Other important aspects being equal, the bid with the lowest priced offer wins (Domberger and Jensen 1997).

appearing due to market failures like asymmetric/insufficient information and failures in the role of the 'principal' who is responsible for establishing and controlling the conditions of competition in the quasi-markets for social services.

Bosch and Lehndorf (2001) have recognised the inclination towards 'service sector Taylorism' resulting from governance reforms which are characterised by the standardisation of tasks, fragmentation of working time, low pay and low job quality. There is also the development of a professional labour market with rising skill requirements and the self-organisation of tasks in social services. Recent years have witnessed an effort to bring down the costs of social services, which has implied a common trend consisting of decentralisation, marketisation and new public management often associated with de-institutionalisation and a flexible mix in service delivery. Strict controls on staffing in the social services and standardisation of tasks has implied cuts in workload standards and unit hours allowed per service. Since part-time, unqualified labour is typically available in many services (easy entry level jobs as a marketised version of domestic tasks, compare Esping-Andersen 2008), this strategy may lead to a 'low road' trajectory of development in social services (that is low pay – low qualification – low prestige – low quality jobs). The above-mentioned effects of governance changes some problems may arise in social services areas with labour shortages, especially in those social services which are affected by the ageing of the labour force (compare European Commission 2008b). A dualisation of the labour market for social services is possible: on the one hand, there is the professionalised segment, where skill requirements and performance standards are a dominant trend, but where the level of employment is very much dependent on public support and/or regulation by the state. On the other hand, the other labour market segment is expanding more with the trend towards cost saving, where labour shortages due to low remuneration and poor job quality are a problem, as well as the uncertain quality of services. This trend might reduce sustainable employment.

For the above reasons, how stakeholders are able to react to institutional reforms is important for the level and quality of employment in social services. The expansion of the private sector helped respond to the growing demand for the care of the elderly in the UK in the 1980s; at the same time, the same objective was achieved with the expansion of NGOs in France (Bönker et al. 2010). Service providers who are no longer supported by institutional arrangements end up undergoing transformation: they reduce their services, or are driven out, as in the case of German municipalities and traditional welfare organisations (see Bönker et al. 2010). Domberger and Jensen (1997) argue that the contracting-out of previously public services leads to a reduction of employment.

In privatised/less subsidised settings, low wages for (mostly low-skilled) care providers make the provision of childcare more affordable for clients (see Bonoli 2006). A good example is care provided by economic immigrants in Mediterranean countries like Spain or Italy (Moreno 2004, Simonazzi 2010, Bönker et al. 2010). Semi-professional private work in households is seen as problematic due to low wages, insufficient training and low career prospects (see

Simonazzi 2010).[2] At least a portion of new jobs in social services (especially in the private sector and contracted services)[3] is created as part-time and/or marginal employment (Domberger and Jensen 1997, Simonazzi 2010), which lessens the real effect of job creation in social services on the economy.

One of the core questions in the future of social services is their continuity and durability from the users' perspective (sustainability). The future scope of employment in social services is based upon the availability of a sufficient number of professional carers in the context of the ageing population. Some authors point to the present and future problems regarding the securing of a sufficient supply of carers in the elder care sector (Timonen 2004, Simonazzi 2010, European Commission 2008b, 2010). Elder care is in some cases very physically demanding, especially for older women who comprise most of the carers. According to Simonazzi (2010) and the European Commission (2008b), long-term care is perceived as a demanding, low-paid, low status, low job quality sector of work and the perceived unattractiveness of caring as a career option is an obstacle to the creation of an adequate supply. In most cases, childcare workers in public facilities are better paid than those in private facilities (European Commission 2008b). In the private long-term care sector, there is a great wage and job quality disparity between high quality (but very expensive) social services and low quality jobs. Pierre (2008) sees low wages as an explanatory factor for the low recruitment of men and the majority of women working in the social services public sector. For a sufficient and sustainable supply of carers, the offer of jobs in social services must be competitive with other similar professions.

Considerations about the Relevance of Factors Influencing Employment in the Social Services in Times of Crisis (and After)

The impact of the crisis, presumably at least temporarily, may change the hierarchy of the factors influencing employment in social services. Long-term drivers, such as changing family patterns, gender roles and preferences, women's employment, dynamic labour markets and new social risks, ageing of the population and path dependency, are not losing their relevance, but they may be outweighed by other short-term factors.

In the short-term outlook those factors that may be expected to gain more strength include the economic implications of the economic crisis, changes in demand for social services, changes in the governance of social services and the changing profile of the users of social services.

---

2   In France a new law was adopted to further professionalise childcare, providing training and improving payment levels (Bönker et al. 2010).

3   Employers in the public sector who are under public control tend to provide more standardised (in accordance to legal standards) working conditions, usually serving as an example for other employers.

First, the changing economic context will prompt governments and policymakers to accept measures which could have implications for employment in social services. In the first phase of the crisis, employment in the public sector and social services serve as a buffer against increasing unemployment and losses of political legitimacy. On the other hand, in the latter phase, the impact of the crisis on job creation in the public sector will be rather negative due to decreasing government revenues and fiscal consolidation measures aiming to diminish the deficit of public finance.

Second, if out-of-pocket fees for services increase as a consequence of cuts in public spending and due to declining incomes and increasing income inequalities in demand for services may become volatile. These impacts may lead to a 'low road', that is, lower quality, higher workload, lower demands on qualifications, lower job quality, more fragmentation and the standardisation of work in social services.

Third, the changes in the governance of social services like marketisation may simply aim prominently at savings of expenditure. This again would have rather negative consequences on their quality and on employment. Furthermore, the economic efficiency is questionable; for example, Esping-Andersen (2008: 104) explains that unit-service costs are often higher in private services than in public/universal services due to profit margins and mainly to transaction costs (administrative, marketing and billing). Recent experience from post-communist countries shows, for example, higher costs of employment programmes financed through the European Social Fund and delivered by non-government agencies when compared to programmes organised by the Public Employment Services, not to mention the high transaction costs of the tendering procedures aiming to select the best suitable providers of specific services (Sirovátka and Winkler 2011).

Lastly the profile of the target groups/users of the services and their legitimacy for the entitlements will matter a great deal, more than in times of economic growth. Several studies have shown that social assistance recipients and the long-term unemployed are exposed to activation programmes often associated with cuts in benefits and more conditionality in the form of workfare measures rather than to human capital development measures (for example Lødemel and Trickey 2001). However, since the elderly and middle class women are typical mainstream users of social services, we may also expect a less restrictive approach in caring services. Finally, increased user fees in health and social care might have negative social repercussions on the less affluent groups and the marginalisation of the most vulnerable groups in society in their access to social services.

Comparison of Employment in Social Services in the EU-27 and an Examination of Possible Explanations

This section will describe the development of employment in social services in the EU-27 between the years 2000 and 2010, and will examine some of the factors which may help to explain this development in social service sector in a broad and narrow approach. The reason for including a broad definition of social services is that mainly at the municipal level, government and social security administration is contributing greatly to the regulation, financing and delivery of social services, and it is difficult to split this sector from the social services sector.

Between 2000 and 2010 the employment rate in the EU increased on average by two percentage points from 62.1 to 64.1 per cent (63.4 per cent in 2005). The growth of employment in social services represented an important contribution to this growth considering that social services represent on average less than one-fifth of total employment (broad definition), or less than 10 per cent of total employment (narrow definition). The increase in the employment rate in social services in 2000–2010 was one percentage point (broad definition) or 0.7 percentage point (narrow definition), which means that social services in the narrow interpretation grew faster than the rest of the social services (government and social security sector), or the rest of the economy.

From the broad definition there is an uneven development in the employment rate in social services in EU countries. In some countries it increased by 2 to 3 per cent, like in Ireland, France, Netherlands, Austria, Spain and Germany. Only in Latvia, Italy and Sweden did the employment rate in social services drop, most significantly in Sweden, where it was already high in 2000 (see Table 6.1).

In 2010 using a hierarchical cluster analysis two large groups of countries emerge: the first one is represented by West and North European countries, where employment in social services ranges between 11.2 per cent (Ireland) and 18.4 per cent (Denmark). Four subgroups may be identified within this group depending on the employment rate in social services. In the leading group, Denmark and the Netherlands have employment rates in social services above 17 per cent; this is followed by Sweden and France, where it is about 15 per cent. In the third cluster, represented by a larger group of countries (that is Belgium, Germany, Finland, Luxembourg and the UK) the employment rate in social services is between 13.7 per cent (Luxembourg) and 14.1 per cent (Belgium). The fourth cluster is represented by Austria and Ireland, where employment in social services is between 11 per cent and 12 per cent. We have a large group of countries where employment in social services is between 6.9 per cent and 9.5 per cent, composed from South European and Central-East post-communist countries. This is followed by Romania, where employment in social services is only 5.8 per cent.

As already mentioned, in most countries, independent of their position in the above clusters, the employment rate in social services grew between 2000 and 2010. In each of the clusters there are very different cases: fast-growing or slow-growing employment in social services, and in some exceptional cases decreasing employment.

This analysis makes it clear that there are two groups of countries in Europe: the North-West group and the South and Central-East group. Employment in social services seems to be more developed in the first group, although Austria and Ireland may represent a transition/intermediate subgroup. According to the narrow definition (health and social services sector), in 2010 employment in social

Innovation in Social Services

Table 6.1   **Employment rates in social services: sectors L, N (O, Q): government and social security + health and social services**

	Government and social security + health and social services				Health and social services only			
	2000	2005	2010	Change 2000–2010	2000	2005	2010	Change 2000–2010
Denmark	17.8	17.8	18.4	0.6	13.3	13.2	14.0	0.7
Netherlands	14.8	16.4	17.1	2.3	9.9	11.3	12.3	3.4
Sweden	17.0	16.0	15.6	-1.4	13.3	12.0	10.6	-2.7
France	12.2	13.9	14.8	2.6	6.5	7.8	8.4	1.9
Belgium	13.4	13.6	14.1	0.7	7.2	7.5	8.4	1.2
Germany	1.9	12.5	13.9	2.0	6.5	7.4	8.6	2.1
Finland	12.8	13.6	13.9	1.1	9.4	10.5	11.2	1.8
UK	12.2	13.9	13.8	1.6	7.8	8.8	9.1	1.3
Luxembourg	12.0	14.0	13.7	1.7	5.1	6.2	6.1	1.0
Austria	9.7	10.6	11.9	2.2	5.4	6.3	7.0	1.6
Ireland	8.3	10.1	11.2	2.9	5.2	6.6	7.7	2.5
Malta	8.3	8.8	9.5	1.2	4.0	4.1	4.6	0.6
Portugal	8.3	9.3	9.2	0.9	3.7	4.5	4.8	0.9
Czech Rep	8.2	9.0	8.9	0.7	3.9	4.4	4.5	0.6
Spain	6.5	7.8	8.8	2.3	3.0	3.8	4.3	1.3
Slovakia	8.3	7.9	8.8	0.5	4.0	3.9	4.0	0
Greece	6.9	7.9	8.5	1.6	2.6	3.0	3.3	0.7
Cyprus	8.3	8.3	8.4	0.1	2.5	3.0	3.0	0.5
Hungary	7.5	8.0	8.2	0.7	3.6	3.8	3.7	0.1
Slovenia	7.1	7.7	8.0	0.9	3.3	3.6	3.9	0.6
Estonia	6.2	7.7	7.9	1.7	2.9	3.6	3.5	0.6
Italy	8.0	7.7	7.7	-0.3	3.3	4.0	4.1	0.8
Bulgaria	6.5	7.0	7.5	1.0	3.0	3.0	3.1	0.1
Lithuania	7.1	7.7	7.5	0.4	3.9	4.2	3.9	0
Poland	6.6	6.5	7.4	0.8	3.6	3.1	3.5	-0.1
Latvia	7.3	8.3	6.9	**-0.4**	2.8	3.4	2.9	**0.1**
Romania	4.9	5.6	5.8	**0.9**	2.1	2.3	2.7	**0.6**
Average	9.6	10.3	10.6	1.0	5.3	5.8	6.0	0.7

Note: Employment rate in social services is measured as numbers of employees in social services to the total number of labour force (full-time or part-time employment).
Source: Eurostat (2012b), own calculations

services rose to 6 per cent of the employment rate on average and increased in the last ten years by 0.7 per cent (see Table 6.1). The differences among EU countries are more remarkable when compared to employment in the broad definition, where they diverge from 14 per cent in Denmark to 2.7 per cent in Romania. Nevertheless, the clusters of countries ranked according to the level of employment rate are very similar to the clusters obtained through the broad definition (see above).

In the first cluster, which is quite distant from the others, are countries where the employment rate is between 10.6 per cent and 14.0 per cent (Sweden, Finland, the Netherlands and Denmark), followed by a group of countries where the employment rate is between 8.4 per cent and 9.1 per cent (Belgium, France, Germany and UK). Then the third, the North-West cluster, where the employment rate is between 6.1 per cent and 7.7 per cent (Luxembourg, Austria and Ireland). All the above countries again have an above-average employment rate, while in the large fourth group, the South-Central-East cluster, the employment rate in social services is between 2.7 per cent (Romania) and 4.8 per cent (Portugal). Again, there is a different pace of change in each cluster: very strong growth of employment in the Netherlands (3.4 per cent), but a remarkable decrease in Sweden (-2.7 per cent) in the first cluster. In the second and third clusters, the growth was rather strong, in particular in Ireland (2.5 per cent) and Germany (2.1 per cent). In the fourth, South-Central-East cluster, only moderate growth prevailed, mostly below 1 per cent, although Slovakia, Hungary, Bulgaria, Lithuania and Poland stagnated.

The financial and fiscal crisis in the period 2008–2010 did not change much in respect to the continuous growth of employment in social services. Using data which capture employment figures year-by-year in the EU-27 there has been an increase of employment in social services each year during 2008–2010 without much variation. Factors which can help explain the differences in the employment rate in social services among the EU countries in the period 2000–2010 are:

- Financing of the welfare state (government revenues, tax on labour, social protection expenditure, social protection expenditure in kind)
- Demographics (ageing of the population – old age dependency, fertility rate)
- Political-economic cycle captured by proxy variables which directly influence the supply and demand for social services (GDP growth, public deficit, unemployment rate total, men, women)
- Employment pattern/modernisation (employment rate total, men, women).

The analysis is done by using the Pearson correlation coefficient of the employment rate in social services with the above variables. The reason for using such a singular measure is that there are very complex relationships among the variables above, which may make the attempts to distinguish the dependent and independent variables misleading. The analysis was conducted in two steps. First, we used the variables above in order to capture the factors which may help explain the differences in employment rates in social services among the EU countries. In the second step, we plotted the variables which characterise the changes in the above variables during 2000–2010, in order to capture the factors which may help explain the changes of employment in social services among the EU countries in this period.

An analysis of three time points during the 2000–2010 period has shown that the employment rate in social services is consistently and strongly correlated with three kinds of variables (see Table 6.2): financing of the welfare state indicated by several variables like government total revenues from taxes and social contributions, tax on labour (except for 2005), expenditure on social protection in total and expenditure on social protection in kind (mostly services) and public finance deficit (except for 2010). The other significant factors are the overall employment rate and fertility rate.

There is a moderate correlation between employment rates in social services and the variables which characterise labour market performance (that is the employment rate of women and employment rate of men, unemployment rate, unemployment rate of women and unemployment rate of men, except for 2005).

The correlation of the employment rate in social services with GDP growth is inconsistent: it was insignificant in 2000, moderate and negative in 2005, and moderate and positive in 2010. Similarly, the correlation with the old-age dependency ratio is insignificant and weak in all the years.

These results indicate that country differences did not change much during 2000–2010, as was also evident from Table 6.1, p. 105. Second, they indicate that the range of factors which influence employment in social services seems to be stable over time. A high level of employment in social services is associated with a higher level of government revenues, expenditure on social protection (total and in kind), a higher level of employment (total, men and women), a lower level of unemployment (total, women and men) and with higher fertility rates. In 2000 and 2005, it was also associated with a lower level of public finance deficit; however, in 2010 this relationship no longer existed. Similarly, while in 2005 stronger economic growth was more associated with a lower level of employment rates in social services, in 2010 the opposite was true.

Besides the correlations among the above variables, an examination of the correlations among the changes in the values of the above variables in 2000–2010, 2000–2005 and 2005–2010 has also been done. These changes in a given period, however, exhibit little association with the change of employment in social services. There is only a moderate correlation between a change of the employment rate in social services between 2000–2010 and a change of the level of public deficit (.455, negative); and between the employment rate in social services and the change of the level of social expenditure in kind (.499, positive) and social protection expenditure in total (.437, positive). However, in the years 2005–2010, significant and positive correlation of the change of employment in social services, the change in the employment rate of women (.418) and also the change of social expenditure in kind (.408) was evidenced. For the period 2000–2005, no significant correlations among the variables contested were found.

Table 6.2   **Correlation coefficients between the employment rate in social services and selected variables in the EU, 2000, 2005 and 2010**

Correlation coefficients PE	with the variable Employment rate in social services total (L, N or O, Q)		
	Strong > 0.66	Moderate > 0.33	Weak, insignificant
2010	Social Protection Expenditure in Kind (.814)**	Employment rate women (.637)**	Public Deficit
	Social Protection Expenditure Total (.777)**	Employment rate men (.636)**	Old Age Dependency
	Total government receipts from taxes and soc.contr. (.798)**	Unemployment rate women (- .502)*	
	Employment rate total (.748)**	Unemployment rate total (- .472)*	
	Fertility rate (.728)**	Unemployment rate men (- .424)*	
	Tax on labour (.670)**	GDP growth (.391)*	
2005	Fertility rate (.807)**	Tax on labour (.646)**	Unemployment rate men
	Total government revenues from taxes and soc.contr. (.787)**	Employment rate women (.627)**	Old Age Dependency
	Social Protection Expenditure in Kind (.786)**	Employment rate men (.574)**	
	Social Protection Expenditure Total (.739)**	Unemployment rate women (- .422)*	
	Employment rate total (.724)**	GDP growth (- .422)*	
		Unemployment rate total (- .411)*	
		Public Deficit (.396)*	
2000	Total government revenues from taxes and soc.contr. (.829)**	Fertility rate (.598)*	GDP growth
	Social Protection Expenditure in Kind (.743)**	Employment rate women (.595)*	Old Age Dependency

Table 6.2   *Concluded*

Correlation coefficients PE	with the variable Employment rate in social services total (L, N or O, Q)		
	Strong > 0.66	**Moderate > 0.33**	**Weak, insignificant**
	Social Protection Expenditure Total (.734)**	Employment rate men (.562)*	
	Employment rate total (.714)**	Public Deficit (.572)*	
	Tax on labour (.704) **	Unemployment rate total (- .507) *	
		Unemployment rate women (- .490) *	
		Unemployment rate men (- .473) *	

Notes: Employment in the public sector and social services:
L (O) Public administration and defence; compulsory social security, N (Q) Health and social work
** significant at 0.01 level
* significant at 0.05 level
Source: Own computations on Eurostat data

There is very strong correlation between employment in social services by narrow definition and by broad definition (PE = .963 in 2010, .956 in 2005 and .956 in 2000). The reason is that the differences between the level of employment in sector compulsory social security and defence are not so wide like in social service sector, and their pattern is not divergent from the pattern of differences in employment in social security (rather both patterns is similar).

The associations of the changes in the values of employment in social services and other variables are observed mainly in the longer period of time 2000–2010.[4] However, these changes are rather moderately associated: correlation coefficients significant at the 0.01 or 0.05 level between the change of employment rate in social services and change in the values of the following variables are evidenced: social protection in kind (.603), social protection total (.575), public deficit (-.504), tax on labour (.449) and employment rate of men (-.407).

---

4   In the 2000–2005 period, we observe a moderate correlation between the change of employment rate in social services (narrow definition) and change in the female employment rate (PE = .408, significant at 0.05 level), and a moderate negative correlation between the change of the employment rate in social services (narrow definition) and the change of public deficit (PE = - .412, significant at 0.05 level).

Table 6.3 **Correlation coefficients between employment rates in social services (narrow definition) and selected variables in the EU, 2000, 2005 and 2010**

Correlation coefficients PE	with the variable employment rate in social services total (L, N or O, Q)		
	Strong > 0.66	Moderate > 0.33	Weak, insignificant
2010	Social Protection Expenditure in Kind (.853)**	Employment rate women (.677)**	Public Deficit
	Total government revenues from taxes and soc.contr. (.782)**	Employment rate men (.574)**	Unemployment rate men
	Social Protection Expenditure Total (.780)**	Unemployment rate women (- .482)*	Old Age Dependency
	Fertility rate (.747)**	Unemployment rate total (- .412)*	
	Employment rate total (.741)**	GDP growth (.383)*	
	Tax on labour (.690)**		
2005	Social Protection Expenditure in Kind (.814)**	Employment rate men (.528)**	Unemployment rate men
	Fertility rate (.799)**	Public Deficit (.488)**	Old Age Dependency
	Total government receipts from taxes and soc.contr. (.776)**	GDP growth (- .415)*	
	Social Protection Expenditure Total (.720)**	Unemployment rate total (- .411)*	
	Employment rate total (.745)**	Unemployment rate women (- .405)*	
	Employment rate women (.690)**		
	Tax on labour (.680)**		
2000	Total government revenues from taxes and soc.contr. (.801)**	Public Deficit (.581)**	GDP growth
	Social Protection Expenditure in Kind (.777)**	Fertility rate (.521)**	Old Age Dependency

Table 6.3   *Concluded*

Correlation coefficients PE	with the variable employment rate in social services total (L, N or O, Q)		
	Strong > 0.66	**Moderate > 0.33**	**Weak, insignificant**
	Employment rate total (.734)**	Employment rate men (.489)*	Unemployment rate men
	Tax on labour (.728)**	Unemployment rate women (- .438)*	
	Social Protection Expenditure Total (.698)**	Unemployment rate total (- .417)*	
	Employment rate women (.677)*		

Notes: Employment in the public sector and social services:
L (O) Public administration and defence; compulsory social security, N (Q) Health and social work
** significant at 0.01 level
* significant at 0.05 level
Source: Own computations on Eurostat data

These findings can be interpreted as follows: fiscal policies have been most important in cases when the previously established patterns changed. On the one hand, sufficient financing (indicated by the increasing level of public social protection expenditure total and in kind in particular) was associated with a positive change of employment in social services. On the other hand, sound public finance indicated by a decreasing public deficit also had relevance both for sufficient financing and for the growth of employment in social services. To some extent, growing employment in social services (narrow definition) was associated with the decreasing employment rate of men. This may be explained both by changing the overall structure of the economy (trends towards post-industrial employment) and through a deliberate policy by government to foster employment by supporting social service employment.

Generally, although the complexity and multi-colinearity of the relationships between the variable employment rate in social services and the other variables reduce the ability to make firm conclusions, the data indicates that higher employment in social services requires both sufficient and sustainable public finance. Furthermore, private out-of-pocket fees, which are not captured in the data on expenditure by Eurostat, are becoming an important source of financing social services. Nevertheless, public finance represents the lion's share of expenditure, regardless of whether the service provider is of the public or private sector.

The expected negative correlation between GDP growth and employment in social services was not proved; on the contrary, in 2010 there is a positive correlation. And finally, negative correlation between employment in social services and public deficit was indicated. On the other hand, the correlation between the change in employment in social services and the change in the public deficit during 2000–2010 (positive) was also evidenced. These findings may indicate that policymaking is becoming more effective in the face of economic austerity and crisis mainly in those countries where social services are better developed and where the new forms of public-private mixes succeed in creating jobs in social services, but do not imply public debt at the same time.

Conclusions and Discussion: What Future is there for Employment in Social Services?

Our analysis has not enabled us to verify the whole range of factors discussed in the previous sections of the chapter. However, some important conclusions are possible. Firstly, path dependency is strong: The established welfare state models which imply this path dependency are best identified by the level and sources of financing – government revenues and expenditure on social services. They represent an important factor which is closely associated with the level of employment in social services and also with other crucial characteristics of the welfare state, like the employment regime, which is visible in the overall employment rate. At the same time employment in social services is not often associated with public debt. This may be explained with a responsible approach to the governance of social services in most of the countries which are ahead in social service employment.

Second, the pattern of female employment, the family model and *'gender order'*, combined with policies supporting a combination of family and work, plays an important role. Higher levels of employment in social services are clearly associated with a higher employment rate of women. In fact, the 'maturation of the revolution in gender roles', which also presupposes strong policies of the work-family combination is strongly associated with a higher level of employment in social services. This appears in the long-term perspective as the most consistent and strongest driver of employment in social services. The development of social services both creates new job opportunities for women and enables them to balance work and family, thus facilitating participation in the labour market.

Third, politics matters: the negative correlation of the employment rate in social services and unemployment rates (overall, women, men) may be due to the overall better performance of the labour market for several reasons like more effective employment services and reconciliation policies. Nevertheless, it may also be a consequence of a deliberate strategy to foster public sector employment in times of economic slowdown and influenced by political considerations in accordance with certain assumptions (Cussack et al. 1989, Tepe 2009). Lastly, there are indications that in recent years social services employment growth has been compatible with GDP growth.

Surprisingly, the ageing of society, indicated by the old-age dependency ratio, did not prove to be significantly correlated with social service employment. This finding contradicts the hypothesis about the decisive influence of demographic changes on employment in social services. Nevertheless, this contradiction could be explained by two circumstances: first, the impacts of ageing on the demand of social services will be more pervasive in the future than it is currently, due to the expected rapid change in demographic structures. Second, as discussed by several authors, welfare state models and family models may imply alternative or informal caring options when public social services are insufficient – like for example in post-communist countries or in the South of Europe, with the negative consequences of a lower female employment rate (compare Jensen 2009, Pavollini and Ranci 2008, Esping-Andersen 2008). Lastly, if life-expectancy is increasing without increases of disability and health and social care supported with new and better technologies, the expected impacts of ageing on employment in social services may be alleviated. As mentioned above, ageing as a factor of employment growth in social services will possibly become more influential in the future in combination with the maturation of the 'female revolution' in the countries which are currently preferring familialist policies (post-communist and Mediterranean models).

In the context of the crisis, however, it is difficult to expect increased public investment into social services, in particular in countries where this expenditure used to be low and which are facing increasing public deficits now. Rather, the innovations in governance (that is, in regulation, financing and delivery of social services) may help overcome the pressures emerging from fiscal consolidation by mobilising available national and local sources, public and private, formal and informal. Sustainable financing requires certain levels of public expenditure.

Chapter 7

The Role of the EU on Welfare States – Focus on Social Services

Bent Greve

Introduction

Welfare states and welfare state policies are argued especially to be national prerogatives, but seemingly there is also an international perspective on the issue. This chapter will focus on and discuss how the interrelated issues combining supranational ideas and policies and national approaches might have an impact on the welfare states and their financing and delivery of social services.

This will be done below, albeit briefly, presenting only the core issue and areas where the EU has an impact on the national welfare state (for example mainly the free movement of workers, but also the equal treatment of men and women, as well as how the free movement of goods and services might influence the delivery and financing of social services). This will be followed by a discussion on the service directive in Section 7.4, which serves as an example of this kind of impact given that it can move the border from what is public governance to market provision and management, thereby also shifting the boundaries between the public and private sectors in relation to delivery.

Theories of Europeanisation will first be touched upon, albeit only briefly, given that the focus here is on impact. Finally, the chapter will also delve into how the OMC (Open Method of Coordination), Section 7.5, can be seen as a new type of governance (for example with a focus on the process of continuing cooperation of national actors and coordination of national and supranational policies (Heise 2008).

Europeanisation

A central issue relates to what can be understood by the impact of the EU. The traditional understanding of the study of the EU and its impact has been revolving around neo-functionalism, neo-federalism, neo-realism, liberal inter-governmentalism, governance or fusion (Wessels 2001). The EU has recommendations and decisions by the Court as instrument directives, but also plays the possible role of agenda-setter. The ability to act as agenda-setter can influence the national welfare states' ability and choice of how to deliver social services in modern welfare states.

A core problem in the analysis is that Europeanisation is not a specific theory, but more 'a way of orchestrating existing concepts and to contribute to cumulative research in political science' (Radaelli 2004). Europeanisation can be understood in at least three different ways:

1. Development of a European level of governance;
2. The process of impact and influence from the supranational level to the national level;
3. Processes focusing on the development of shared beliefs and norms that might be then transferred to nation states, but also in both a bottom-up and top-down understanding (Börzel and Risse 2007).

However, in general Europeanisation will be understood here as the impact of the EU on European integration and member states, in line with Radaelli (2003), as this implies a focus on the link between the supranational development and national welfare state development (for example impact can go in both directions based on the uploading or downloading of ideas and policies).

Another approach is to see that:

> Subjective Europeanisation refers to Europe's growing role in the cognitive, affective and normative perceptions and orientation of people, and the weakening of the fixation on the nation state. Europe appears as an additional frame of reference, superimposed on the level of the nation state but without necessarily replacing it (Mau and Verwiebe 2010: 329).

The impact from Europeanisation can be direct (that is stemming from directives and court decisions depending on national reactions to these decisions), but also indirect through the gradually more integrated European economies. A core argument is that, 'most of the effects of economic and political integration within the EU: on social insurance and social services appear to have been indirect, with high unemployment serving as the main catalyst' (Korpi 2003: 604). Another distinction is between positive and negative integration (Kühnle 1999). It has been argued that EU social policy is driven mainly by negative integration, or by courts and markets. Furthermore, that positive integration is not moving by the transfer of sovereignty from national states to the EU level, but more through collaboration among the member states (Kvist and Saari 2007). Europeanisation thus is also argued as something that 'walks on two legs – market efficiency and political voluntarism' (Verdier and Breen 2001). The OMC seems to be in between these different understandings given the possible impact of the formulation of European policies while at the same time opening space for national implementation and allowing a role for the market. The relation to how the EU might influence, not only through 'hard' law (such as directives) but also steering through the OMC, social services will therefore also be touched upon.

A simple model of the Europeanisation of social protection looks into how development at the EU level regarding policy processes, internal market and so on is mediated by the welfare regime, country size, and so on – this then might imply different kinds of responses and welfare reforms. The conclusion is that since 2000, the EU has had an increased influence on social protection, but also that, 'in sum, EU developments have influenced national welfare reform, but in varied ways and to different extents' (Kvist and Saari 2007: 238).

National governance and change herein is part of the focus of the analysis of change in the case analysis, but this has to be seen in the light of supranational governance, which can be defined as, 'a situation/condition that describes the competence of the European Community to make binding rules in any given policy domain' (Rosamond 2009: 89). This in line with the fact that governance can be understood as rules and methods to ensure and coordinate the delivery of, in this case, social service, but also sometimes related to the 'softer' methods (compare also the section on the OMC). This implies that governance in a broad understanding tries to capture changes in authority and policy-making.

The impact has often been measured by looking into whether or not convergence or divergence takes place. In Chapter 4, the measure of convergence (coefficient of variation) has been used as an indicator of development in the last ten years; from 1985 to 1999 there seems to have been a trend towards convergence (Alsasua et al. 2007). In Chapters 8–11, this will be supplemented by information on changes in the governance, employment and tax-structure of four different countries representing four various welfare regimes. Convergence can be related to factors such as ideas, structure and spending; it might be equally argued that it is easier to agree upon ideas than implementation (Radaelli 2005), which indirectly also can be seen to be confirmed by the fact that a common understanding of the concept of flexi-curity and policy aims of transforming labour market policy from passive to active are positive without looking more into the details of the understanding of these issues.

Convergence has been one of the expected outcomes of a more common approach and integration of the European economies, also revolving around issues such as policy innovation, diffusion and transfer. There have therefore also been several approaches to try to find out whether there has been an impact from examples of using different dependent variables such as goals, content, instruments, outcomes and style of policy-making, also arguing that 'policy output were strongly correlated with levels of technological and economic development' (Jordan 2005: 948). In the same vein, there has been an attempt to analyse whether there is convergence in convergence research (Heichel et al. 2005). The conclusion is that there has been only limited convergence in the field of policy analysis; however, sigma convergence (that is coefficient of variation), as used in Chapter 4, is one of the classical ways to analyse convergence. This in combination with the use of case studies (compare Chapter 8–12) should thus be a good way to make a comparison possible.

Core Areas in the EU in Relation to the Welfare State

Historically, the EU in principle has had only limited influence on the structure of the national welfare state. The demand for fiscal prudence can implicitly influence the options available in nation states. This is not included in the analysis here. Furthermore, the possible impact stemming from the use of the European structural fund and pressure to take specific actions is not analysed here (for example for a possible scenario compare Verschraegen et al. (2011) for the impact on activation in Belgium).

From the early days till the present, the core influence of the EU has been related to the free movement of workers. Rules were laid down in the now-changed Directive 1408/71 (Regulation 883/2004) as the core instrument for ensuring the easy free movement of workers; in combination with the case law of the European Court, this has increased internal migration (within the EU) especially in the wake of EU enlargement and the fiscal crisis. This regulation originally covered employed and self-employed people, but was later broadened with Regulation 883/2004 so that all those 'who are or have been subject for the legislation of one or more Member States' are covered (Pennings 2009: 6).

The general idea was that if a worker moved from one country to another, the rules should not be a hindrance, but instead should support free movement. For example, this should make it possible to combine the earned right to pensions from different countries; the right to welfare benefits should also be given to workers; child benefits should be available even if the child is not residing in the country where the work takes place. Rules preventing people with disabilities have also been said to hinder free mobility, given the restrictions on exporting benefits and non-legal barriers in several areas such as transport and housing (Morgan 2005).

As an example of the impact, the Laval judgement of 2007 implied a break with the Danish labour market model in that the Parliament created legislation in areas that had previously been taken care of by labour market partners by including a new rule on how to define minimum wages in the law concerning the posting of workers in 2008 (Kristiansen 2011). Kristiansen also argues that the EU rules concerning the free movement of workers, seen from the employee organisation point of view, generally imply the possibility and risk of social dumping.

The use of regulations and other attempts to harmonise has been the main approach for a long time, until it became clear in the mid-nineties that due to the fact that most areas needed unanimity, it would be difficult to decide on binding directives. There have, for example, been directives on social security (1997/7/EEC) and equal treatment (1976/207/EEC) that could have an impact on the nation state's ability to pursue welfare policies. Later there was also a directive with regard to leave in relation to the birth of a child (Parental leave 1996/34); nevertheless, in general the EU has not been the main player in relation to having a direct impact on a nation state's welfare policies, although the indirect influence due to free movement can be witnessed (compare above on the Laval case).

Since the Amsterdam Treaty and with an increased focus on how to promote employment, there has also been a concern with regard to the reconciliation of work and family life. This has included a focus on gender equality policy, equal treatment at work, parental leave and child care. There have been directives on equal opportunities, on services in the internal market and on equal treatment (also being one of the cornerstones of the Rome Treaty), communication on a better work-life balance, council conclusions and targets related to the employment rate of women, and so on, and also increased funding (European Social Fund) in these areas (Jacquot et al. 2011). Thus the EU in general has not had a strong role with regard to welfare services; nevertheless, the interaction between EU policy and national policy has gradually become stronger, and case law has moved the boundaries between the EU and the nation states (compare next section). The lack of success with regard to implementing 'hard' law (that is binding directives) is part of the reason why there has been a movement and discussion in relation to the implementation of 'soft' law as is the case for the use of the OMC.

Recommendations have been used as a way of influencing national developments, cf.

Box 7.1   EU viewpoint on childcare services based upon ecommendation 92/241/EEC of 31 March 1992 on childcare

'In this context, efforts should be made in particular to ensure that:

- The services offered to parents are reasonably priced;
- The services combine reliable care from the point of view of health and safety with a general upbringing and a pedagogical approach;
- The services take into consideration the needs of parents and children as far as access is concerned;
- The services are available in all areas and regions of the Member States, both urban and rural;
- The services are accessible to children with special needs, for example from the linguistic point of view, and to children in single-parent families, and meet the needs of such children.'

Source: http://europa.eu/legislation_summaries/employment_and_social_policy/ equality_between_men_and_women/c10916_en.htm (accessed 3 October 2012).

Furthermore, when they met in Barcelona in March 2002 the Council recommended that childcare facilities for 90 per cent of children over three years old and 33 per cent of children under three years old should be reached by the year 2010. This has not proven to be the case and indicates a weakness in the indirect approach through recommendations.

Nevertheless, the difficulty in reaching consensus also helps to explain why the EU in several areas often is more driven by court decisions than by EU formal decisions (for example in the area of health care services – Greer 2011). Given that the Court's starting point has been the Treaty, this also implies that the EU is more effective at liberalising than making formal decisions about how and to what extent to regulate welfare issues, including job creation.

Part of the reason why there have been court decisions in the area of health care is that there has been difficulty in drawing a line between hospital and non-hospital care services. This presumably also explains why health care was taken out of the Service Directive at the end; implicitly this meant that the Court was still left with the free movement of goods and services as the main guideline when regulating health care. The distinction made differed based upon whether the person needing treatment has to be in hospital for more than one day. The implication is that day-to-day services can be treated as part of the free movement of services, thereby reducing a nation state's option to regulate the area as part of a welfare approach (compare next section).

To state this more strongly, 'there is essentially no evidence of economic, political, or social supporting coalitions behind the ECJ's move into health care services' (Greer 2011: 191).

In at least the area of disability and employment there is no formal legal base, among other things, as a result of the fact that both the EU and member states have used supranational rules, including UN and ILO standards (Morgan 2005).

The Service Directive – A Case and Possible Impact on Social Services

The Service Directive provides a case, which will be described below, illustrating how the principles of state and market involvement sometimes interact and can lead to different outcomes. This is due to the fact that a central issue related to social services is whether the service is a good that should be provided by the market and be available for purchase on the market at a given price, or whether it is a public good provided as a result of some of the rationales for providing public goods (compare also Chapter 2). In principle, the limits are clear, but a closer look reveals that not only goods have changed over time (for example television signals and lighthouses have moved from being public to being private goods). The same can be questioned in relation to social services. Care for the elderly could in principle be provided not only, as earlier, mainly by the family but also as a private good delivered by the market. Given that it is very difficult to estimate the precise need for care (compare also Chapter 2), this has been coped with financially by the welfare state in one way or another. The same is, to a large degree, the case in health care, where recent years of development have seen some changes (compare below).

Part of the reason for the development of the Service Directive has been the change in case law, or more importantly that a number of cases gave a clear indication of the fact that 'judicial activism has clarified that the Community principles of free movement of goods and service apply to health care policy field' (Martinsen 2005: 1031). The author even more strongly formulated the idea that national rules regarding the authorisation of who to provide non-hospital care for was a barrier that was not in accordance with the rules of the free movement of services. In general this has implied that, since the end of the 1990s, a number of cases have expanded the citizen's right to planned health care in other countries beyond that of their home country (Kumlin 2010). The idea is that people could travel or use services in neighbouring countries in areas such as physiotherapy, dental and medical treatment, including visits to a general practitioner and having prescriptions delivered. Nation states supporting this economically will therefore have to pay the same amount even if the treatment takes place outside the home country. One possible risk is that quality control is more difficult. Individuals also have the right to move to another country to search for a job and claim unemployment benefits in another country. This also raises issues of how to ensure quality and use other types of services.

In principle, the starting point is that the EU in general only has a limited role in welfare state areas, although at the same time the court has, by referring to the free movement of goods and services, changed the rules and the way the system is working (compare for example the three cases regarding Kohl, Decker and Peerbooms). Another example was the Watt case from 2006 (Martinsen and Vrangbæk 2008), where the court came to the conclusion that Mrs. Watt could get the cost of a hip operation reimbursed, despite the fact that it took place outside the physical borders of the UK. The court also argued that medical services are within the scope of freedom with regard to the provision of service. Other important cases include the Decker and Kohl cases, which changed at least the Danish perception that health care was not clearly outside the scope of the internal market. This led to a change in the Danish legislation allowing for the purchase of specialist services (for example dental assistance) abroad and then being reimbursed with a fixed amount of money equal to what the Danish providers would get; there was also the interpretation that 'services as services normally carried out in return for remuneration' (Danish report – here quoted from Martinsen and Vrangbæk 2008: 179).

In this way at least some national welfare state services are more open to international competition, and by this also a change with regard to steering and governing the social services in these areas. The debate concerning the Service Directive (labelled the Bolkenstein Directive) also, at least implicitly, implies the possibility of a movement away from and difficulties for the universal welfare states to provide specific services. If a national welfare state cannot provide without too much delay (and this is not precisely defined) health care services, then a citizen may have the right to go to another country to obtain the treatment.

The debate over the Bolkenstein Directive was one of the first to be launched after the Lisbon Agenda in 2000. The Directive on service in the internal market shows the ongoing debate and struggle between state and market led development.

The draft directive from 2004 '…aimed to reduce national regulation of services, unless they were non-discriminatory, justified with respect to public interest and proportionate' (Grossman and Woll 2011: 346). One debate revolved around the country of origin for setting up a business in the sense that those having residence in one country should only abide by the rules in that country. Another issue was related to the inclusion of public service in the suggestion for the Directive, including services of general interest (Crespy 2010). A third issue revolved around the position of posted workers, where the understanding in the Posted Worker Directive from 1996 was that working conditions and pay should be in accordance with the rules in the country where the work was carried out; the suggested Directive was seen as 'being de facto ruin of these provisions by making controls impossible' (Crespy and Gajewska 2010: 1191). After changes reducing and amending these elements, including explicitly to exclude services of general interest, the Directive was adopted on 12 December 2006.

However, there can and presumably will continue to be cases where the borderlines between state and market, and thereby the role of the welfare state, can come into question.

The OMC – Another Way?

The Open Method of Co-ordination (OMC) has been central since the Amsterdam Treaty and was an attempt to move forward with a supranational impact in development in the core welfare state areas. The theoretical underpinnings were building upon new institutionalism on path-dependency (Pierson 1996), or the impact of learning effects to alter beliefs and practices (Knill and Lehmkuhl 1999). This was seen early as the best approach to coping with this complex issue with many actors and countries involved (Roth and Schmidt 2000); since then this complexity has not been reduced due to the enlargement of the European Union. OMC can also be seen in the light of the EU understanding of governance as focusing on rules, processes and behaviour that might also have an impact on the way there is an option for openness, participation, and so on (Heise 2008).

Despite changes that have resulted in moving away from 'hard law' through directives to this 'softer' approach, the aim is convergence, but with respect for national institutional diversity (Teague 2001). Teague also points to the fact that OMC might ensure the Europeanisation of the employed working in the different welfare states in various policy areas. However, it is also obvious that the capacity of convergence policy is lower within the OMC given the focus on bench-marking, recommendations and peer-pressure compared to situations where direct legally binding regulations are available (Citi and Rhodes 2007).

The real impact of the OMC has thus often been questioned, as has the direction from which it came (that is impact from below or from above). Another issue was how strong the pressure was, ranging from very mild in most programs, such as the European Employment Strategy, to stronger pressure concerning issues in the

EMU. A core question, also raised earlier, was whether the OMC would be a sea-change or standstill in the development of Europe (Falkner 2000).

The OMC revolves around issues such as recommendation, bench-marking, communication, peer-review, opinion and guidelines. The general aim is to try to reach a common understanding and interpretation of societal development. The differences and history of the development of OMC will not be shown; rather, there will be emphasis on whether or not one can argue that this has had an impact on welfare state policies and development, including how to measure and discuss convergence/divergence in welfare states. One of the central issues relates to the employment area, also given the central role this has had, including fixing targets since Amsterdam and later with the 2020 plan. Already here it was clear that part of the success could involve the integration of various types of labour market and welfare state strategies, so that more interventionist policy elements could be found and, at that same time, both regulation and deregulation (Magnusson and Ottosson 2002).

It has often been difficult to disentangle the impact of the various national and supranational actors from economic and political development. Therefore the results are not always the same. Consequently, the impact of the European Employment Strategy (EES) on national active labour market policy has been questioned. Armingeon thus argued that there has been an impact on ALMP from a higher level of spending as a result of the EU strategy (Armingeon 2007). This is confirmed in a study from 2011 that OMC has had an impact through the mutual learning of the peer-review program, although not supporting the arguments that recommendations have an impact (van Vliet and Koster 2011, Mailand 2009).

A possible explanation for the variation of impact is that the EES has several different types of governance objectives. They include the promotion of learning and convergence (although maintaining respect for diversity), the integration of separate policy areas, and increasing participation (Trubek and Mosher 2003). These authors also argue that the 'EES has had an influence on such policy fields as social exclusion, education and training, fiscal policy and family policy' (Trubek and Mosher 2003: 51). This is, however, based upon the Commission's viewpoint, which is not necessarily an objective opinion.

A more normative viewpoint states 'On the other hand, it is inevitable that in a converging Europe, national politics will lose its importance. If we want to build up a European society, we cannot afford big social discrepancies. For reasons of social cohesion, there must be a minimum standard for all European citizens in old age.' (Reinhard 2010: 213). The author also argues that the Green Paper on Pensions, published by the EU Commission on 7 July 2010, might play the same role as the papers on the single European currency did around 30 years ago. The agenda-setting role of the Commission in combination with the OMC might thus be a way to move the decisions forward. So far no strong and clear impact on the EU in core welfare areas can be witnessed from this OMC approach, although court decisions have seemingly had a stronger impact.

Conclusion

There has been a movement towards a larger role for the EU in the core area of welfare state services, although the way to a higher impact on welfare policies has been very diverse. In some areas, this has been achieved through court cases (for example Laval); in others through agenda-setting as part of the communication of viewpoints and the OMC (active labour market policy); still other areas used gradual economic integration, implying a gradually weaker role for individual member states in the field of social policy. Finally, the use of directives has opened the discussion, as is seen in the case of the service directive, for example. Generally, the impact has been stronger where there have been directives or court decisions.

However, given the financial crisis pressures from convergence and tendencies towards it (see Chapter 4), the role of the European Union (taken more as a common set of options and possibilities rather than as a specific entity) can imply further development towards welfare state models moving in the same direction. The demand for fiscal consolidation thus acts as pressure on the decision-makers also in relation to social service. This theme will be further pursued in the chapters dealing with the developments of welfare policies of national states.

The financial crisis has further aggravated financial problems and the EU has strengthened its demand on what proper fiscal policy is. This then implies a further limit on the abilities of a nation state to pursue its own fiscal policy.

Chapter 8

Governance, Financing and Employment in Social Services in the Czech Republic

Pavel Horák, Markéta Horáková, Ondřej Hora and Tomáš Sirovátka

The Czech Republic represents a post-communist hybrid welfare state (Cerami 2006), shaped by the 'layering' of the Bismarckian, communist and liberal elements into its specific current combination. It is a low social expenditure welfare state influenced by imbedded liberalism after 1989 (Armingeon 2006) and is moving slowly towards neo-liberalism (Saxonberg and Sirovátka 2009). Specifically, the challenges raised by the new social risks have been neglected (Sirovátka 2007). This overall context has had important consequences for the developments of social services, as will be shown in this chapter.

Change in the Financing of the Czech Welfare State

The Czech Republic is a country where social protection expenditure is clearly below the EU average, which in 2010 was 28.2 per cent of GDP, including both expenditures in cash/benefits and in kind/services (see Table 8.1). This pattern has not changed much since the year 2000. The increases of total social protection expenditure as a percentage of GDP in 2010 is partly due to the drop of GDP by 4.5 per cent in 2009 after which in 2010 growth of only 2.5 per cent of GDP followed. This was partly due to the increases of expenditures, both in cash benefits (pensions) and in kind (health care). In social services the decrease in expenditure is clear.

Since 2000 it is mainly health care expenditure that has increased; meanwhile, other expenditures have stagnated and expenditure on services for the elderly and disabled have dropped. Those that have remained especially low are expenditure on family services, housing and active labour market policies.

Table 8.2 shows the overall structure of how the Czech Republic finances the welfare state. On average there is a lower level of taxes and duties than in the EU. This is especially prevalent in the area of capital and labour taxation.

The Czech Republic has followed many of the same traits as other EU member states by lowering the tax rate for companies. Since 2000 it has been reduced from 31 per cent to 19 per cent in 2010. The top-level tax has been reduced dramatically from 32 per cent to 15 per cent. However, the overall revenue from taxes and duties has remained stable with the implication that there has especially

Table 8.1   **Social protection expenditure as per cent of GDP in the Czech Republic (2000–2010)**

	2000	2005	2010
Social protection total	18.2	17.8	19.5
Social protection in cash	12.3	11.6	13.1
Social protection in kind	5.9	6.2	6.4
Health care and sickness in kind	4.9	5.2	5.7
Invalidity in kind	0.2	0.2	0.1
Old age in kind	0.5	0.3	0.3
Survivors in kind	0.02	0.02	0.00
Family in kind	0.1	0.2	0.1
Unemployment in kind	0.03	0.03	0.02
Housing in kind	0.1	0.1	0.1
Social Exclusion in kind	0.06	0.07	0.04

Source: Eurostat (2012b)

been an increase in the revenue coming from taxes on consumption. Environment taxes (such as those in Germany and the UK) play only a limited role in the provision of revenue and have been stable since 2000 at around 2.5–2.6 per cent of GDP.

It follows that there are overall tax and duty burdens (including social security contributions), thus the revenues from different types of taxes and duties to the Czech state budget have been relatively stable within the last ten years. The comparison with the overall level of taxes and duties of the other surveyed countries shows that the revenues in the state budget were the lowest in 2009/2010. Although the private out-of-pocket payments for health as a percentage of GDP

Table 8.2   **Development in overall tax and duty revenue on labour, capital and consumption as percentages of GDP in the Czech Republic (2000–2010)**

	2000	2005	2010
Total receipts from taxes and duties	33.9	35.7	33.8
Taxes on labour	17.1	19.1	17.5 (2009)
Taxes on capital	6.2	6.8	5.8 (2009)
Taxes on consumption	10.6	11.3	11.2 (2009)

Source: Eurostat (2012b)

have moved up from 10.2 per cent in 2000 to 14.4 per cent in 2009 (OECD 2012b), this ratio is actually below the EU average, although above the average of the UK, Germany and Denmark.

The presented data show that the total revenues to the state budget from taxes and duties have been stable in the Czech Republic in recent years, in fact, the lowest of all the countries surveyed in 2009/2010. Hand-in-hand with low revenues to the state budget, the expenditure on social protection was consistently low in the monitored period (there was an increase only in the area of pensions and expenditure on health services; the other types of expenditures remained low or even decreased).

Change in the Governance of Selected Social Services in the Czech Republic

Childcare

During the era of communism, Czech women were encouraged to participate in the labour market through special incentives which included *inter alia* a wide palette of publicly provided childcare services for all age groups of preschool children. After the collapse of communism, the Czech government began to promote the male-breadwinner model, in which a woman should stay at home with the children, while her husband works (Szelewa and Polakowski 2008). Giving less priority to publicly provided childcare services is presented by policymakers in these countries as offering 'more choice' or 'the right to care' (Szelewa and Polakowski 2008). As a result, state and municipal authorities started to close many childcare facilities, especially nurseries, and eliminated financial support to parents (Saxonberg and Sirovátka 2006).

Nurseries were drastically reduced and currently are unavailable to most of the Czech population of women with very young children because of their small number, their concentration in big cities and high financial costs. There has been a gradual reduction of the child population from the mid 1990s to 2007. Responding to this trend, many Czech municipalities cancelled day care for children of pre-school age (kindergarten). The subsequent rise in the birth rate has led to the situation whereby in some municipalities and regions there is insufficient institutional support for care for the youngest generation and for parenthood. The consequence of this is the decreasing employment rate of women – mothers at the time of their highest fertility. While in 2002 the employment rate of women with one or two children up to six years of age was 69.4 per cent, in 2005 it was only 36.3 per cent; in 2010 it dropped to 21.1 per cent. This is almost half the average employment rate of all EU countries (Eurostat 2012c, UNECE 2012). Moreover, women returning from parental leave belong to the groups with the highest risk of becoming unemployed (compare Kuchařová and Svobodova 2006, Kuchařová et al. 2009, Sokačová 2010, Vláda 2011, Mejstřík et al. 2011).

Despite the aforementioned trend in the reduction of childcare facilities, contemporary Czech family policy can be characterised as a more conservative model with universalistic and liberal elements, where the universalistic elements are the result of both the conservative tradition of the pre-war era and the universalistic policies of the communist regime. In this context especially kindergarten for children aged three to five has gained great popularity (Saxonberg and Sirovatka 2009).

Regulation and Delivery

Childcare services are regulated in the Czech Republic by the Ministry of Labour and Social Affairs and by the Ministry of Education. A role is also played by the Departments of Finance and the Interior, which set policy for the operation of local and regional governments.

Three kinds of childcare services exist that are mostly publicly funded and managed in the Czech Republic (MLSA 2009, Kuchařová et al. 2009, OECD 2011c): care services for children up to three years of age (day nursery and private childcare facilities); care services for pre-school children aged from three to six years (kindergartens and private childcare facilities); and care services for primary-school age children (school nurseries designed to primarily assist parents of primary-school age children in reconciling their professional and family life). To a limited extent, some parents use the services of private nannies and babysitters, however, these are too expensive for most parents. The network of maternity and parenting centres designed for the common residence of parents with children is also significant; some provide regular or one-time 'baby-sitting' services for a regular or one-time payment. There are only a few company kindergartens, because of the large financial and organisational demands the companies must meet (Sokačová 2010).

Financing

Childcare services are mostly financed from the state and municipal budgets and various national and supranational grants. However, the extent of public expenditure on childcare services has been very low in the Czech Republic over a long period and consistently reaches about half of the average costs of the EU member states (0.14 per cent of GDP in 2005, 0.12 per cent of GDP in 2008; OECD statistics 2012). Moreover, while governments of many EU countries financially support facilities for children under three, the funding of day nurseries in the Czech Republic is fully in the hands of municipalities. The enrolment fees for nurseries are therefore very high and the parents' payments must cover more than half their costs (Kuchařová et al. 2009): the fees represent between 6 and 22 per cent of the average wage (Vláda 2012).

On the other hand, public childcare services for children from three to six are fully supported by the state, and parents contribute at only minimal levels (between 3 and 5 per cent of the average wage in the economy). Even though the financial participation of parents has increased in the last decade, it has had no significant effect on the placement of children in Czech kindergartens (Kuchařová et al. 2009). Under the current legislation, the director of each kindergarten has the choice to reduce or waive the fee for younger children in pre-school education with respect to the financial situation of the nursery and parents (Vláda 2011).

The costs of non-state institutions caring for pre-school children differ according to the type of services provided. Although private kindergartens receive state subsidies for educational activities, they require quite high tuition fees from parents (about 44 per cent of the average wage in the economy). Similarly, the enrolment fees in private kindergarten are significantly higher as compared to public kindergarten (from 21 per cent to 83 per cent of the average wage in the economy) (Vláda 2011, Novotná 2012, Jak do školy 2013, Jesle-jesličky 2013).

Outcomes
The accessibility of pre-school education is a key element in the competitiveness of the Czech economy (Mejstřík et al. 2011, Strategie 2011). The recent analysis and media debates related to childcare reveal great problems in the regional capacity and accessibility of childcare facilities (Kuchařová et al. 2009, Vláda 2011), especially of public and private nurseries, whose current number is only a few dozen (there were 46 facilities in 2010; ÚZIS 2011). In addition, both public and private nurseries are extremely expensive, as mentioned above. Likewise, babysitting services, which are available only in large cities, are also expensive and therefore of very limited accessibility (Sokačová 2010). For the above-mentioned reasons, the enrolment rate of Czech children under three attending nurseries has been considerably undersized for a decade in comparison to other countries surveyed – about 4 per cent of all children in this age group in 2005 and 7 per cent in 2010, (OECD 2011c, UNECE 2012).

In contrast, the number of children attending kindergarten for children from three to school age is at a relatively good level in the Czech Republic even though there was a decline of these facilities in the years 2005–2010 (the enrolment rate dropped from 85 per cent to 72 per cent, which is about 6 per cent below the EU average (OECD 2011c)). However, there was a more than four-fold increase in the number of Czech children who were unable to enrol in kindergarten in the last ten years (the number of pending requests was 29,600 in 2010, Vláda (2011), ÚIV (2012). The increase in the demand for kindergarten services has not only been caused by the higher number of children in each age group, but also by the increase in the proportion of children below three years of age who have been recently admitted to kindergarten (one third of all children attending Czech kindergartens were under two in the 2009/10 school year (Vláda 2011)).

Childcare services (nurseries and kindergartens) in the Czech Republic are good quality. In the case of nurseries, Czech legislation requires nursery employees to have, as a minimum, qualification from a 4-year course at a secondary nursing school. OECD statistics also show that the quality of formal day-care services for children under three is at a satisfactory level in terms of the child-to-staff ratio at the level of other countries surveyed (see Chapter 12, data by OECD 2011c).

Research conducted in nurseries in the Czech Republic in 2007 confirms that these facilities are of high quality both in terms of care and staff training, as well as the actual psycho-social development of children (Kolářová 2007). Even though there are differences between particular facilities (Sokačová 2010), the hygiene and spatial requirements set by legislation are usually followed.

Similarly, there is a requirement for kindergarten workers to have undergone four years at secondary pedagogical school or three years of tertiary education. In fact, workers with secondary school graduation have been dominating in the Czech pre-school services over a long period, although their share has been falling slightly in recent years; by contrast, the share of workers who are university graduates has increased (from 4.4 per cent in 2006 to 7.8 per cent in 2009; ÚIV 2012). The child-to-staff ratio in pre-school services is at a good level in the Czech Republic in comparison to the other countries surveyed, as in the case of nurseries. Furthermore, public and private kindergartens are responsible not only for compliance to pedagogical but also hygienic standards. Checks are implemented through a special body called the 'Czech School Inspection'. Kindergarten teachers are required by a Decree on the Additional Training of Teaching Staff to expand their professional qualification.

Trends and Innovations
As we have shown, facilities for the youngest children have gradually disappeared in the last two decades and the number of places in kindergarten for children aged three to six years has dropped in the Czech Republic. This is the opposite trend to that of the other countries surveyed (that is Denmark, Germany and the United Kingdom). In addition, due to the higher birthrate in recent years, interest in these facilities has increased, which is currently reflected in the almost zero availability of nurseries and in the limited availability of kindergarten.

Faced with the increasing demand for childcare during the last decade, the Czech government has started to consider some solutions which would be cheaper than expanding the capacity of public childcare facilities. Since 2007 alternative forms of childcare have been discussed: services provided at home by private child-minders or neighbours and children's groups and enterprise facilities. The Czech government submitted a draft law on child groups (nurseries) in August 2012, which should increase the childcare services alternative to public childcare.

Elderly Care

There has been a gradual increase in the number of people over 65 in the Czech Republic since 2000 (from 13.8 per cent to 15.4 per cent of the population). According to OECD data, the ratio of economically inactive elderly to the total labour force almost reached the level of the OECD average in 2010 (30.7 per cent in the Czech Republic compared to 31.3 per cent in the OECD). The available data show that the proportion of inactive people aged over 65 has been gradually increasing over the last ten years. Comparing the situation in 2000 to 2010, the increase in the proportion of economically inactive older persons exceeds the increase in the share of the number of people aged over 65 to the entire population (that is, there was a 3.3 per cent increase in the inactive and a 1.6 per cent increase in those aged 65). It is expected that the current number of seniors will increase by more than one third in the Czech Republic within the next 13 years (Průša 2011). As the improving health and economic activity of older people can be expected in the future, the state expenditure on old-age security will certainly increase as well.

Regulation and Delivery
In the Czech Republic, no single body is responsible for integrated long-term care policies or benefits. The responsibilities are divided across social services, the health-care sector and among different levels of government (local, regional, national). While the health sector (including long-term care) has remained largely centralised, responsibilities in providing and, in part, funding social services have been increasingly shifted towards regional and local levels (Österle et al. 2010).

From the emerging welfare mix in the long-term care point of view, public sector care clearly dominates the formal provision of care in Central-East Europe – including the Czech Republic – more than in most other European countries. There is, however, a general trend towards strengthening and incentivising the role of private actors, in particular non-profit organisations. A broader welfare mix has developed rather modestly due to the relative weakness of civil society in this region (by comparison with Western Europe), the limited accessibility of public funding and the regulation of underlying funding regimes that limit the degree of pluralisation of social services and their expansion (Österle et al. 2010).

Caring for the elderly is provided in three ways, which differ by whether the care is provided within social services, health care facilities or other facilities. Social services coordinated by the Ministry of Labour and Social Affairs include residential services ('senior citizens homes' and 'special regime homes'), field-based services (community care service ('*pečovatelská služba*') at home users or 'nursing home'('*domov s pečovatelskou službou*') and out-patient services (including day centres of different type). Health care facilities managed by the Ministry of Health include 'hospitals for the chronically ill' ('*léčebny pro dlouhodobě nemocné*') and 'geriatric departments (centres)' at hospitals. Other facilities include community care services ('*domovy s pečovatelskou službou*') that are built and managed by municipalities with a financial contribution from the Ministry of Regional Development.[1] While social services are governed by the Act on Social Services and include care services performed by social workers ('*pečovatelské služby*'), health services are governed by the Act on Health and are provided by nurses who perform nursing services ('*ošetřovatelské služby*'). All of these services can be publicly or privately provided. Furthermore, NGOs

---

1   These facilities are houses, often located in residential areas where seniors using community care services are accommodated. The community care centre (pečovatelská služba) is present either in the house with seniors or outside the complex.

can operate at the interface between social and health services and can therefore provide both day-care services provided by social workers and nursing services provided by medical professionals.

The founders of institutional care are mostly higher local government bodies (the regions comprise 90 per cent) and municipalities. In neighbouring Germany, the situation is reversed: providers of social services are private companies and the non-profit sector. The Czech self-government model is criticised for a variety of complications such as conflicts of interest and slower responses to environmental changes.

The most frequently used services by Czech senior citizens are the home-care services: available statistics show that around 20 per cent of seniors over 65 obtain help from their families (APSS 2010) while about 70–80 per cent of seniors require long-term care[2] from their family members (Jeřábek 2005).

The social innovation that aimed to reduce institutional care and create a market for elderly services is the 'care allowance', which was defined by the Social Services Act of 2006. The allowance may be used by the entitled elderly person – according to the primary intention of Social Services Act – for purchases of services from service providers and from people close to the seniors. However, experience shows that most of the seniors consider this allowance to be rather low;[3] it appears to them as a supplement to their pensions, therefore, they do not use it to purchase professional social services. For example, in 2007 an amount of 14.6 billion CZK was paid for care allowance to the elderly in need of home care while 2.4 billion was used for the purchase of services. In 2012 the respective figures were 18.4 billion CZK and 6.4 billion, respectively. This is about one third of the allowance used for purchasing the service, although it is assumed that it partly serves as a reward for informal care to family members. Since this allowance is not means-tested, but is considered a categorical benefit to those who need assistance, the question discussed in the Czech Republic revolves around its targeting efficiency. Another difficulty for those who need assistance and cannot afford to pay for it is the time-consuming administrative procedures associated with the claim for the allowance.

The quality of social services (including the control of user rights) is supervised by the state through social services inspectors comprised of employees of regional offices and the Ministry of Labour and Social Affairs. Moreover, from June 2010 to November 2011, the European E-Qalin Management quality system was introduced in many Czech public facilities for elderly people (APSS 2013).

---

2   What is important is that the long-term care term is not legislatively or conceptually anchored in the Czech Republic and therefore it is not usually used. Nevertheless, within the existing network of services, we can identify facilities that have the character of long-term care (e.g. special regime homes or hospitals for the chronically ill).

3   The level of the care allowance is between 800 CZK (in the case of light dependency) to 12,000 CZK/440 Euros (in the case of full dependency) – this maximum amount is slightly less than half the average wage.

Financing

The current Czech elderly care system is financed by the state as well as through contributions from the founders (regions and municipalities), health insurance companies, care allowances and pensions (Průša 2011). Medical services and social institutional care have different sources of funding, although health care services in both sectors are covered by health insurance funds. Social services, which are a responsibility of the Ministry of Labour and Social Affairs, are financed by a mix of general taxes, regional budgets and individual contributions. While nursing homes for the elderly are paid by the region, retirement homes are funded by individual municipalities. For residential care in particular, individual contributions by clients make up 35 per cent of total costs while state budgets (30 per cent) and local authorities (25 per cent) cover over half of all costs. Health insurance finances comprise on average 3 per cent of total long-term care costs in the social sector. Client contributions for care in social services cannot exceed 85 per cent of individual income (Colombo 2011).

In the case of social care provided in the home, the financial participation of service users is often only a fraction of the total cost (for example in 2008 this share was 25 per cent on ambulatory care services and 20 per cent on personal assistance; APSS 2010). By contrast, costs paid by clients for stays in care institutions are very high (50 per cent in the case of homes for the elderly and about 33 per cent of total costs in the case of the facilities with special regimes; see APSS 2010).

At present, the system of financing social and health services is criticised as being ineffective. Many experts consider the sources of their funding to be random, voluntary, non-transparent, non-systematic and/or discretionary (Průša and Horecký 2012). Furthermore, there are two problems associated with the new care allowance. First, this allowance does not distinguish the different costs generated by formal and informal home care service providers. For this reason, it seems to be too low to allow the person to hire professional services (the purchase of professional service is low, as explained above). Second, in the case of institutional care, the allowance is cut to the lower level; however, the state subsidy to service providers is not high enough to cover the costs of care. The service providers are allowed to charge the clients: the problem is that their pensions plus the care allowance received do not cover the costs of care that remain after the state subsidy is provided. Service providers often invest their own money in order to prevent dismissals of clients from care.

Outcomes

Of all the above-mentioned services for the elderly, care at home delivered by female family members dominates in the Czech Republic in the long term (care in informal networks represents 80 per cent of all care delivered in the Czech Republic; see Jeřábek 2005, APSS 2010, OECD 2011d). In the case of other social services (that is residential care, field- and out-patient services) there are differences in the scope and quality of provided services between the regions and municipalities. Whereas care services in small communities are often not established due to the little political support or the insolvency of municipalities (which rely on senior citizens homes paid by the regional authority), large municipalities often provide well-funded social services which are at a level of good quality (compare Habart 2007, APSS 2010, Průša 2010, 2011, Průša and Horecký 2012).

The trend of gradual improvement in service quality can be seen especially in residential social care facilities where EU subsidies enabled the new construction or reconstruction of buildings and the introduction of quality standards in 2007, influencing the increase of individual care of seniors by care workers. On the contrary, health care facilities focused on long-term care ('hospitals for the chronically ill') have often been criticised in recent years for the poor conditions of buildings and the lack of staff and resources needed for adequate treatment, rehabilitation and care (Princová 2009, MLSA 2010a).

The accessibility of social and health institutions delivering long-term care in the Czech Republic is at a good level. The ratio of long-term care beds in social institutions and hospitals per 1000 of the population aged 65 years and over is close to the OECD average in the long-term (for example in 2010, 42 beds in institutions in the Czech Republic compared to 50 beds in OECD countries on average and 7 beds in hospitals in the Czech Republic compared to 5.8 beds in OECD countries; OECD 2012b).

Trends and Innovations
Summing up, the Czech Republic ranks among the countries representing the conservative model of social policy with elements of the social democratic model. In this context, the trend of greater preference of home-care over institutional care prevails. Moreover, the limited public funding of Czech institutional services has resulted in the capacity of these facilities to remain insufficient for many years (although there are bigger problems in regions with smaller communities that are characterised by limited local resources and limited political support).

Expectations in care for the elderly have been connected to the Social Services Act of 2007 which brought three crucial changes that can be considered as social innovations with respect to the criteria set in Chapter 5. First, the active participation of service users was introduced, which is reflected in the possibility that (a) users can participate in decisions on the planning of social services at the community level and (b) in the setting of individual services (individual plans). Users can also (c) use a care allowance, which enables them to pay for home (informal) or professional (formal) carers. Another innovation is related to the introduction of quality standards, the categorisation of different types of social services and the possibility of sharing them by different groups of clients. However, the profits from these innovations are not very high due to insufficient financing. The purchase of professional home care has not increased very much; at the same time, the combination of state subsidy and care allowance does not sufficiently cover the costs of institutional care for care providers. Moreover, while the quality of residential social services and home care services improves, the quality of long-term health facilities is not sufficient due to the outdated legislation from the 1990s (the result is an insufficient number of poorly-paid nurses and social workers).

Employment Services

From the long-term perspective, the unemployment rate in the Czech Republic has ranged between 4 and 8 per cent over the last decade, always slightly below the average unemployment rate in EU countries. In 2011, the unemployment rate was 3 per cent below the EU average (that is 6.7 per cent in the Czech Republic compared to 9.7 per cent in the EU).

In 2009, the most significant economic downturn occurred in the Czech Republic since its transition to a market economy in 1990 (a decrease of 4.7 per cent of GDP). However, during the years 2009–2011 the unemployment rate did not reach the levels of 2004 and 2005. This reflects the fact that the Czech labour market has become more flexible since 2006 in terms of the inflows and outflows of unemployment in spite of the deep recession (Sirovátka and Šimíková 2013). Evidently, the long-term structural problems of the labour market are more significant than the cyclical fluctuations of the economy caused by the recession. Nevertheless, new groups of unemployed were registered at the labour offices during the global recession and the disadvantage of the traditionally vulnerable groups in the labour market intensified due to the competition of a larger number of unemployed for the declining number of available jobs (Sirovátka and Šimíková 2013, Hora and Sirovátka 2012).

Regulation and Delivery
The governance of Czech labour market policies is concentrated in the hands of the Ministry of Labour and Social Affairs as well as the Labour Office of the Czech Republic, which is its subordinate administrative body with nationwide coverage in particular regions. The ministry is responsible for four areas: designing the national program of reforms, implementing active labour market policies (ALMP), administering unemployment benefits and monitoring and evaluating active labour market policies (Sirovátka and Kulhavý 2008, Kalužná 2008).

Since 2010, the ongoing reform of employment services has reversed the originally heavily decentralised system into a fully centralised system when regional and local employment offices with great discretion were established as bodies (regional offices with detached local subsidiaries) with minimum power and fully-dependent on the allocation of resources and staff by the ministry (compare Sirovátka and Kulhavý 2008). At the same time, social assistance, which had formerly been in the jurisdiction of the municipalities, was merged to the labour offices. The number of staff dealing with clients in social assistance was reduced as were the counselling activities of office workers, which were newly contracted (within national or regional individual projects) to non-governmental institutions from the private sector. However, the Public Procurement Act of 2012 tightened the conditions for obtaining and implementing contracted services; therefore, the flexibility and potential innovations resulting from these projects have been limited. While the cooperation between public and private actors (NGOs, private agencies, and so on) is often rather formal, based mainly on mutual legislative obligations, the cooperation of the state labour offices with regional employers has remained at a good level in many regions (compare Horák 2010, 2011, 2012).

Financing

In the Czech Republic, active and passive employment policy measures are financed from the state budget based on mandatory contributions by employers to the social insurance system and from the European Social Fund (ESF).

Budgets for active labour market programmes are determined annually by the Ministry of Labour and Social Affairs at the central level and allocated to individual district labour offices that formulate their financial needs and expectations. Although their requests are taken into account, their needs are not always fully covered (Kalužná 2008).

National sources are allocated by the centre of the Labour Office to the regional labour offices according to several criteria (namely the number of registered unemployed, the unemployment rate, the number of job seekers under 25 years of age and those above 50, the number of disabled job seekers, the number of job seekers per job vacancy and the number of long-term unemployed). Although overall spending priorities are determined at the central level, the regional/district labour offices have some freedom in deciding how the allocated resources are to be spent.

In the case of funding from the European Social Fund (ESF), the programs financed by the ESF are approved by the Ministry of Labour and Social Affairs in the Czech Republic. The individual projects must meet all the formal requirements and conditions as specified in the Public Procurement Act of 2006 (revised in 2012). They are often very inflexible and limit the service suppliers from the private sector concerning the specific activities and number of participants in each activity/measure.

In recent years, the total expenditure on the labour market has grown (from 0.50 per cent GDP in 2005 to 0.72 per cent GDP in 2010), which is still well below the EU average (2.17 per cent of GDP in 2009). In addition to increased spending on labour market services, spending on active measures also increased in 2005 and 2010 in the Czech Republic from 0.13 per cent of GDP in 2005 to 0.23 per cent of GDP in 2010. These costs amounted to under half the average of the EU-27 (0.54 per cent of GDP; OECD 2012c). The share of ESF expenditure of the total active labour market policy expenditures has consistently been between 60–70 per cent since 2007 (see MLSA 2012).

However, in recent years the Czech Republic has cut expenditure on active labour market policies: in 2011 expenditure on active employment policy declined by 38 per cent compared to 2010. Simultaneously, the volume of spending on active labour market policy financed by the ESF decreased substantially (see

MSLA 2012). These changes are compatible with the liberal reforms of the Czech welfare state implemented by the centre-right government after 2008, which intensified during 2010–11 with cuts of public expenditure on social services.

Outcomes

The OECD data show that the share of the unemployed using active employment policy measures was constantly around 1 per cent of the labour force between 2004 and 2010. This ratio is consistently three to four times lower than the OECD average (OECD 2012c). At least the evaluation of the Czech active labour market programmes shows that they were targeted at the regions with the highest unemployment rates, especially in times of economic crisis (2009–2010) where they are relatively well targeted on the most vulnerable unemployed (that is mothers with children, people with disabilities, recent graduates and the long-term and chronically unemployed; Hora and Sirovátka 2012). On the other hand, the Czech system of public employment services faces the problem of insufficient staffing in the long-term: Kalužná (2008) refers to an average of 202 clients per front-line staff in 2006. This number increased to about 300 during the crisis.[4] The result is that the performance of Czech public employment services manifests a certain kind of formality and schematisation (for more details see Sirovátka et al. 2007, Horák and Horáková 2009, Sirovátka and Šimíková 2013).

The proportion of the unemployed who were recipients of unemployment benefits was in the range of 2 to 4 per cent of the labour force between 2003 and 2010. The indicator of participant inflow was the lowest in 2007 and 2008, that is, during the end of the economic boom and the beginning of the global economic crisis. The reason for this is that recent graduates are not entitled to benefits (since they do not fulfil the condition of having an employment record). Secondly, the benefits are provided for a period of only five months (or 8/11 months in the case of people above 50/55). After that the unemployed may be entitled to social assistance benefits that are funded from general revenues, not from unemployment insurance.

Trends and Innovations

To summarise, reforms in employment services have followed over recent years. In the recent history of the Czech employment services, we can identify two key time periods in which reform changes have occurred. The first period (2003–2006) is associated with legislative and institutional changes resulting in the introduction of new tools, practices and non-governmental agencies enabling the fulfilment of principles of client activation and individualisation and the contracting out of delivered employment services. The second period is related to reforms of the Employment Office that are aimed at saving money through the centralisation

---

4   Own estimates based on the fact that unemployment went up by about 50 per cent and the number of staff was cut by 12 per cent in 2011.

of decision-making and streamlining the overall management, administration and delivery of social benefits and services.

These reforms have included measures like compulsory deliverred Individual Action Plans, increasing the scope of ESF projects, project-based management and the outsourcing of a wide range of labour market policies, including job mediation and the individual choice of re-qualification measures by the unemployed. These attempts of social innovation, however, were implemented under conditions of diminishing personnel at labour offices, restricted scope of active labour market policy measures, insufficient incentives for private agencies in job mediation and within rigid conditions for the implementation of ESF projects. Under these circumstances, the attempts to innovate have not brought a significant increase in the effectiveness of meeting client needs or in decreasing expenditures.

Nevertheless, many examples of social innovations may be found in the form of individual projects of active labour market policies financed by the ESF where counselling, training and job creation measures are combined with other social services which are typically implemented by private agencies or NGOs, often providing better treatment of clients than is possible from Public Employment Services.

Employment in the Health and Social Work Sector in the Czech Republic

For the discussion of employment in social services we use data collected in Chapter 3 supplemented by data from national administrative sources. The Czech Republic is a country where employment in HSW was 333,500 and the share of HSW in total employment in the economy was 6.90 per cent in 2010 (the share is rather low compared to the other countries in focus). Most employment in the HSW sector (73 per cent) is concentrated in health. Residential care activities constitute 17.7 per cent and social work without accommodation 9.4 per cent of the sector. The employment in social care without accommodation is very low when compared to the other countries. The employment in HSW grew by 18.7 per cent between 2000 and 2010; most of this growth occurred between 2000 and 2005 (Eurostat data) in full-time jobs.

The national data in Table 8.3 (based on LFS and published by ČSÚ) confirm a trend of employment growth in the HSW sector in the Czech Republic (in the data provided by Eurostat). The growth of HSW employment started in 1999 after a period of stagnation (1993–1998); from 2000 to 2011 this growth was about 20 per cent. The growth in women's employment was more substantial than the growth in men's employment.

The sector is highly dominated by women (especially in residential care and social work). The workforce in the HSW sector is ageing quite rapidly. The share of workers aged over 50 increased from 26.3 per cent in 2000 to 31.3 per cent in 2010. The prevailing education level of workers in the HSW sector is at the medium level (69.1 per cent), which is the most typical education level for the

Table 8.3   **Employment in Health and Social Work Sector in the Czech Republic, in thousands (2000–2011)**

	2000	2001	2002	2003	2004	2005
Total	285.1	298.5	298.3	300.9	317.3	321.7
Men	57.4	62	63	63.2	60.9	66.7
Women	227.7	237.7	235.3	237.7	256.4	255
	2006	**2007**	**2008**	**2009**	**2010**	**2011**
Total	323.4	331.6	321.3	326.3	339.9	324.8
Men	63.8	65.9	59.3	60.5	68.7	60.3
Women	259.6	265.6	262	265.8	271.2	264.5

Source: ČSÚ (2012)

whole Czech workforce; the share of low educated workers is rather small (5 per cent). Most workers are qualified in health and welfare or social sciences, but among the medium qualified there are also some industry qualified workers. Younger workers usually have a higher level of qualification than older cohorts of HSW workers. Similarly, men usually have a higher level of qualification than women.

Data for childcare services are provided by the Ministry of Education. Nurseries (crèches) for children under three years of age are very rare, and consequently there were only 447 workers employed in nurseries in 2005 in the country (Kuchařová and Svobodová 2006); nevertheless, kindergartens are used widely. According to ČSÚ (2008) and Kuchařová et al. (2009), the number of pre-school teachers in kindergarten has declined from over 32,000 in 1990/1991 to about 22,000 in 2004/2005.[5] The decline in the number of teachers accompanied the decline in kindergarten facilities. This reduction was connected to two trends: a decrease in the number of children (low fertility) and the merging of kindergartens (ČSÚ 2008). Most kindergarten workers in the Czech Republic work in facilities which are established by the municipalities (only about 400 teachers worked in private or church facilities in 2005/2006; see Kuchařová and Svobodová 2006). The number of teachers started to grow slightly in 2005 with a further increase in 2007–2009 (see Table 8.4). From 2005 to 2007 there were also about 10,000 to 10,500 out-of-school teachers who took care of young school children in special facilities of after-school classes called '*družiny*'.

In other words, the data presented show that the number of employees in public kindergartens in childcare has increased since 2000/2001 (compare Table 8.4).

---

5   Kuchařová and Svobodová (2006) declare that of the 21,621 teachers in kindergarten, 100 per cent were women and most of them were from 30 to 49 years of age.

Table 8.4   **Number of teachers in kindergarten in the Czech Republic (2000–2010)**

School Year	2000/2001	2001/2002	2002/2003	2003/2004	2004/2005
Kindergarten	6 007	5 881	5 795	5 067	4 994
Children	286 085	282 642	284 950	286 340	286 230
PST	22 906	22 451	22 332	22 158	21 840
School Year	2005/2006	2006/2007	2007/2008	2008/2009	2009/2010
Kindergarten	4 834	4 815	4 808	4 809	4 826
Children	282 183	285 419	291 194	301 620	314 008
PST	22 485	22 368	22 744	23 567	24 584

Note: PST = pre-school teachers (working in kindergarten) are recounted to full job standard
Source: Kuchařová et al. (2009); Institute for Information on Education (Education Yearbook)

The increase in the number of children in 2002–2005 caused a rise in the number of teachers in existing facilities in 2007–2009; new facilities were not established due to related financial costs.

Data on social and employment services are provided in Table 8.5. The data confirm the overall trend of social services growth (employee total) and show a shift from pedagogical and medical employees to social care employees and social workers. These trends are the result of the reaction of the Ministry of Labour and Social Affairs, which seeks to expand the number of services for the growing senior population, and the Ministry of Health, which seeks to streamline the existing medical services in healthcare by reducing the number of services.

Work in employment services and social security is less stable; however, there is still an overall trend of employment growth or stagnation rather than reduction. Nevertheless, the main cause of employment expansion is the reform of social benefit administration rather than advancement in employment services like job mediation or counselling: the administration of some (social assistance and family) benefits has been transferred from the municipalities to employment offices.

Mean annual earnings of workers in the HSW sector amounted to €12,154 in 2010 (Eurostat data). This is about 7 per cent less than the reference category of manufacturing (see Chapter 3). Young workers were usually the group with the lowest wages in HSW (13.6 per cent below average). The Czech Republic has one of the highest numbers of weekly working hours in the HSW sector (due to the low use of part-time work). According to national data, in the period 2000–2009, the total wages in the HSW sector (Table 8.6) were about 4–11 per cent below the wages in the total economy (the lowest in 2000, the highest in 2003); nevertheless, there are substantial differences among various professions in the HSW sector (see below).

Table 8.5   Number of employees in social services, ministry, employment services and social security (2005–2010)

	2005	2006	2007	2008	2009	2010
Number of employees in social services and specific categories of workers						
Employees (total)	36 079	36 516	37 152	38 115	39 497	40 384
Social care workers	10 031	11 172	13 832	15 168	16 599	17 970
Social workers	1 038	1 213	1 381	1 499	1 594	1 540
Pedagogical workers	1 254	1 201	1 046	967	870	777
Health care workers	10 391	9 403	7 450	6 963	6 698	6 449
Technical and manual workers	13 193	13 703	13 293	13 321	13 567	13 620
Number of employees in ministry, social security and employment services						
Ministry (MLSA)	712	721	738	764	807	836
Employment offices	8 024	8 008	8 200	8 229	8 184	8 276
Social security workers	7 902	8307	8397	8 176	8 273	8 754

Source: MLSA (2006, 2007, 2008, 2009, 2010b, 2011), own calculations

Table 8.6   Average gross monthly wages of workers in Health and Social Work Sector, in CZK (2000–2009)

Sector	2000	2001	2002	2003	2004
Total	13 594	14 750	15 911	16 905	18 025
HSW	11 754	13 354	15 051	16 311	16 770
HSW/Total	0.86	0.91	0.95	0.96	0.93
Sector	**2005**	**2006**	**2007**	**2008**	**2009**
Total	18 940	20 158	21 621	23 430	24 242
HSW	17 518	18 977	19 892	20 903	22 401
HSW/Total	0.92	0.94	0.92	0.89	0.92

Note: data for 2010 are not available because of substantial changes in methodology
Source: ČSÚ (2012)

Innovation in Social Services

Table 8.7   **Average gross monthly wages in social services, ministry, employment services and social security, in CZK (monthly) (2005–2010)**

	2005	2006	2007	2008	2009	2010
Gross wages of employees in social services and specific categories of workers						
Employees (total)	14 479	15 207	16 350	16 822	17 817	18 377
Social care workers	13 015	13 453	14 496	15 048	15 631	16 106
Social workers	16 244	17 132	18 706	18 515	19 946	20 605
Educators	16 666	17 454	19 757	19 759	20 632	21 109
General nurses	18 767	20 835	22 987	24 009	25 165	26 404
Manual workers	10 934	11 428	12 206	12 556	13 919	14 990
Gross wages of ministry, social security and employment services workers						
Ministry (MLSA)	27 095	28 702	31 509	34 995	36 762	37 778
Employment offices	19 340	20 222	22 074	22 610	23 576	22 659
Social security workers	19 742	21 301	22 196	22 905	24 049	22 613

Source: MLSA 2006, 2007, 2008, 2009, 2010b, 2011 (own calculations)

The gross wages of workers in social services (Table 8.7) are available for the period 2005–2010.[6] There are substantial differences between different professions in the social services sector. General practice nurses, educators and social workers are usually better paid than social care workers and manual workers (who can be considered to be low paid). The wages of employment office and social security workers are usually just below the average wage in the economy (about 23,542 CZK in 2008; 23,951 CZK in 2010).

In 2010, for example, we see that the salaries of workers in social care are more than 12 per cent lower than the average wage of social service social workers, educators or people at employment offices, who get more than the average wage by 12–24 per cent.

Conclusions

The presented data on the development of childcare, elderly care and employment services show that the Czech social services are financially undersized: the level

---

6   The table is not fully comparable to the table on employment above because data for more general categories are not available. Instead, data about specific professions (usually most numerous in a given category) were used (e.g. general practice nurses represented healthcare workers).

of expenditure on childcare, elder care and employment services is low. While the number of employees in social services has increased in the last decade, the increase has been very small in childcare and employment services, where wages are slightly below the average wage in the Czech Republic. On the contrary, a significant increase in the number of employees has occurred in elder care, where jobs are the worst paid and the salaries often do not even reach two thirds of the average wage in the country. However, this increase is rather a compensation for the decrease in the number of health workers.

The low public spending on social services clearly implies the slow pace of development of jobs in the social service sector. In recent years, some reforms have been introduced in the field of elderly care and employment services, although in childcare there has been stagnation and certain new measures have been merely considered. The attempts at innovation which have occurred in the Czech Republic were strongly influenced by ideas of marketisation and public-private mix; they were aimed at diminishing the role of the state in service delivery and increasing the role of private profit and non-profit providers or relatives (in elderly care). These attempts, however, have brought little employment growth. The reason is that the finance provided and incentives used with respect to non-state service providers have not been strong enough and have not enabled expansion of the services. Furthermore, sometimes the governance reforms have not been carefully or appropriately designed and/or implemented.

Specifically, in elderly care the quality of low-paid services provided to seniors in social services has increased. On the other hand, care allowance implemented in 2007 has not brought the expected expansion of individually purchased services by the elderly. Secondly, centralisation steps and some reforms in employment services, which should lead to higher system efficiency, have led to the greater unification and bureaucratisation of the provided services as well as to less access to active labour market policy measures.

The importance of the non-governmental sector is explicitly supported particularly in the field of employment, where many services are contracted out by private organisations; however, mutual cooperation is quite rigid. In elder care in the Czech Republic, the largest proportion of seniors use public services, which are increasingly co-financed from their own pockets; the financial support to purchase services is not sufficient considering the low purchasing power of the elderly. Dependence on public services is also very high in childcare; this is because there are just a few private facilities and they are affordable only to wealthy citizens.

Chapter 9

Governance, Financing and Employment in Social Services in Denmark

Bent Greve, Pavel Horák, Markéta Horáková and Ondřej Hora

Denmark represents a Nordic/social democratic welfare regime which to a large extent is perceived as a service welfare state, where welfare services are available as a universal element (that is access is based on the criteria of the need for services more than being on the labour market).

Change in the Financing of the Danish Welfare State

Social protection expenditures, both in cash and in kind, are among the highest in the EU due to the emphasis on the policies of de-familisation (childcare, elderly care), employment services and other policies responding to new social risks (housing, social exclusion). The expenditure on social services was 11.5 per cent of GDP in 2005 and increased even further in 2010 to 13.3 per cent.

Table 9.1   Social protection expenditure as per cent of GDP in
Denmark (2000–2010)

	2000	2005	2010
Social protection total	28.1	29.4	32.4
Social protection in cash	17.3	17.9	19.1
Social protection in kind	10.9	11.5	13.3
Health care and sickness in kind	4.7	5.1	6.2
Invalidity in kind	1.1	1.3	1.5
Old age in kind	1.7	1.8	2.0
Survivors in kind	0.01	0.01	0.00
Family in kind	2.2	2.3	2.5
Unemployment in kind	0.10	0.10	0.18
Housing in kind	0.7	0.7	0.8
Social Exclusion in kind	0.27	0.23	0.29

Source: Eurostat (2012b)

Table 9.2   Development in overall tax, duty revenue and taxes on labour, capital and consumption in Denmark as per cent of GDP (2000–2010)

	2000	2005	2010
Total receipts from taxes and duties	50.2	51.7	49.1
Taxes on labour	26.1	24.8	27.1 (2009)
Taxes on capital	7.2	10.0	5.9 (2009)
Taxes on consumption	15.7	16.2	15.2 (2009)

Source: Eurostat (2012b)

On the other hand, public health care and sickness in kind expenditures are relatively modest, lower than in Germany or the UK. Nevertheless, health care expenditure increased from 5.1 per cent GDP to 6.2 per cent GDP between 2005 and 2010. Most importantly, expenditure on family in kind (childcare services), old age and invalidity in kind (caring services) and employment services, including active labour market policies, grew consistently in the periods 2000–2005 and 2005–2010. Social expenditures on housing and services for social inclusion were also relatively high and growing as per cent of GDP (see Table 9.1).

The Danish welfare state is mainly financed from general taxation: the tax structure is different from those of other EU member states, with more emphasis on direct income taxation.

Table 9.2 is clear indication of the overall deviation of the tax-structure compared to other countries in the EU in that taxes on labour are the central element in the tax-system and that taxes on consumption play an important role. In line with development in the EU, there has been a decline in the top statutory rate on corporate income and on the highest marginal taxes.

The overall long-term trend has been the lowering of income taxation to the state, an increased focus on labour market contributions and green taxes, and a broadening of the tax base. In spite of that, from 2006 to 2012 the overall tax burden was reduced from 49.8 per cent to 46.7 per cent of GDP; especially from 2009 to 2010 the level of income tax (compare Table 9.2) also decreased. Part of the development has been due to a tax-freeze since 2002, which committed the government to 'abstain from raising any tax or duty either as a percentage rate or as a nominal account'.[1]

Part of the trend since 2000 has also been to lower the marginal tax-rate in the tax-system, while at the same time broadening the tax-base, especially by reducing the tax-rebate for income tax-exemptions and integrating the working-tax credit in the system since 2004. Without the tax-freeze and lowering of taxes on labour,

---

1   www.skm.dk/foreign/english/2177.html, accessed the 15th of May, 2012.

the overall public finance situation in Denmark would have looked much better, by presumably even having had a surplus on the public sector budget.

There has been stability in the overall tax-structure, although a change between the central and de-centralised income taxes is evident in the wake of the administrative reform of 1 January 2007. At the same time, there have been important structural changes in the tax-system. Thus the overall corporate tax-rate declined from 32 per cent in 2000 to 25 per cent in 2010 (European Commission 2011a), although this has been combined with the continued effort to broaden the tax-base (compare Chapter 4).

Nevertheless, one central argument has been the growing inter-dependencies and mobility of capital and income as an argument for lowering the tax-rate. The same tendency can be witnessed with regard to the top statutory tax-rate moving from 59.7 per cent to 51.0 per cent in 2000–2010 (European Commission 2011a). Although one of the highest in the EU the taxation stemming from environmental taxes and duties has risen only slightly from 5.3 per cent of GDP to 5.7 per cent in 2008 (European Commission 2011a).

To summarise, the tax system is still to a large degree using income tax as the main tax base, although VAT and payroll tax (at around 22 per cent) and green taxes (around 9 per cent) also play a role in the overall method of financing the welfare state. Denmark thus has a higher proportion of taxes coming from the use of green taxation than most other EU member states, albeit the main part relates to duties on gasoline. With the exception of payment for certain aspects of health care (medicine, dental care, and so on) and day-care for children, user charges do not play a central role. Nevertheless, the payment for day-care is considerable: it may be 25 per cent of the cost, although there is a reduction for low-income earners.

Change in the Governance of Selected Social Services in Denmark

The Danish welfare state is often depicted as a universal welfare state with the ambition of full employment, a high degree of equality (including gender equality) and being mainly financed from general taxation (Greve 2007b). Furthermore, it is a highly decentralised system where local municipalities have the right (within certain overall macro-economic limits) to pursue local strategies and local combinations of the level of service and especially the level of income tax. Despite the fact that profound changes have been witnessed, the core characteristics still seem to prevail; nevertheless, there is increasing focus on and development in occupational welfare related to being or having been on the labour market (Kvist and Greve 2011).

The welfare state, like others, has been influenced by rapid economic development since the year 2000. At the same time, this has also been a period of recession and increased pressure on the welfare state, implying reduced options for the public sector and higher levels of unemployment. However, as the data show, there is a high degree of public sector involvement in the Danish welfare state, even though there has been more pressure on the universality of the welfare state.

Municipal authorities have a responsibility for taxation, childcare, education of children between seven and 16, voluntary adult education, libraries, cultural and sporting facilities, home help and elderly care. County responsibility mainly focuses on hospitals. Upper secondary education is a state responsibility often provided by what are, in principle, labelled independent institutions, still having to fulfil state rules.

Over the last decade, fundamental changes have occurred in the sectors of social care and health care in Denmark: decision-making structures have been reformed to become more consumer-oriented (Højlund 2009). Both private enterprises and organisations from the non-profit sector have been invited to participate in the delivery of services. Traditional means of government based on hierarchy, financial budgeting and formal contracting have been combined with new governance arrangements, such as partnering and network organisation (Ahonen et al. 2006, Andersen et al. 2008, Christensen and Lægreid 2007, Entwistle and Martin 2005, La Cour and Højlund 2007).

A core fundamental change in Denmark has been the structural reform of 2007, where the previous 14 counties were reduced to five regions. In contrast to the situation prior to the reform, the new regions have no right to decide on the tax level and have fewer areas of responsibility. At the same time, the municipalities, which were reduced from 275 to 98, have been given new tasks in relation to preventive health care, environment, public transport and the active labour market policy. This in general can be argued to be a continuation of the decentralisation of responsibilities in the Danish welfare state while still implying some level of concentration: for many, having fewer local municipalities implies a larger geographical area and higher number of people to cover. Furthermore, from 1 January 2013, there has been increased centralisation of payment for most social benefits, as it is now done by the state instead of the municipalities.

The state is still central both in financing social services and welfare state issues; however, the last decade has seen development in that increasingly more people also have private sickness insurance paid by their employers, especially with the purpose of faster treatment in the case of sickness.

The last 10-year period has also seen increasing choice in different providers in the Danish welfare state (Greve 2002, Greve 2010). The greater availability of choice was said to contribute to the strengthening of citizens' influence on service, but it has also implied that in some areas private providers now play a larger role than they did before implying higher use of market elements.

The number of people with private sickness insurance is still a deviation from the universal, given that they only provided a limited part of the service it could be said that the financing of the social services has generally remained universal. Nevertheless, there is an increasing number of people retiring from the labour market who have a job-based pension as well as the basic public pension. Thus the universality of the welfare state is less strong than it used to be. The fact of being on the labour market has an increasingly important function for most people.

Childcare

In Denmark, as well as in other Nordic countries, childcare is an essential part of social policy, therefore the provision of childcare services is rather extensive (European Commission 2009a). One purpose of childcare is to encourage women's labour market participation and to promote gender equality both in the family and at work. Hence there is a well developed system of day-care for young children, which simultaneously should ensure the child's well-being through the introduction of more formal and structured learning in day-care institutions (see Gíslason and Eydal 2011). The childcare services are flexible especially during the day; however, several municipalities have 'closed days' around Christmas and during the summertime.

The employment rate of women with one or two children up to six years of age has, for a long time, been at the highest level of all European countries. Specifically, the Lisbon target of the year 2000 to raise the employment rate of woman to 60 per cent by 2010 has been reached and surpassed by more than 10 per cent for over a decade (OECD 2013). At the same time, fertility rates have been relatively high in the past ten years: 1.7–1.9 children per woman.

Regulation and Delivery
The legal regulation on childcare policy is the responsibility of the Danish Government. Childcare is a right for all children aged between six months and six years; access to childcare has been legislated (Productivity Commission 2011). The childcare system is well-established (over 170 years ago) and its activities are delegated to municipal authorities which ensure that the flexibility of the system meets local needs through many types of services. The system is predominantly a public service, supervised by local authorities and funded from local taxes and central government grants.

In Denmark there are key childcare services (day-care facilities – '*dagtilbud*') for children from six months to six years. Of these, about 70 per cent are operated by public community services (compare OECD 2006, FOA 2009, European Commission 2009a, OECD 2011c). Family day-care ('*kommunal dagpleje*') represents local authority childminding where childminders take care of children in private homes (one childminder may take up to five children). This kind of service covers 43 per cent of children up to the age of three. Centre-based day-care is offered through local authority day-care centres focused on children from 0 to school age. They are local authority owned institutions such as crèches ('*vuggestuer*'), nursery schools ('*børnehaver*') and age-integrated ('*aldersintegrerede*') institutions. Crèches and age-integrated centres together enrol 15 per cent of children under three and about 38 per cent of children from three to six years of age; nursery schools enrol 58 per cent of children from three to six. Independent day-care facilities are institutions that are owned by private individuals and supervised by the local authority, from which they receive subsidies to cover their costs. Private day-care centres owned and operated by private individuals must be approved by the local authority, which grants a subsidy per child.

While the Ministry of Children and Education has the main responsibility for Early Childhood Education and Care Provision for children 0–6 years old, local authorities have the overall responsibility for providing day-care facilities to ensure a sufficient supply of places, and to take all the necessary initiatives in relation to children in need of special support (Hiilamo 2008).

Local authorities provide between 70–75 per cent of all day-care services, determine their own day-care structure on the basis of local needs and requirements, decide on the age-groupings to be made and the combination of the various types of day care facilities to be used and promote co-operation. They may subsidise 'pool' schemes, where groups of parents come together and make an agreement with the local government. Some local authorities provide financial support for parents who choose 'private' childcare facilities that are not subsidised directly by local authorities (nannies, family members, another private person, or a private childcare facility).

Financing

Public expenditure on childcare has been well above the OECD average in the last few years, regardless of whether it is childcare (nurseries/crèches above all), or pre-primary services (especially kindergarten), alltogether 1.4 per cent of GDP (see Table 12.4 in Chapter 12) and remained stable between 2000–2009 while OECD average was 0.7 per cent of GDP. Especially high is expenditure on childcare (children 0–2) which amounts to 0.7 per cent of GDP which is more than twice that in OECD in average (OECD 2012d).

For childcare services parents pay a maximum of 25 per cent of the costs for pre-school children from their own pockets (that is from family income) (European Commission 2009b). The fees that parents must pay for childcare facilities are rather low: on average, they represent 11.2 per cent of the average wage in the country (the OECD average is 18.4 per cent; see OECD 2011c). Fees paid by parents for family day-care and crèches vary according to family income: lower income families pay a reduced rate, or receive the service free of charge. Municipalities provide the majority of funding for relevant services.

Outcomes

The broader public policy context in which the governance model operates can be described by means of the principles of universalism, quality, affordability, public-financing and accessibility (CCCABC 2007). The main point is that the local government takes a universal entitlement approach to childcare. Municipalities guarantee access to childcare for children at the age of one at the latest; most offer a place for children at the age of six months. It is thus the municipalities which have the responsibility for providing spaces to all children in their community;

they are also responsible for setting standards for the relevant services that they enforce and resource. The primary purpose of childcare is social development, rather than education.

Most children remain exclusively in parental care until they are at least six months old. Generally, they begin using public childcare services when they are one year old when parental leave expires. About 80 per cent of Danish children between six months and nine years have a place in a publicly supported day-care facility (64 per cent of all children between six months and two years, 91 per cent of those from three to five years) (Eurochild 2010). Use of services for children up to three years of age is huge; in fact the level is more than twice as high in Denmark than that of the EU-27 (that is 66 per cent and 28 per cent, respectively; see Table 12.3 in Chapter 12). This means that Denmark (as well as Netherlands, Sweden, Belgium, Spain, Portugal and United Kingdom) reached the Barcelona target that recommended a rate of 30 per cent coverage of children up to two years in formal childcare facilities (European Commission 2009a). These services are often used on a full-time basis (at least for 30 hours/week). However, only 10 per cent of children below the age of one are in public day-care and 5 per cent in crèches, because newborn children spend an average of 11 months with their parents on maternity or parental leave. Moreover, there are some nurseries and kindergartens that offer care even during the evening and night hours. The coverage of children from three years to school age is over 92 per cent, which is 20 percentage points above the OECD average (see Table 12.4 in Chapter 12).

Whereas in many European countries the supply of high-quality and affordable childcare facilities may be insufficient (especially in the case of formal childcare facilities for the youngest children), in Denmark (as well as in other Nordic states) childcare is considered a social right (European Commission 2009a). For this reason, Denmark is often considered to be a world leader in positive child outcomes and is among the top-rated nations for child well-being (UNICEF 2007, Productivity Commission 2011), however, with a decline in recent years.

While approximately 60 per cent of staff in the Danish childcare services are qualified pedagogues/teachers (OECD 2006) the rest of the staff comprises teaching assistants, for whom no formal qualification is required. There is regular training of employees providing care for children of up to three years of age (childminders). Moreover, the annual income of childminders who complete the training increases.

Data by Eurostat show that in 2008 the Danish child-to-staff ratio was the lowest of all surveyed countries, more specifically, about half that of Germany and the Czech Republic and almost one-third compared to that of the UK (see Tables 12.7 and 12.8 in Chapter 12). According to the OECD, this ratio is 3:3 in the case of care for children under three years and 7:2 in the case of care for children aged three to school age (OECD 2011c). From the above, it is clear that Denmark belongs among the countries with the greatest potential to meet the specific needs of individual children.

Trends and Innovation

Summing up, the labour market has long been characterised by a high participation rate of parents with young children. For this reason, the system of care for children is very mature because it has been developing for more than four decades, when the female employment rate began to rise. The high female employment rate is accompanied by a high level of children attending predominantly public childcare facilities (although one third is private services). Most of the costs for childcare are paid by municipalities, although family allowances are paid by the state (even to private providers, whose role is important especially for children aged 0–3).

Elderly Care

Regulation and Delivery

Long-term care provides comprehensive coverage for a wide range of social services, including homecare and institutional care.[2] The extent of Danish homecare exceeds institutional care more than three-fold. In the case of homecare services, personal care (ADL) and practical assistance (IADL) are publicly available to all dependent individuals when in need, especially to a person with reduced physical or mental capacity (but not only to them). Home adaptation, assistive devices and home help are among the main aims of the Danish social services so as to ensure that the elderly can manage in their own homes (see Höhnen 2011, Colombo et al. 2011).

Institutional care in Denmark includes senior citizen residences, gated communities, assisted living units and nursing homes.[3] The pivotal principle is that all eligible individuals have a free choice of care providers (including those who do not wish to move permanently). Older and disabled people pay the rent for living in a non-profit or conventional nursing home corresponding to the costs of running the housing estate; however, they have access to benefits compensating part of the costs, depending on the assessment of their incomes (Schulz 2010a).

Informal caregivers play a relatively small role in the Danish long-term care system, although family members often have a role. Only about 8 per cent of the senior population use the help of these workers, which is one of the lowest rates among the EU countries (Colombo et al. 2011). The eligibility criteria for obtaining the benefits (which can be used to purchase services from informal

---

2   The local authorities offer substitute care or respite services to a spouse, parent or other close relative caring for a person with impaired physical or mental function. These services may be granted for a few hours up to full-time, depending on the needs and preferences of the primary caregiver and the person with disability.

3   Another typology of Danish institutional care distinguishes conventional nursing homes (care homes), on the one hand, and modern close-care accommodation (subsidised housing for older persons with care facilities and associated care staff), on the other hand (Schulz 2010a).

carers and compensate them for the loss of wages if they work) are based on a Needs Assessment performed by the local authority. Eligible individuals may receive a cash benefit to employ the necessary assistance (see Kvist 2011).

Financing

The long-term care is free of charge; nevertheless, there may be user fees on food and various other services such as rent in care institutions, hair-styling and laundry services, equal to what would have been the case when living in one own apartment and in several homes for the elderly they rent their own apartment.

The costs of long-term care are financed by local authorities through block grants received from the government, local taxes and equalisation amounts received from other local authorities. Public and private elderly care is covered by similar collective agreements. Only a small part of the total long-term care expenses is paid by the user (out-of-pocket payments represent about 4 per cent of total expenditures) (compare Schulz 2010a, OECD 2012b). Publicly provided, domiciliary elder care is free of charge (tax financed) (Höhnen 2011).

In long-term care, Denmark belongs among the countries with the highest level of spending. In 2010, these expenditures amounted to more than twice the EU average (4.5 per cent of GDP in Denmark compared to 1.84 per cent of GDP in the EU 27 countries) (see Table 12.8 in Chapter 12).

One of the key objectives of the long-term care (LTC) system is to encourage and enable the elderly to stay at home for as long as possible. Personal care (ADL) and practical assistance (IADL) are available to all dependent individuals and are not subject to co-payments (home-care services also include support for technical aids and consumer durables, assistance for home or out-of-home adaptations for individuals with reduced physical or mental capacity, the purchase of a car and so on). For those who do not wish to move permanently, day-care centres are available.

The actual service provision is handled in local settings: local centres are in charge of the administration and regulation, while public and private providers carry out services (Højlund 2009). More specifically, the local authorities are responsible for the delivery of long-term care services, for designing and implementing long-term care policy and for deciding how long-term care resources are allocated (Colombo et al. 2011). Decision-making concerning rights and needs is enacted locally, although based on general rules and national laws. There are three sub-systems pivotal in decision-making (Højlund 2009): 1) formalised needs assessments (based on the entitlement of all people in need of services); 2) free choice of service provider (where citizens are included through an act of self-determination); and 3) preventive home visits (where citizens are included through acts of dialogue).

Wages in Danish elder care are, to a large extent, regulated by collective agreements between a few large unions and employer organisations. The largest and most influential union (but not the only one) in Danish elder care is the Trade and Union (FOA), which represents approximately 100,000 care workers in elderly care (that is 80 per cent of total care workers in Denmark) (Höhnen 2011).

Outcomes

Denmark has a relatively high level of care coverage for the elderly. There were 9.5 formal long-term care workers per 1,000 of the population over the age of 65 in 2007 (while the OECD average was 6.1 workers) (OECD 2011d).

On the other hand, in 2010 there were 51 long-term care beds per 1,000 of the population aged 65 years old and over, the same as is the OECD-average (see Table 12.10 in Chapter 12). Denmark belongs among the countries with the highest proportion of people over 65 who are granted long-term care (in Denmark, 16.9 per cent, compared to 12.2 per cent in the OECD average in 2010). More than 4 per cent of the Danish population of elderly people used institutional care (similar to the OECD average) (see Table 12.9 in Chapter 12).

The rules on long-term care are part of the Consolidation Act on Social Services (CASS), which respect the individual needs of the clients considerably. The quality standards and price requirements for both public and private services must be adopted by the local authority, which follows up on the quality and management of the services provided at least once a year.

During the last decade, elder care has become more professionalised, notwithstanding that the number of care workers has been relatively stable (between 110,000 and 125,000 – Höhnen 2011). The majority of care workers are currently trained as 'care helpers' or as 'care assistants'. Although the share of skilled care workers gradually increased until 2007 (from 50 per cent in 1997 to 65 per cent in 2007), more unskilled workers seem to have entered the sector since. According to Höhnen (2011), this development probably reflects an increase in the differentiation of care work which consists of practical help (mainly cleaning) and personal care, where practical care is increasingly carried out by unskilled employees. Of the total number of skilled care workers, one in six is employed in domiciliary elder care and the rest are employed in institutions for the elderly, in hospitals, or in other sectors. Moreover, in reaction to the introduction of the free-choice model, there has been high turnover in the care sector between 1998 and 2006 (in this period, about 2,000 people have changed employers and moved from the public sector to the private).

A range of decisions about work, such as the quality of care, type of care, amount of care and time allocated to the provision of care, have become standardised (Höhnen 2011). The reform initiative on the quality of care also included a reduction in the number of different assistants visiting the individual citizen; clear and measurable objectives for the services are stated in the local council's contract with the care provider (including home care); there was the introduction of a quality fund for improving the physical infrastructure and introducing new technology for old-age care; an accreditation model supports staff quality through ongoing learning; and there was a reduction of long waiting times for places in nursing homes (compare Council of Europe 2008, Government of Denmark 2008, Schulz 2010a).

Trends and Innovations

During recent decades, two key changes have occurred in Danish long-term care for the elderly: firstly, the free-choice of service by the beneficiaries was introduced in 2003; secondly, there was a structural reform of the Danish municipalities in 2007. Although private provision in elderly care has been made possible, the responsibility for providing and paying for care has remained within the municipality, which also makes the decisions about the type and amount of care. In other words, privatisation has generally not taken place. Out-sourcing to one or more private providers is not based on competition of price and quality, but rather (like in Germany) on the fixed-price arrangement of municipalities, which enable private suppliers to provide care in a free-choice system (Höhnen 2011). All eligible elderly people in Denmark have the free choice of care providers; however, they mainly choose private providers with regard to cleaning in private homes.

The establishment of the 'free choice reform' in 2003 allowed private entities to provide their services in the long-term care sector on the condition that they meet the quality standards and price requirements established by local authorities (Colombo et al. 2011). The free choice reform enabled the development of a 'purchaser-provider' model whereby not only the general quality level has been strengthened but a range assessment of very specific issues around care work has been introduced in the municipalities. At the same time an increase in standardisation and the reduction of influence and flexibility for care workers has gone (Höhnen 2011). Furthermore, the Consolidation Act of Social Services implemented in 2010 gives the local authorities an option for arranging services by providing a user with a service certificate which allows a person to employ his/her own personal helper.

The long-term care system for the elderly and people with disability is a universal system, although it has undergone change whereby new management ideas and technologies have been implemented in the last 10–15 years (Højlund 2004, 2006). New Public Management reforms have promoted, among other things, standardisation, performance management and increased efficiency (Szebehely 2005, Ryberg and Kamp 2010 in Höhnen 2011).

In the last decade, a great development of new technologies has been implemented in Denmark, particularly in care for the elderly. These technologies assist in many ways: they ensure a clean home environment and sufficient hygiene for older people (robotic vacuum cleaners, washing robots, automatic toilets); they increase personal safety for seniors by preventing or dealing with injury (sensor technology installed in bathrooms); they can call for medical help in the case of need (patient briefcase with videophone); and they provide new technologies for everyday activities (technology for reminding seniors of daily activities, robotic therapeutic pets for people with dementia, robotic assistants, and so on). They also include Social Technologies for communication support in creating social networks in virtual space (see OECD 2012a). Welfare technology is seen as a way of innovate the system towards better service also implying that elderly can live a more independent live, the working conditions can be improved, but also that fewer elderly will be in need of care within the public sector. Rehabilitation to ensure that the individual can live an independent life is part of this development.

To conclude, long-term care for the elderly is a universal system which is financed from public funds (mostly local taxes). Home care, which is usually free of charge, is very well developed and the most-used kind of long-term care service. Two innovative changes have occurred during the last decade. They were based on the possibility of the client being able to choose from a wide palette of services ('free choice model' of 2003), whose operation and quality is ensured by local municipalities either through their own local centres, or through private providers on the basis of mutual agreements between municipalities and providers (Structural Reform of 2007). Management reforms placed great emphasis on standardisation, performance management and increased efficiency through the quality management of delivered care.

The increase in the quality of delivered services was secured not only through the introduction of an accreditation system and the supervision of operating procedures of service providers, but also in a standardisation of needs investigation and the establishment of a quality fund for improving physical infrastructure and introducing new technology for old age care.

Employment Services

The labour market regulation is considered to be the most successful model as a result of high labour market dynamism combined with a general level of social protection (that is the 'flexicurity' model). The dynamism of the Danish labour market model is secured by a high degree of job mobility of low and high status jobs (due to limited employment protection legislation), relatively generous but declining unemployment benefits and a well developed active labour market policy.

State interventions are seen as necessary to ensure adaptability among both employers and employees, which is crucial for the effective functioning of the labour market. The Danish government is trying to create an environment to support the creation of more jobs and the promotion of active and universal inclusion in the labour market by helping individuals to adapt and take advantage of new opportunities. Public employment services and other actors in active labour market policies (ALMPs) play a substantial role.

Even though long-term unemployment has doubled in the last ten years, the long-term unemployment rate was more than half the EU-27 average in 2010 (1.5 per cent in Denmark compared to 3.6 per cent in EU-27; see Eurostat 2012c). The general unemployment rate during the crisis increased from 3.3 per cent in 2008 to 7.6 per cent in 2010 (see Table 12.12 in Chapter 12). By contrast, the employment rate is high (73.4 per cent in 2010) and the employment rate of women is exceptionally high (72.1 per cent), with a high share of Health and Social Work Sector employment (see Chapter 3).

Regulation and Delivery
The system of employment services is based on both the duty of the unemployed to actively seek work through their participation in mandatory full-time activation

programmes and on comprehensive unemployment insurance (UI) benefits, a voluntary scheme complemented by a basic state-financed social security benefit system. The Public Employment Service (PES) is responsible for the activation of the unemployed through education and training programs. The majority of unemployed receive benefits at the rate of 90 per cent of their previous income, but with a ceiling from the first day of unemployment and up to a maximum of two years. These benefits are administered by the 36 state-approved unemployment insurance funds, which are managed by trade unions. There are also two groups of unemployed that receive social assistance benefits from the municipality (they are either people considered not able to work by the municipalities or require special support).

Danish labour market policy is coordinated with local economic development policies at the central and regional levels (Hendeliowitz 2008) and also coordinated between the national, regional and local levels (OECD 2011e). The system of labour administration is therefore considered to be corporatist, which means that the social partners participate in regulatory and decision-making processes at all levels of public administration (Andersen and Pedersen 2007). While the benefit system is administered by the trade unions, employment services are subordinated to the Ministry of Employment and include job placement services and active labour market programs organised at the municipality level.

A feature of the Danish labour market model is the tripartite co-operation between trade unions,[4] employer organisations and the state, implying that the Danish labour market model is a combination of an agreement and of regulation.

The Local Employment Councils are a weak type of governance network in the sense that they bring together interdependent policy actors who engage in institutionalised negotiations that produce public value in terms of policy advice, policy surveillance and the initiation and funding of projects (Sørensen and Torfing 2007). They are a peculiar form of governance network since they are mandatory and embedded in a hierarchical governance structure in which the basic parameters for the negotiated interaction are defined by the central government and the overall policy decisions at the local level are taken by the Municipal Council and the directors of the Job Centre (Damgaard and Torfing 2010). The Agency for the Modernisation of Public Administration in Denmark supports and supervises modernisation, the improvement of efficiency and performance of tasks in the public sector and public employment services.

The Danish employment system can be depicted as a triangle which consists of flexible rules (governing the hiring and dismissal of employees), security for wage earners (in times of unemployment) and the active labour market policy (activating the unemployed to work). Contemporary labour market policy is the

---

4   More than 80 per cent of Danish employees belong to trade unions that are grouped into national confederations (e.g. Trade Unions (LO) representing workers from both the public and the private sector, or The Confederation of Danish Employers (DA), representing 13 employer organisations) (Hendeliowitz 2008).

result of the labour market reforms of the 1990s and the 'More People at Work' program of 2003, which shifted a part of the system from a focus on welfare to a focus on work first. The particular reform steps were aimed at ensuring a flexible labour market, combined with generous unemployment benefits and the right and obligation to participate in activation measures. Newly introduced measures included upgrading the skills of the unemployed and eliminating restrictions on any opportunities to remain outside of the labour market while receiving benefits. The activation of the unemployed became not just a right but a duty for all the unemployed (Hendeliowitz 2008). Further legislation in 2005 ('A New Chance for All') and 2006 ('Welfare Reform Agreement') introduced benefit cuts and even more restrictive work requirements for social assistance and unemployment recipients (mostly migrants and young people) (Andersen and Pedersen 2007). From 2007, the overall management strategy of employment services has been systematised and homogenised: job centres have gained more freedom in planning and implementing their employment measures, while increased attention has been paid to performance outcomes. In December 2010 a reform of the financial system in the employment area, indicating a sharper focus on the outcomes of employability enhancement measures rather than the volume of employability enhancement, should influence the flexibility of the local level to plan local measures and financial incentives (OECD 2011e).

Financing

Passive labour market policy in Denmark has traditionally been financed by contributions to a voluntary unemployment insurance scheme and by taxation. The regulation and delivery of labour market services falls largely within the public domain, although elements of marketisation have been introduced (in 2003, through contracts for services with private enterprises, which represented 57 per cent of all contracts; with trade unions – 25 per cent; and with public institutions – 18 per cent). Furthermore, the introduction of a 'taximeter' system has linked payments for labour market training providers to the number of participants in the programs (OECD 2011e).

Spending on active labour market policies in Denmark declined slightly after 2002, yet in 2010 the percentage was still three times that of the EU average (see Table 12.13).

Outcomes

Summing up, the employment policy can be perceived as a highly effective system which is often referred to as a 'flexicurity' model because of the successful combination of flexible hiring and firing rules and a generous social safety net; it also makes it possible to increase qualifications and job finding chances for the jobless. Although the labour market has been severely affected by the Great Recession, from a comparative perspective overall performance is still characterised by below average unemployment and large job gross flows; nevertheless, there are also tendencies for unemployment to become persistent (Andersen 2011). The scope, quality and effectiveness of ALMP measures seems to be good in international comparison (see Chapter 12).

Trends and Innovations

The recent governance reform in the field of active employment policy has created a more decentralised multi-level governance system which matches the public agencies at the national and local levels with a corresponding set of governance networks involving key stakeholders. The municipal reform which came into force in 2007 withdrew managerial labour market competences from the corporatist-governed regional labour market councils to the municipalities (Andersen and Pedersen 2007). The new one-stop Job Centres are anchored in Local Employment Councils replacing the former Regional Labour Market Councils. The main task of these centres is to establish a quick and efficient match between job-seekers and enterprises; therefore, job services and the payment of benefits are kept separate (Hendeliowitz 2008, OECD 2011e). The extent of delivered services is to a limited extent dependent on the decision of the municipalities. In the case of the job centres, there is limited freedom in the planning and implementation of employment measures.

Employment in the Health and Social Work Sector in Denmark

Eurostat data show that employment in HSW comprised of 508,300 people and the share of HSW employment of total employment was 19.1 per cent in 2010. Denmark has the highest share of HSW sector employment in the EU-27. Employment in the HSW sector grew by 8 per cent between 2000 and 2010 (most of the employment growth was in part-time work).

The relatively high number of workers in HSW has a clear relation to the central role of social services. This sector prevails in HSW – the share of residential care activities was 23.9 per cent, the share of social work without accommodation was 39.1 per cent, while the health sector constituted only 37 per cent of the HSW sector in 2010. Work in social services implies employment of a broad and very diverse type of staff, from highly specialised people (for example doctors) to people with some specialisation (for example nurses, social workers and educators) and to some extent to those with other types of skills, such as cleaning and cooking.

The presented information on the development of employment in the HSW sector from national data (Table 9.3) is based on 'The register-based labour force statistics' (RAS). RAS are annual status observations of the population's attachment to the labour market at a given point in time, that is, at the end of November (Statistiks Denmark 2013). The HSW sector is divided into four basic categories (hospital activities, medical and dental practice activities, residential care activities and social work without accommodation). There are two breaks in the statistics (in 2003 and 2009). When considering this fact, there was a clear trend of growth

Table 9.3   Employed persons in social services in Denmark (2000–2010)

	2000	2001	2005	2008	2009	2010
Hospital activities	:	102 444	104 904	109 247	109 946	113 139
Medical and dental practice activities	:	42 251	48 995	52 099	55 159	57 122
Residential care activities	:	140 796	151 361	147 153	140 604	143 926
Social work activities without accommodation	:	180 116	175 509	185 212	188 366	195 928
Social institutions for children	145 278	149 865	147 901	146 223	:	:
Social institutions for adults	168 066	169 098	178 645	185 322	:	:

Note: There are data breaks in the statistics in 2003 and 2009. From 2009, a new data source for the employment of employees is used. As a consequence, the employment level is lower.
Source: Register-based labour force statistics (RAS statistics), STATBANK

of employment in social service activities (residential as well as activities without accommodation) in all three periods: 2001–2002, 2003–2008 and 2009–2010.

From the last two rows in Table 9.3 and from Table 9.4, it is possible to conclude that while employment in services for children stagnated, employment in services the adults (including the elderly) grew in the 2000–2010 period. Overall, the RAS data confirm the trend of social service employment expansion in Denmark presented in Chapter 3.

According to these data, employment in health and social services grew between 8–10 per cent in the specific sub-sectors, more rapidly in the medical and dental practice activities (13.5 per cent), but less (1 per cent) in social institutions for children (where it was already high).

The HSW sector is highly dominated by women (more than 80 per cent of workers). As in other countries in focus, the workforce is ageing quite rapidly – the share of workers over 50 increased from 24 per cent in 2000 to 31.4 per cent in 2010. HSW workers are a very diverse group of people with all types of qualifications, from highly specialised people to unskilled workers. The prevailing education level of workers in the HSW sector is high (42.8 per cent), with a significant proportion at the medium level (36 per cent); however, the share of low educated workers is also substantial (21.2 per cent) compared to other countries. Men have a very similar level of qualification to the women.

The mean annual earning of workers in the HSW sector was 47,342 Euros in 2010 (Eurostat SES data; see Chapter 3, Table 3.4), which is the highest in the EU and at the same time 22 per cent above the wages in manufacturing. Young workers were usually the group with the lowest wages in HSW (17.9 per cent below the average

Table 9.4   **Earnings of local government employees (average income per working hour in DKK) (2000–2009)**

	2000	2001	2005	2008	2009
The whole economy	189.1	194.9	222.1	239.4	254.4
Midwife, leading nurse work	220.8	228.3	258.9	277.7	297.4
Assistant work in healthcare, except nurse	186.2	191.6	218.2	231.2	246.5
Nurse work	212.8	217.6	247.5	261.2	270.6
Care and pedagogical work	185.4	188.6	210	225.9	242.1
Care work	155	159.8	182.1	198.7	212.5
Child minding	139.1	143	162	175.8	186
Social and health care workers at institutions	176.9	182.5	209.3	221.6	239
Care work in private home	154.1	158.9	177.8	200.8	215.6

Note: Wages were rounded up to one decimal
Source: STATBANK, table LON42x

wage); middle-aged workers have wages that are 7.5 per cent below average while workers over 50 receive above-average wages. The difference between women and men is small: women earn about 4 per cent less. The average number of hours worked per week is 32.5, reflecting the prevalence of part-time work.

National long-term statistics are available for the earnings of local government public employees (Table 9.4). Primary statistical data are submitted by those agencies engaged in the operation of the public sector's computerised pay transfer systems (Statistiks Denmark 2012). The time series are not fully comparable due to some changes of methodology (see metadata). For the same reason data is not available for 2010. Wages of healthcare professions are usually higher or similar to the wages of all local government workers; however, the wages of care workers (for example child-minders and care workers in private homes) are substantially lower.

Wage positions of particular professions are very similar throughout all the period in focus. Data for Denmark regarding wages in specific professions in all sectors (not only in the public sector) are available only for 2010; nevertheless, the overall results are very similar to those of the public sector in previous years (see Table 9.4). The data confirm the Eurostat SES information presented above that social service workers are relatively low paid compared to the average wage and the wages of other selected professions. Usually the wages are about 20 per cent (in the case of childcare workers more than 28 per cent) below the national average wage.

Table 9.5   Earnings of social services employees (average income per working hour) and difference from average wage in total economy (in per cent in brackets) (2010)

	Total economy (average wage)	Nursing and midwifery professionals	Personal care workers	Childcare workers	Personal care workers in health services	Home-based personal care workers
2010	274.7 (ref.)	284 (+3.4)	214 (-22.1)	197.6 (-28.1)	222.4 (-19.1)	214.1 (-22.1)

Source: STATBANK, table SLON21

Conclusions

The universal welfare model still seems to be prevailing in Denmark; however, there have been changes making the model less distinct than it used to be. There is less emphasis on universality and more focus on 'work first'. At the same time, although the process of decentralisation has continued, in recent years there has been greater state involvement and recentralisation. The implication is that the model still has a high focus on service and local influence, but with compared to historical development less impact from the labour market partners.

Social protection expenditure was among the highest in the EU in 2010. Especially expenditure in kind (services) on old age, invalidity, child care and employment grew consistently in last ten years.

Denmark has a well-developed system of day-care for children in early age: childcare is a right for all children aged between six months and six years. The system is predominantly a public service, supervised by local authorities and funded from local taxes and central government grants. Parents pay for childcare services from their own pockets in average 11.2 per cent of average wage which is much less than OECD average 18.4 per cent. The quality of services is higher than in most of the other countries and coverage is extraordinary high, especially with children below 3 years of age.

Long-term care for the elderly is a universal system which is financed mostly from local taxes. Innovative changes which have occurred during the last decade were emphasising the possibility of client´ s choice from a wide range of services. Although privatisation in elderly care has been enabled, the responsibility for providing and paying for care remained within the municipality. Denmark has achieved outstanding developments in care for the elderly and belongs consistently among the countries with the highest proportion of people over 65 who are granted long-term care. Permanent long-term care is free. Only a small part of the total long-term care expenses is paid by the user while publicly-provided domiciliary elder care is free of charge (tax financed).

The delivery of labour market services falls largely within the public domain, although elements of marketisation have been introduced. Spending on active labour market policies was three times the EU average in 2010. The recent governance reform has created a more decentralised multi-level governance system which is matching the public agencies at the national and local levels with a corresponding network involving key stakeholders. The municipal reform which came into force in 2007 withdrew managerial labour market competences from the corporatist governed regional labour market councils to the municipalities (Andersen and Pedersen 2007). Vocational training programmes take place mainly in educational institutions, which form part of the public labour market training system and which are the product of cooperation between the organisations of the social partners and the public authorities (Dingeldey 2009).

Social innovations have been implemented in social and health services which increased consumers' choice, most visible in long-term care accompanied with emphasis both on the quality of services and efficiency, with use of new public management instruments. The other stream of social innovations was the implementation of welfare technologies in long-term care which help to use human labour in this field more effectively and to improve the quality of service.

Denmark is a country with the highest share of HSW sector employment as part of the total employment in EU-27 (19 per cent in 2010). As in other countries in focus, the workforce is rather rapidly ageing – the share of workers aged over 50 increased from 24 per cent in 2000 to 31.4 per cent in 2010. Employment in the sector is still highly genderised with four fifths being women; most work part-time and at lower wages than those with jobs in the private sector.

Chapter 10

Governance, Financing and Employment in Social Services in Germany

Pavel Horák, Markéta Horáková, Ondřej Hora and Bent Greve

Germany represents a Christian Democratic welfare state characterised by a strong tradition of subsidiarity and corporatism associated with decentralised welfare services. However, New Public Management methods have been applied in recent years, with increasing emphasis on accessibility of services and marketisation. The delivery of welfare services is a public-private mix, where the combination of formal and informal services is typical.

Change in the Financing of the German Welfare State

The view on expenditure on social protection shows that Germany is slightly above the EU average (about 29 per cent of GDP). This is a consequence of the traditionally high expenditures on social insurance benefits and in the area of social services, which involve the relatively high expenditure on health care services (between 7 and 8 per cent of GDP during the 2000s and increasing to 8.0 per cent in 2010).

Table 10.1   Social protection expenditure as per cent of GDP in Germany (2000–2009)

	2000	2005	2010
Social protection total	28.6	28.9	29.3
Social protection in cash	19.5	19.7	18.8
Social protection in kind	9.0	9.2	10.6
Health care and sickness in kind	6.8	6.9	8.0
Invalidity in kind	0.8	0.8	0.9
Old age in kind	0.0	0.0	0.0
Survivors in kind	0.01	0.01	0.00
Family in kind	0.8	0.8	1.0
Unemployment in kind (employment services)	0.21	0.08	0.07
Housing in kind	0.3	0.6	0.6
Social exclusion in kind	0.06	0.04	0.03

Source: Eurostat (2012b)

Table 10.2   Development in overall tax and duty revenue and taxes on labour, capital and consumption as per cent of GDP (2000–2010)

	2000	2005	2010
Total receipts from taxes and duties	2.8	39.7	39.5
Taxes on labour	24.5	22.6	22.7 (2009)
Taxes on capital	6.8	6.0	5.9 (2009)
Taxes on consumption	10.5	10.1	11.1 (2009)

Source: Eurostat (2012b)

Expenditure on family policies in kind increased from 0.8 per cent to 1.0 per cent of GDP between 2005 and 2010, which indicates some change in the approach. Similarly, expenditure on housing increased from 0.3 per cent to 0.6 per cent of GDP between 2001 and 2005 and remained at this level in 2010. Conversely, expenditure on employment services dropped between 2001 and 2010 from 0.21 per cent to 0.07 per cent of GDP, in spite of the crisis; nevertheless, this is still relatively high. The other categories of expenditure on social services remain quite stable. Expenditure on elderly care is zero since this area is financed through a special social insurance cash benefit to the elderly (*Pflegegeld*).

Germany's way of financing the welfare state follows the continental tradition with a high reliance on labour taxes collected through obligatory social insurance contributions. The last 10 years have had a relatively stable composition in the overall tax and duty revenue (compare Table 10.2).

Germany is slightly above the European average in relation to taxation, although there has been, as in other countries, a relative decline in the overall level of taxes and duties to slightly above 3 per cent. From a level of 51.6 per cent in 2000, Germany lowered the top tax rate on companies to 29.8 per cent in 2010, a very dramatic reduction; nevertheless, Germany has a higher level than that of the average EU-27. Furthermore, the top personal tax-rate was lowered from 53.8 per cent to 47.5 per cent following the developments in other European countries.

Taxes and duties coming from environmental taxation were slightly reduced from 2.4 per cent in 2000 to 2.2 per cent in 2008 (European Commission 2011b). Despite discussions on the possibility of a double dividend by moving towards a higher level of taxation in this area (compare Chapter 4), this has not been the case in practice, as is also true in other EU member states.

However, lower incomes to the state budget have not been accompanied by a reduction in public expenditure on social protection: except for reduced expenditure on employment services (due to reform of the system), other expenditures on social and health services and housing have increased, hand in hand with the increase of GDP. Furthermore, expenditure on health care also increased in the case of out-of-pocket payments as percentages of total costs in the area from 11.2 per cent in 2000 to 13.1 per cent in 2009 (OECD 2012b). Thus, user fees especially in this area also play a role in the financing of the welfare state.

Change in the Governance of Selected Social Services in Germany

Childcare

Since the 1990s, dramatic changes have occurred in German family policy: legislators have replaced the traditional 'male-breadwinner/female-caregiver' model with a model that supports work/family life balance. The unification of East and West Germany played an especially large role in the evolution of the reconciliation of family and work: the bilateral unification contract (*Einigungsvertrag*) supported the maintenance of the East's extensive childcare infrastructure and promoted the participation of women in labour markets (Fagnani and Math 2010).

In the last decades, childcare services in Germany have been provided within a 'sustainable family policy' (Hübenthal and Ifland 2011), which is characterised by the fact that the current conservative-liberal government (since 2009) seeks, among other things, to implement measures aimed at increasing the birth-rate of children and the participation of their mothers in the labour market, thereby contributing to the economic growth of the whole of German society. The employment rate of German women with children up to six years of age has gradually been increasing in the last ten years, both for full-time and part-time employed women (in the case of part-time jobs, the number of employed women increased from 49 per cent in 2005 to 57.3 per cent in 2010). Currently, the number of employed German mothers is higher than the EU average (64.9 per cent in Germany compared to 38.5 per cent in the EU in 2010; see Eurostat 2012c, UNECE 2012). The increasing number of working mothers occurred in Germany even during the global economic recession 2008–2009, to which the German government responded by adopting measures that increased family support through extending the duration of maternity and parental leave, related benefits and delivered services.

Regulation and Delivery
Although the German government has for more than two decades supported the mother's choice as to whether to stay at home or enter the job market, including part-time work (compare Evers et al. 2005, Rüling 2010, Fagnani and Math 2010), childcare was a relatively neglected area of family policy until 2001. In the following years, the red–green coalition began to support the activities of private childcare providers (2001). Similarly, many benefits were introduced: child care provisions for children under three years of age delivered by local authorities were extended (2002, 2005); parental fees were reduced; and it became possible to deduct the childcare cost and the parental leave allowance (Elterngeld) from income tax as a non-taxable benefit (2007) (Fröhlich 2006).

The German system of childcare includes both nurseries ('*Krippen*', '*Kindertagespflege*') for children under three years of age and kindergarten ('*Kindertageseinrichtungen*') for children between 3 and 6. It is governed at the local level where there are Youth Welfare Boards composed of representatives from the municipality, voluntary providers and parent associations. This system, financed from local public funds at the discretion of local corporatist governments, represents a universal, mixed-market model where public and voluntary providers dominate over private providers, which are minimal. In 2009, private commercial centres covered only 2 per cent compared to religious, not-for-profit and public providers, which each covered one-third of all services delivered (Mühler 2010,[1] see also Evers et al. 2005, Mühler 2008, BMFSFJ et al. 2013).

Financing

Financing of child care is decentralised in Germany to the level of the municipality and the district where both public sector and voluntary providers are encouraged and financially supported by local governments. Even though the range of providers that receive financial support from the German state is large, the overall public expenditure on child care has been below the average of EU countries in the last decade (that is expenditure on nurseries/kindergartens was 0.1 per cent/0.4 per cent of GDP in Germany in 2009 compared to 0.3 per cent (0.4 per cent of GDP in the EU, respectively).[2] Whereas publicly provided child-care centres are funded to an extent of around 70 per cent by public sources, non-public providers gain only about 10 per cent of the operating costs from the state (Mühler 2010). Germany is also a country where parents pay a relatively low share of the total costs of childcare (about 18 per cent; Gathmann and Sass 2011).

Outcomes

Even though available studies proved that there has been some progress in the quantity and quality of subsidised childcare facilities during recent years (Hübenthal and Ifland 2011), the number of children under 3 years of age using formal childcare has been low in Germany for decades. The increase of the number of children enrolled (from 14 per cent in 2000 to about 25 per cent of all German children of this age group in 2010, OECD 2011c, UNECE 2012) has been due to the higher demand of German mothers and to government efforts to extend the current number of childcare provisions (for example commitment to create 750,000 places for children under three between 2008 and 2013; European Commission 2009a).

On the contrary, the amount of services for older children has covered almost the entire population of children aged from 3 years to pre-school age in recent

---

1   About 10 per cent of all childcare facilities in Germany are formed both by parent-run centres (operated by a parent board) and company centres (mostly organised as a registered membership association) (Mühler 2010).

2   See Chapter 12, Table 12.4.

years (over 92 per cent of all children in 2010, which is 14 per cent more than the EU average; see Chapter 12, Table 12.6). Moreover, there are huge regional differences, especially in the case of services for children under three years old. These services are less accessible in smaller cities, in regions with low population density and in the former West Germany. For example, the enrolment rate of children under three is 4.5 per cent in Lower Saxony in West Germany compared to 49.9 per cent in Saxony Anhalt in the former East Germany (European Commission 2009a). For this reason, empirical studies confirm the increased demand of parents for the expansion of capacity in both types of existing public facilities (nurseries and kindergartens) and for an increase of company nurseries (BMFSFJ 2013). In addition, empirical studies concerning children between the ages of 3 and 6 demonstrate that the children of migrants are under-represented in early childcare facilities (Nauck et al. 2008, in: Hübenthal and Ifland 2011).

Not only accessibility but the quality of services is also regionally differentiated. Individual states (*Länder*) address the quality of childcare services through uniform licensing standards and the pedagogical programmes ('*Bildungsprogrammen*') of childcare employees: child carers ('*Kinderplfelgerin*') must have completed secondary vocational training, and in the case of children's governesses ('*Erzieherin*'), an internship is required (OECD 2011c). However, the average quality of German child-care is evaluated as medium to low by international comparison, because only minimum quality standards are imposed and there is considerable heterogeneity in the availability and quality of services among different kinds of providers within particular regions (Mühler 2010). The number of children per teaching staff in pre-school facilities dropped from nearly 12 to 10 between 2005 and 2010, which is 6 per cent below the OECD average. Currently, the parent fees for childcare facilities are below the EU average (that is 14.1 per cent of the average German wage compared to 18.4 per cent of that in the OECD in 2010; OECD 2011c).

Trends, Changes and Innovations
Summing up, the female employment rate in Germany is relatively high. In recent years, especially part-time jobs have been systematically supported, resulting in an increase in women's employment of this kind. The rising employment of German women is the result of the transition from the male-breadwinner model to the model supporting family/life balance. The key changes include the universal delivery of childcare to pre-school children, the gradual strengthening of services focused on children under three years, providing access to parental allowance for fathers, but also the shortening of the parental allowance. Since 2000, there has been a great emphasis on the expansion of childcare providers operating in the market.

Childcare in Germany is traditionally funded by the state through local public funds, which are at the discretion of local governments, and by parent contributions, which cover up to one-third of the total costs. While public spending on childcare for children between 3 years and school age is slightly below the

EU-27 average, spending on services for children under 3 years is consistently three- to four-times lower than the EU-27 average. Available services cover almost the entire population of German children of pre-school age and about one fifth of children under 3 years of age (these services have been constantly increasing since 2000). Service quality differs from region to region because of the lack of central regulation of childcare staff.

Elderly Care

The worldwide demographic trend in the aging of the population is also occurring in Germany, where the number of economically inactive people over 65 has increased by almost 6 per cent in the last decade (in 2010 the rate was 40.3 per cent in Germany compared to 31.3 per cent (OECD 2011d). In line with the Bismarckian tradition, social assistance benefits for care were replaced in 1995 by a compulsory social insurance scheme (Long Term Act/LTA 1995). The new system of long-term care was based on the principles of universality in coverage, social solidarity across generations and equality, which is evident in the standardised benefits of all recipients and in the standardised costs of care packages (Theobald 2004). The main objectives of present long-term care insurance are to secure the risk of the need for care; to enable people in need of care to stay in their home for as long as possible; to improve social security for carers who are not employed in order to promote willingness to provide care at home; and to support the expansion and consolidation of the care infrastructure (Schulz 2010b).

Regulation and Delivery
The current German system of elder care is regulated by the federal government: both kinds of delivered services and their price and scale of fees are defined by the government, rather than being determined by the market. Simultaneously, individual Länders are responsible for service infrastructure and care delivery. Therefore, care practice varies greatly among the 16 German states. The development of services for the elderly is supported by municipalities whereby the services are provided under the legislatively set rules of the Health Care Fund Organisation (according to the Long-term Care Further Development Act – LCFD). Some states (*Länders*) directly finance investments in nursing homes, while others only provide subsidies for dependent older people who are living in nursing homes and relying on social assistance (Schulz 2010b).

Although informal care provided at home by family members or non-professional private persons still plays a significant role in current elderly care in Germany, a general trend towards institutionalisation is evident in the last ten years. In this period, the number of elderly receiving care in institutions has increased (mainly in nursing homes). In 2011, nearly 98 per cent of all beneficiaries of institutional care were living in private or public nursing homes (Schulz 2012). Institutional care is often provided by non-profit organisations that ensure housing options for the elderly like sheltered housing and old age homes. Simultaneously, the effort to enable care in a home environment for as long as possible is strengthened by the development of formal home care services that are provided both traditionally by family members and by professionals who are licensed and supported by the Long-term Care Insurance funds (Rothgang 2010); 73 per cent of both groups of these workers were female (see Heinicke and Thomsen 2010). Since the introduction of the Long-term Care Insurance scheme the number of professional home care services has shown great dynamic, in particular the number of private home care services. For example, in 2007 a total of 11,530 companies provided home-care services for 504,230 persons in need (Schulz 2010b).

Long-term care benefits are set by law (Social Code Book), whereby in addition to cash allowances and benefits in kind for home (informal) care, financial support for institutional care is also provided (Schulz 2010b; Heinicke and Thomsen 2010). These benefits are paid from existing public and private health insurance funds, which are legally independent entities that provide the mandated tasks under government supervision and are responsible for capacity planning, monitoring, organisation, quality control and assessment of care provision (Schulz 2010b). All providers are monitored and advised by the Medical Review Board of the social health insurance funds.

Financing
The current public long-term care system in Germany is based on the statutory Long-Term Care Insurance scheme (LTCI), representing a pay-as-you-go system that is almost entirely financed from contributions and premiums. These contributions are income-dependent and are shared equally between the employee (50 per cent) and employer (50 per cent). The amount of contributions increased from 1 per cent of salary in 1995 to 1.70 per cent in 2000 and 1.95 per cent in 2009, subject to a wage ceiling of €3,600 per month since 2008 (Schulz 2010b). Employees with higher long-term earnings (more than €4012 per month in their last three years of work) can be better insured because they can opt for private health and long-term care insurance that offers at least the same level of benefits and often more than the public mandatory LTCI system (Schulz 2010b). German seniors can purchase services from any provider; however, if they make use of care by family members or non-professional private persons, the costs are covered by cash allowances that are not tied to the purchase of care.

In 2007, the highest amounts of the social LTCI funds were spent on full-time institutional care (€8.83 billion), on cash benefits for people receiving informal care (€4 billion) and professional home care services (€2.47 billion; Heinicke and Thomsen 2010; Schulz 2010b). Although elder care benefits are uniform across Germany and are adjusted periodically to compensate for fluctuations in inflation, there are regional differences between fees because wage and income levels are different in the individual states (*Länders*) to account for general wage levels and income differences among individual *Länders*. While the benefits for home-care cover the costs of personal care almost entirely, the benefits for institutional care cover only about half of the total costs of nursing homes. Private co-payments for institutional care are needed because of the high costs: beneficiaries in nursing homes have to pay 'hotel costs' and in some states (*Länders*) there are also investment costs on building and modernising care facilities.

Outcomes

The proportion of beds per 1,000 people over 65 years of age in Germany greatly exceeds the average in OECD countries; this number is the highest of all the countries surveyed (see Chapter 12, Table 12.10). Compared to the home-based care that is traditionally a well-developed area of elderly care in Germany, residential care facilities have expanded and improved in recent decades in both the former East and West Germany. The number of employees in these facilities has increased as well, especially part-time workers. The LTCI scheme implies universal coverage for people in need. Therefore the extent of people receiving long-term care benefits has been a growing trend and traditionally relatively high – from 2 million in 1999 to 2.34 million in 2009 (Schulz 2012).

The quality of elderly care, which is monitored and controlled by social LTCI funds and the Medical Review Board of social health insurance funds, is ensured in Germany through annual inspections whose evaluations ('*care marks*') are publicly accessible. Moreover, some national governments stimulate the transfer of innovations and good practices as well as nationally developed guidelines and standards for better care (Nies et al. 2010). Vocational training of caregivers is standardised at a comparatively high level; for example, there are entrance requirements and a compulsory three-year training programme (Theobald 2004). The measure aimed at improving the delivery of long-term care came in May 2008 when a new act on long term care was passed (*Long-term Care Further Development Act*). This law focuses on five key areas: (1) the introduction of a new instrument called 'nursing care time' (which regulates activities and benefits for caregivers; for example time to vacation or have unpaid leave from work for informal family carers); (2) the promotion of rehabilitation, case management and counselling; (3) quality improvements; (4) adjustment of benefits; and (5) financing (see Rothgang 2010).

Trends, Changes and Innovations

Summing up, care for the elderly is based on universal, non-means-tested contribution-financed social insurance for long-term care that is intended to provide comprehensive coverage. The range of benefits and tools is relatively broad and allows both informal care for older persons at home as well as professional care through a network of private (profit, non-profit) and public providers. However, the key principle of the German care system for the elderly is short-term rehabilitation care at home instead of full-time long-term care in institutionalised facilities.

The delivery of elderly care in Germany is based on the self-administration of long-term care insurance funds. In this context, some experts claim that the German system of long-term care is not sufficiently networked or coordinated, as the long-term care insurance system is threatened by financial instability in the long run (compare Theobald 2004, Schulz 2010b). On the other hand, the quality of elderly care services and the sustainability of this quality is perceived as good both in the home and in residential care thanks to vocational training of its staff.

Employment Services

Contemporary German labour market policy can be characterised as 'a mix of governance modes: rule-oriented modes co-exist with New Public Management models supported by quasi-market mechanisms and network relations between public and private providers' (Konle-Seidl 2008: 31). Growing long-term unemployment, the unlimited duration of benefits, training and public job creation measures and the low priority placed on individual work with the unemployed were the main problems that led the German government to radically reform the existing system of public employment services ten years ago through the Hartz Reforms. The German National Labour Office was restructured and what were previously separate systems of active and passive labour market policy were integrated. These changes occurred even though the unemployment rate in Germany was oscillating around the EU average. The years 2004 to 2006 were exceptions, where the unemployment rate rose to 2 per cent above the EU average, that is, to 10–11 per cent (see Eurostat 2012b).

Regulation and Delivery
Public employment services are supervised by the Ministry of Labour and Social Affairs and administered by the German Federal Employment Agency ('*Bundesagentur für Arbeit*'), which is organised into ten decentralised regional directorates and 180 large local offices. Individual organisational units are largely autonomous both in decision-making and in resource allocation for active programmes, and their supervisory bodies are strongly influenced by their social partners (Tergeist and Grubb 2006, Dingeldey 2011a, 2011b).

Since 2002, the Job-Activ Act and four subsequent acts (the Hartz I-IV laws) were negotiated and implemented step-by-step between 2003 and 2005. The key point of the Harz Reforms was to transform the Federal Employment Agency into a service provider with private management structures. Public employment services were modernised through the introduction of New Public Management methods (performance targets); the accountability of local employment offices was strengthened; there was more outsourcing of many services as well as open competition between private service providers. At the same time, new activation strategies were implemented in the tightening of suitable job requirements, the targeted use of benefit sanctions, more intensive contact and the follow-up of the unemployed. However, the newly introduced two-tier system, including Public Employment Offices (PES) for the short-term unemployed and Employment agencies (*Arbaitsagenturen*, ARGE) for the long-term unemployed, is regarded as too complex and sometimes impracticable. Especially criticised are the separation of benefit entitlements and the fact that the system is not based on client service needs (compare Benhard and Wolf 2008, Räisänen et al. 2012). Although training and similar measures have always been provided by private actors (often non-profit actors) before the Harz Reforms, the number of market-based actors has increased, as well as the level of efficiency tests of service providers after the reform. Furthermore, New Public Management methods have been implemented not only in private employment services but also in public employment services (Dingeldey 2011a, 2011b).

The former benefit system changed significantly and can be considered a shift from the dominance of contribution-based financing towards tax-based financing (Dingeldey 2011a, b). The former three-tier system was changed into a two-tier system, whereby the first tier is financed by contributions and the second one, which newly dominates and covers two-thirds of all the unemployed, is means-tested and financed by taxes. Simultaneously, the level of unemployment benefits and their durations have been reduced; eligibility for subsistence allowances began to be determined according to a person's ability to work; and sanctions for inactivity have been introduced (see Tergeist and Grubb 2006; Jacobi and Kluve 2007; Konle-Seidl 2008). Services for long-term unemployed recipients of unemployment assistance and social assistance have been integrated (into Unemployment Benefit II) and administered by a newly created institution ('joint associations', or 'consortia' – '*Arbeitsagenturen*', ARGE) composed of representatives of local employment offices and local authorities.

Financing
During the last decade, there has been a gradual decline in public expenditure on active and passive employment policy (from 3.39 per cent GDP in 2002 to 2.26 per cent in 2010), although it is still somewhat above the EU average. In the case of active labour market policy, the shift towards the activation of the unemployed was accompanied with stricter cost-benefit calculation for active programmes, with a subsequent reduction in training programme expenditure and public sector job creation schemes. At the same time, the German benefit system changed from one dominated by unemployment insurance funding to one dominated by tax funding (Jacobi and Kluve 2007, Konle-Seidl 2008).

Outcomes
The number of participants involved in active labour market measures dropped from 7.4 per cent in 2002 to 3.6 per cent in 2010, below the OECD average (see Chapter 12, Table 12.14). The Harz Reforms have led to a gradual decline in the number of unemployed per one case-worker which is lower predominantly in ARGE offices. The legislator has set targets of 75 unemployed per one case-worker for youths and 150 for adults: in 2011 these targets were nearly achieved (86 and 158), see OECD (2011f). The professionalism of these workers is ensured by the existing system of education and recruitment, which takes between 14 and 15 months and where each state ('*Länder*') has its own colleges of public administration (for

example the Federal Academy of Public Administration, or '*Bundesakademie für öffentliche Verwaltung*'; CEDEFOP 2011). The professionalism of employment workers is also ensured through the National Management Information System and reciprocal dialogues between the state and regions, allowing the local agencies to enter a comment alongside their performance information, identifying weaknesses, providing explanations and approving measures to improve the performance of the PES.

The German system seems to be successful especially due to its shift to management-by-objectives and the introduction of market mechanisms in the public sphere (Konle-Seidl 2008). The effectiveness of active labour market policy measures has improved only modestly after the implementation of the Hartz Reforms; nevertheless, the redesigned training programmes, wage subsidies and start-up subsidies show significantly positive effects. However, for the long-term unemployed, the new scheme labelled Unemployment Benefits II has not led to an increase of incentive to work (compare Kemmerling and Bruttel 2005, Bruttel 2005a, 2005b, Mosley 2005, Tergeist and Grubb 2006, Jacobi and Kluve 2007, Kolne-Seidl 2008, Benhard and Wolf 2008, Räisänen et al. 2012).

Trends, Changes and Innovations
Summed up, the changes in the German employment services have mainly entailed a reduction in welfare benefits and a promotion of flexible forms of employment (Dingeldey 2009). The key point of the Harz Reforms, which began in 2002, was to transform the Federal Employment Agency into a service provider with private management structures. Public employment services were modernised through the introduction of New Public Management methods (performance targets). The accountability of local employment offices was strengthened, as was the outsourcing of many services and the open competition between private service providers. At the same time, new activation strategies were implemented both in the form of more intensive contact and the follow-up of the unemployed (through employment offices as customer-orientated one-stop-shop centres operating in collaboration with private providers) as in the form of tightening suitable job requirements and the targeted use of benefit sanctions.

The former benefit system has changed significantly: the level of unemployment benefits and their durations have been reduced; eligibility for subsistence allowances has been newly delivered according to a person's ability to work (rather than according to their previous contribution payments); and sanctions for inactivity in the form of withdrawal of enrolled unemployed from the labour offices have been introduced (see Tergeist and Grubb 2006, Jacobi and Kluve 2007, Konle-Seidl 2008). This means that there has been a shift from contributory to non-contributory benefits; therefore, the relative importance of tax-funded unemployment assistance has increased as well (Dingledey 2009). Labour market programmes have always been delivered mostly by non-public, third-sector organisations and (to a minor extent) by profit-making organisations; thus the trend towards further marketisation is rather limited.

Employment in the Health and Social Work Sector in Germany

For the discussion of employment we use data collected in Chapter 3 (Eurostat data) supplemented by data from national sources. According to Eurostat, employment in HSW was 4,619.9 thousand and the share of HSW employment in the total employment of the economy was 12.1 per cent in 2010 (similar to other western European countries). Employment in HSW grew remarkably (by 28.1 per cent) between 2000 and 2010.[3] The growth in part-time jobs was more than twice that of full-time jobs. Most employment in HSW is in the health sector (59.4 per cent); 22 per cent of workers in HSW work in residential care activities and 18.6 per cent work in social work without accommodation. Germany thus holds an intermediate position in the extent of social services compared to the other three countries in focus.

National data on employment usually comes from the German Microcensus (Table 10.3). Most data are in WZ (2003) classification; the latest data use WZ (2008) classification. There is a clear trend of growth in the number of workers employed in the HSW sector for the whole period 2000–2010 when using both classifications. This is confirmed by the Microcensus data on social services professions from detailed employment publications (Statistisches Bundesamt 2005–2011). According to this data, the number of workers in HSW grew by 21 per cent between 2000 and 2010 (that is from 3,568 thousand to 4,329 thousand). This is almost by 7 per cent less growth in HSW employment compared to Eurostat data by Labour Force Survey (LFS), although the base numbers in 2000 were similar: 3,585 thousand employees in LFS and 3,568 thousand in the national data.[4] According to LFS, in 2010 employment grew to 4,620 thousand, while in the national data it grew to 4,329 thousand. The reason is that from the total 1,024 thousand new employees, 734 thousand were part-time worker (that is over 70 per cent). This means that in the full-time equivalent numbers, the national data show a smaller increase in HSW sector employment.

In social professions the number of employees grew from 1,394 to 1,784 between 2005 and 2010 according to the national data; this is an increase of 28 per cent over a 5-year span. There was more growth in the number of workers caring for the elderly (from 397 to 532,000, that is, by 34 per cent) and less growth in the number of educators (from 465 to 547,000, that is, by 18 per cent) between 2005 and 2010.

---

3 We should recall that pre-school education services are not counted in the HSW sector in Germany, which influences both the growth and structure of the sector in the Eurostat data.

4 LFS data counts the number of employees in the sector regardless of whether they are full-time or part-time covering just resident households. The national data count employees in full-time equivalent numbers. On the other hand, this national data include cross-border workers and persons living in institutional and collective households (conscripts).

Table 10.3   Workers in Human Health and Social Work Sector and specific professions (2000–2010)

	2000	2005	2009	2010
All workers (WZ 2003)	39 144	38 835	40 271	40 483
HSW (WZ 2003)	3 668	4 037	4 355	:
HSW (WZ 2008)	3 568	3 889	:	4 329
Social professions	:	1 394	1 692	1 784
Social workers, social pedagogues.	:	255	304	316
Educators, instructors	:	465	519	547
Social carers for the elderly	:	397	493	532

Note: Classifications used: Klassifikation der Wirtschaftszweige, Ausgabe 2003 and 2008 (WZ 2003, WZ 2008), Klassifizierung der Berufe 1992.
Source: Statistisches Jahrbuch Für die Bundesrepublik Deutschland (2001–2011), Mikrozensus: Bevölkerung und Erwerbstätigkeit.

The development of employment in specific social service professions is also evidenced in data from the administration of compulsory social security. The first line of Table 10.4 shows the development of employment in social affairs – '*Heime und Sozialwesen*' (excluding healthcare) according to WZ 1993 (2000–2002), WZ 2003 (2003–2008) and WZ 2008 (2009–2010) classification. In the other lines, the *Klassifizierung der Berufe* (1988) is used. There was a substantial growth of employment (workers paying contributions) in all the professions in focus. For example, the total number of workers in residential care and social work grew from 1,020.8 thousand to 1,426.6 thousand (by 40 per cent); the number of workers in kindergarten grew from 367,000 in 2000 to 459,000 in 2010 (by 25 per cent); and the number of social workers and carers grew from 358 to 538,000 in the same period (by 50 per cent).

Data available on public employment in social services are provided as both a headcount and full-time equivalent (WTE). Unfortunately, the statistics were provided in the same classification but not in the same groups for the period in focus (for example social facilities for the young category published in 2000–2005 include day facilities for children published in 2006–2010, but also children's homes and children's information centres). Data on the facilities for the young and for adults refer only to the local level, while data on Agency for Work include all levels. The number of people working in facilities for adults (including care of the elderly) was relatively small and roughly stable in the period 2006–2010. The decline in the number of workers in childcare facilities between 2002 and 2005 was reversed by the trend of growth in employment in day childcare facilities between 2006 and 2010 (there may still be a decline

Table 10.4   Employees paying compulsory social insurance by 30th June of given year, in thousands (2000–2010)

	2000	2005	2009	2010
Residential care and social work	1 020,8	:	1 350,6	1 426,6
Helper in hospital care	220,6	234,9	254	266,7
Social care	:	:	1 242,6	1 314,9
Social workers and social care workers	357,9	408,1	502	537,7
Housemasters (wardens) and social pedagogues	215,4	245,4	279,4	291,1
Workers in kindergarten, carers of children	366,7	393	436,8	458,5

Note: All data were rounded to the nearest hundreds.

Source: Statistisches Jahrbuch Für die Bundesrepublik Deutschland (2001–2011)

in the remaining part of the sector of social facilities for the young). At first, there is stagnation and then strong growth (in the second part of the period) in employment in Agency for Work (from approximately 95,000 in 2002 to 124,000 in 2010). Summed up, there is evident growth in public sector employment in social services.

Table 10.5   Public employment in selected professions (2002–2010)

	2002	2005	2009	2010
Social facilities for adults Headcount	:	:	29 719	26 839
Social facilities for adults WTE	:	:	23 537	20 849
Social facilities for the young Headcount	150 174	144 880	:	:
Social facilities for the young WTE	120 006	112 900	:	:
Day facilities for children Headcount	:	:	143 559	151 677
Day facilities for children WTE	:	:	112 325	118 227
Office/agency for work Headcount	95 490	96 578	118 261	124 579

Source: Finanzen und Steuern: Personal des öffentlichen Dienstes (2002–2010)

Table 10.6   **Gross annual wages of full-time workers in Health and Social Work Sector and specific social services professions, in Euro (2007–2010)**

	2007	2008	2009	2010
Total economy	40 134	41 260	41 468	42 515
Human health and social work	37 614	38 522	39 836	40 439
Residential care	31 303	32 077	32 708	32 915
Residential nursing care	:	:	31 427	31 662
Residential care activities for elderly and disabled	:	:	32 773	32 854
Social work activities without accommodation	32 259	33 229	33 790	33 969
Pre-primary education	:	:	34 931	35 116
Employment activities	19 987	21 018	22 021	21 912

Source: Verdienste und Arbeitskosten: Arbeitnehmerverdienste (2007–2010)

According to Eurostat data in HSW, women dominate the sector (about 75 per cent of workers). Surprisingly, this number is slightly lower (by about 5 per cent) than in other nations. Similar to the situation in the other countries in focus, the workforce is quite rapidly ageing – the share of workers aged over 50 increased from 19 per cent in 2000 to 31.9 per cent in 2010. The prevailing education of workers in the HSW sector is at a medium level (52.8 per cent) and high level (34.2 per cent); the share of low educated workers is average (13 per cent) compared to the other countries. Most workers are qualified in health and welfare and/or social sciences. Younger HSW workers (15–29 years old) are less likely (20.3 per cent) to have a high level of qualification and more likely (23.6 per cent) to have a low level of qualification than their older cohorts (30–49 years, 50+ years). Men are more often highly qualified than women.

    The mean annual earnings of workers in the HSW sector were 35,819 Euros in 2010 (Eurostat SES data). This is 19 per cent less than in the reference category of manufacturing. Young workers were on average very low paid compared to other age groups (31 per cent below average). The number or weekly worked hours is 32.8, reflecting the substantial use of part-time work. The national data about wages have been published by the German Statistical Office only since the year 2007 (*Statistisches Bundesamt* 2007–2010). Wages in HSW are close to the national economy average, although the wages of the social care professions overall (excluding healthcare) are substantially lower. The lowest wages are found in employment services (€21,912 a year) and residential nursing care (€31,662 a year). Compared to the average €42,515 in the total economy in 2010, they represent 51.5 per cent and 64.5 per cent of the average wage, respectively. It is notable that in the national data, only wages for full-time workers are published, which may bias the real situation, that is, the fact that many workers in social services work part-time (if it were possible to take into account part-time jobs, the wages would be even lower).

All these data indicate considerable growth of employment in health and social services, in social services in particular in the period 2000–2010. Employment grew slightly even in the public sector social services. The level of wages in social services is substantially lower than the country average.

Conclusions

The German welfare state in the long-term is characterised by public expenditure that overall surpasses the average level of the EU-27. However, spending on services for children of pre-school age is much lower than the EU-27 average, although it has been increasing in the last few years. The social insurance scheme, which is the base for financing the long-term care of the elderly, has been strengthened in the 2000s. The trend in employment services has shown declining expenditure on active labour market policy measures, while personnel capacities have been strengthened.

In the case of family policy and childcare, the reforms aimed to replace the traditional male-breadwinner model with a model that supports the work–family life balance. Childcare is traditionally funded by the state from local public funds (at the discretion of local governments); financing out-of-the-pockets of parents is relatively low. The contemporary German model of care for children represents a mixed-market model, whereby the predominant providers are religious groups, public centres and not-for-profit centres. Almost one fifth of children under three years of age use these facilities, which is double the number of ten years ago. Services are at a good quality level, but differ from region to region.

Care for the elderly is based on universal, non-means-tested contribution-financed social insurance and on a wide pallet of tools enabling predominantly informal care at home and professional care through a network of private and public providers. The organisation of elderly care is based on the self-administration of health and social insurance funds. However, although there are many of these funds and public and private providers delivering services of high quality, long-term care is often criticised for not being sufficiently networked or coordinated.

In employment services, great emphasis has been put on labour market participation and activation associated with cuts in unemployment benefits for the long-term unemployed in recent years. Labour market programmes are often delivered mostly by non-public third-sector organisations; involvement of profit-making organisations is rather limited. The Hartz Reforms have brought improved case work and the greater outsourcing of programmes.

The last ten years have seen growth in employment in health and social services by more than 20 per cent, especially in social services as well as in child care, elderly care and employment services. The employment level has grown slightly even in the public sector of social services. Nevertheless, the level of wages in social services is substantially lower than the average wage.

Chapter 11

Governance, Financing and Employment in Social Services in the United Kingdom

Markéta Horáková, Pavel Horák, Ondřej Hora and Tomáš Sirovátka

The United Kingdom represents a liberal welfare state (Esping-Andersen 1990) characterised by predominantly targeted state support in welfare services which are strongly marketised. New Public Management methods are applied in the governance of public services. Public-private mix in service delivery is typical, mixing public-private resources and formal and informal services (Dingeldey 2009).

Change in the financing of the UK welfare state

In the UK, a relative decline in cash benefits has been observed between 2000 and 2010, while expenditure on social services has been on the increase due to rapidly growing expenditure on health care. Table 11.1 shows that social expenditure is slightly below the EU average (28.2 per cent), while it increased from 25.5 per cent of GDP in 2000 to 25.8 per cent in 2005 and to 27.1 per cent in 2010.

Table 11.1   **Social protection expenditure as per cent of GDP in United Kingdom (2000–2010)**

	2000	2005	2010
Social protection total	25.5	25.8	27.1
Social protection in cash	17.0	15.4	15.8
Social protection in kind	8.5	10.4	11.3
Health care and sickness in kind	5.8	7.4	8.0
Invalidity in kind	0.3	0.4	0.4
Old age in kind	0.4	0.6	0.2
Survivors in kind	0	0	0
Family in kind	0.3	0.4	0.7
Unemployment in kind	0.13	0.15	0.17
Housing in kind	1.4	1.4	1.5
Social Exclusion in kind	0.19	0.0	0.02

Source: Eurostat (2012b)

Table 11.2   Development in overall tax and duty revenue and taxes on labour, capital and consumption as percentages of GDP (2000–2010)

	2000	2005	2010
Total receipts from taxes and duties	38.1	37.6	37.4
Taxes on labour	14.1	14.3	14.0 (2009)
Taxes on capital	10.8	10.7	10.5 (2009)
Taxes on consumption	11.8	11.2	10.4 (2009)

Source: Eurostat (2012b)

There has also been an increase in childcare services, disabled care services and employment services, while in kind expenditure on old age/elderly dropped due to changes in financing between 2005 and 2010. Expenditure on housing has traditionally been high. The above trends in social protection expenditure, especially the decreasing cash benefits, correspond to the model of the liberal welfare state; nevertheless, social services as a whole have gained more weight than in Germany, for example, where cash benefits still dominate. Facing an increasing deficit of public finance (47 per cent of GDP), the new conservative-liberal government proposed, among other things, cuts in the working age tax-benefit system (welfare reform) in the amount of £7 billion per year, which is likely to affect social services due to losses in benefits tied to the services. On the other hand, the government has committed itself to protecting the funding for Sure Start services (childcare) and adding £2 billion to social care support, as well as providing more personalised support in employment services (HM Treasury 2010).

The tax structure in the UK and its development in many ways follows the lines of other EU member states, although with some differences. One is the increase in the top personal income tax rate in 2010 to 50 per cent, making it close to the top rate in Denmark, even though it has already decreased to 45 per cent. Since 2000 the revenue from taxes and social contributions has remained remarkably stable as percentages of GDP (for example 38.1 per cent in 2000 and 37.4 per cent in 2010). Table 11.2 shows the overall development in total taxes and duties, as well as the development in the taxation of labour, capital and consumption.

The implicit tax rate on labour and consumption has remained stable, whereas there has been a reduction in the implicit tax rate on capital, implying that the total tax paid as a percentage of the potential tax base has been reduced over the years. Taxes on property contribute a relatively large amount in the UK compared to that of the other countries – at 12.1 per cent of total taxation in 2010 (OECD 2011b). Part of the reason for this is that local taxation to a large degree is based upon property tax. Furthermore, there has not been any dramatic change in the out-of-pocket payments to healthcare in percentages of total expenditure; in fact, they have even been reduced from 13.5 per cent in 2001 to 10.5 per cent in 2009 (compare OECD 2012b).

Despite the few changes, as remarked above in the overall structure, there has been a rise in the public sector deficit in the wake of the financial crisis and as of 4 January 2011, the VAT rate has been increased from 17.5 per cent to 20 per cent. Theoretically, the UK has better options for using duties due to the fact that cross-border trade is less likely to occur than in countries having a direct border with

Thus there is generally remarkably stable development in the ways that the welfare state is financed in other member states. The reason for the higher level of property tax is due to the fact that since 1993 a council tax was imposed on property based upon a value for Scotland and England as of 1 April 1991, whereas in Wales a revaluation was made in April 2003 (Adam and Browne 2011).

The distribution of tax is set up in that the top 10 per cent of income tax payers contribute over half of the income tax, and the top 1 per cent (that is, those also paying the 50 per cent tax) pays 28 per cent of all income tax. Official documents reveal (HM Treasury 2010) proportion of personal income paid in total taxes is slightly higher for the poorest fifth than it is for the average and richest fifths. However, recent changes since 2010, including the increase of indirect taxes, are likely to worsen the impact for the very poorest groups, even though the income tax threshold has been raised considerably. Furthermore, it can be argued that 'income tax has moved away from providing support for marriage and towards providing support for children' (Adam and Browne 2011: 42).

Environmental taxation plays only a limited role and the main area where this tax is used is with regard to motoring: environmental taxes and duties amount to around 2.4 per cent of GDP. Taxes on companies have in general had a downward trend and will be further reduced to 23 per cent in 2014/15.

Summarising the above, from the perspective of stage budget revenue, the UK welfare state has been stably financed in recent decades. In comparison to the other surveyed countries, in the UK most funding has flowed from the pockets of the rich; taxes on property have always played a significant role; the out-of-pocket payments have decreased in the last years; and the public sector deficit caused by the financial crisis was mitigated by the increase of the VAT rate in 2011. On the other hand, social expenditure (traditionally around the EU average) has increased significantly since 2000, even during times of economic crisis in 2008 and afterwards, due to the growing demand for health care, elder/disabled care and childcare services; nevertheless, there may be some reversal of the trend with the coming public expenditure cuts. Since 2010, the UK government has decided to cut public expenditure on the welfare state and has been committed to planning and implementing the reform of the welfare system (especially the Universal Credit Reform of Benefits and Tax Credits) in order 'to make it fairer, more affordable and to tackle poverty and welfare dependency, whilst continuing to support the most vulnerable in society' (DWP 2010:6).

Changes in the Governance of Selected Social Services in the UK

Childcare

According to Nygard (2012: 18), 'traditionally, British government have generally been quite reluctant to engage in extensive family policy interventions due to the dominant cultural and ideological divide between the public and private sphere'. However, social and economic changes together with demographic development in recent years have highlighted the importance of re-examining gender relationships in labour market, family and welfare state policy (Finch 2008). Since 2000 family policy in the UK has become more explicit and shifted towards a higher level of gender equality and the possibility of reconciling work and family life. These shifts are often considered as a 'modernisation' of the old family care model (Daly 2010). Fundamental changes occurred under New Labour rule (1997–2010): an expansion of childcare and early education services; better financial support and more effective tax credits enabled more parents to return to work; better services for young children and (poor) families together with a focus on employment activation (through tax credits and the promotion of employment among single parents) combat unemployment, poverty and social exclusion; work–family reconciliation (through an extension of maternity leave, the introduction of paternity leave, and rights to flexible working hours) reinforcing gender equality; and social cohesion and emphasising the social rights of citizens (see Daly 2010: 441).

The recent demographic developments in the UK could be considered to be relatively positive because the fertility rate has been rising in the last ten years and is considerably higher than most of the other EU countries today. The higher fertility rate is associated with the long-term stable employment rate of women, which has been in the range of 64 per cent to 66 per cent in the last ten years (OECD 2012b). In this period, however, the proportion of employed women – mothers of young children (with one or two children under the age of six) – has significantly declined by nearly 10 percentage points per cent (from 71.5 per cent in 2002 to 63.1 per cent in 2010, Eurostat 2012c).

Regulation and Delivery
The UK represents a typical traditional model of the family and there is a significant role played by the market in childcare provision. Public childcare services are financed by central government (through general taxation) and organised by local authorities. In 2001 the UK government began its move to implement a nationwide programme of Sure Start Children's Centres, working with the parents' right to childcare from the birth of their child. The Children's Centres have been developed in line with the needs of the local community since 2011, when there were more than 3,600 children's centres; however, the significant cuts made recently within local authority budgets have caused a reduction in the level of services in some areas (Government 2012). Since 2011, the Sure Start centres have been more oriented to providing services for disadvantaged groups in

deprived areas. Nevertheless, the children's centres remain a top priority of local governments (Sure Start Children's Centres Census 2012).

The framework for the operation of UK childcare has traditionally been set by central government. On the other hand, the administration of social care services was historically a matter for local government. However, the neo-liberal strategies of marketisation pursued since the late 1980s have resulted in the extensive growth of private-sector provision (Land and Lewis 1998). As Caluori (2009) points out, the childcare market has mainly expanded over the past ten years, fuelled by increased demand and increased government subsidy, each one feeding the other. Within the childcare market, there are few large providers and the private, voluntary and independent childcare market is comprised of a mosaic of small businesses of various sizes. The supply and quality of childcare services vary according to the individual providers. Although the UK system of Early Childhood Education and Care (ECEC) has recently been integrated under education, it still suffers from fragmentation as to the diversification regarding philosophy, curriculum and programme focus (The Clearinghouse 2008).

Parents have a statutory right to childcare, integrated with early education for young children and out-of-school hours care for older children (The Clearinghouse 2008). Local authorities play a crucial role by managing the childcare market in their catchment area and have the statutory responsibility of ensuring that sufficient childcare is available. Nevertheless, as shown by Caluori (2012), Rüling (2010), Daly (2010) and others, they need to be given the funds, support and powers from the central level to ensure that they are able to fulfil their duties.

Besides the Sure Start Children's Centres there are some early education and childcare places which are free of charge for all 3 and 4 year olds for 15 hours per week (Government 2012). Children under the age of 5 are entitled to day nurseries and classes and/or pre-schools and playgroups. Day nurseries provide care and learning activities for children from their birth and they are often based in workplaces and run by businesses or voluntary groups; 3 and 4 year olds can obtain their 15 hours a week of free early education. Nursery schools, which are the basic provision for working parents, provide early learning and childcare and are often based at Sure Start Children's Centres, or linked to an infant or primary school (Government 2012).

Financing
Funding UK family policy is largely based on indirect financial support for low income families through the concept of means-tested tax credits (Child Tax Credit and Working Tax Credit – WTC) which are refundable: the WTC will be replaced by the Universal Tax Credit over the next few years (by about 2016). This implies that families will have the right to a reimbursement even if the amount exceeds what the family has to pay in tax (Adam and Browne 2011). Since 2003, the WTC has extended in-work support to adults without children, as well as providing subsidies for childcare expenditure for some working parents (Daly 2010). Government

effort to save money has led to the decrease of entitlements in households with incomes below £58,000 a year in 2009/2010 to £41,000 in 2011; there was also the abolishment of the extra £545 for a baby under one year old (HMRC 2013). At the same time the British government has also recently announced that it will introduce a new Tax-Free Childcare scheme for working families that will provide 20 per cent of working families' childcare costs (that is up to £1,200 for each child). This measure would support families with children who want to work through covering part of the high cost of childcare (HMT and HMRC 2013).

Although the overall amount of public financial support for childcare had been increasing until 2010, the total sources have decreased since then as a result of government cuts. Simultaneously, the childcare costs of public and private services increased significantly from 2011 to 2013 (for example in the first half of 2013, nursery care for a child under two and a child over two increased by 4.2 per cent and 6.6 per cent, respectively; childminder costs increased by 5.9 per cent and 5.2 per cent compared to the previous year – DT 2013). Moreover, experts have shown that there is low take-up and poor targeting of this financial support (compare Daly 2010, Finch 2008, Caluori 2009). The typical British family spends more than a quarter of its disposable income on childcare (compare Daly 2010, OECD 2011c).

The increasing costs of childcare in the last three years, cuts to the Childcare Tax Credit and to relief on corporate childcare vouchers in 2011 have caused a significant decrease in the overall demand for childcare and the increasing use of informal childcare by parents, relatives or friends (Blackburn 2011). Over one-third of parents (36.9 per cent) use this kind of care for children aged 3–5 years (Rogers 2012).

Outcomes: Accessibility and Quality
Until recently, local authorities provided only 6 per cent of children with day nursery places; the majority of children were provided with childminders (compare Truss 2012). Eurostat data show that only 5 per cent of the population in the youngest (up to three years) age group of children were in formal care in 2005 and only 4 per cent in 2010 (Eurostat 2012a). The high costs of private services and small scale of public funding lead British parents of up to three-year-olds to use primarily informal childcare, namely, unofficial care from relatives or friends (representing 80 per cent of cases in 2012) (Eurostat 2012a).

When it comes to caring for children over the age of three years, the situation is different. Data suggest a noticeable increase in the UK child population using the services of childcare: from 25.8 per cent of up to three-year-olds in 2005 to 40.8 per cent in 2008, and from 68.9 per cent of 3 to 5 year olds in 2000 to 92.7 per cent in 2008 (OECD 2011c). According to the information of the OECD study (2006), half of all 3 year old children enrolled in early education were placed in the private and voluntary sector in 2005; nearly three quarters of 4 year olds had public provision. Although a significant proportion of the 3 year olds are in pre-school programs today, most are part-day and part-week programmes (The Clearinghouse 2008).

The quality of childcare services in the UK is focused on the institutionalisation of minimal standards of education for staff especially. OECD data show that the child-to-staff ratios are rather high in the UK. In 2008, there were more than 17 children per worker for both children under 3 years and from 3 to 5 years (OECD 2011c).

Moreover, the childcare workforce in the UK (which is 98 per cent female) has low pay and lacks training and development opportunities (Caluori 2009, Truss 2012). A reduction in the number of care workers has resulted in both the declining range and quality of services, and the increasing use of volunteers to work with children. Many institutions try to find other alternative ways to provide professional childcare.

Trends, Changes and Innovations
Summed up, the wide variety of providers of childcare has caused fragmentation in the provided services that differ in various local areas. The trend in governmental provision points towards more early-years educational provision and longer hours of opening (focused on disadvantaged areas). Since 2010, the prices of public and private services have increased significantly, as the government has reduced spending on childcare by cutting tax credits.

Elderly Care

The number of people older than 65 years has gradually increased since 2000 in the UK. Although this increase was the lowest of all the surveyed countries (0.7 per cent compared to the OECD average of 1.8 per cent), the proportion of people over 65 to the total UK population slightly exceeded the OECD average (16.5 per cent compared to 14.8 per cent in the OECD) (OECD 2013).

Regulation and Delivery
Care of the elderly in the UK is mainly achieved by a system of long-term care that can be characterised as a residual (Brodsky et al. 2003) or safety-net (Fernández et al. 2009) system that only supports those with very severe needs who are unable to meet the costs of their care. In 2012 the vast majority of services for older people (residential care and nursing home care) were provided by private (78 per cent) and voluntary institutions (14 per cent), compared to local authority services (5 per cent) and National Health Service (NHS) (3 per cent) (Laing 2012). The UK elder care system has evolved incrementally from earlier systems of welfare for the poor by developing specific services to meet the long-term care needs of older people and the limited application of the means tests (Ikegami and Campbell 2002 in Comas-Herrera et al. 2010).

In 1999 the Royal Commission on Long Term Care proposed that 'personal care' should be provided free on a similar basis to health care; this suggestion was accepted in Scotland and in Northern Ireland (see Mooney and Wright 2009, Bell and Bowes 2012, Longley et al 2012, Scott and Wright 2012). In England, on the contrary, personal care continues to be means-tested, whether provided in residential or domiciliary services (Land and Himmelweit 2010). The UK, in fact, has a dual system, within England and even further varied by devolution. The 'primary' care system is largely run by local authorities and health authorities, funded by the devolved administration (through the Department Expenditure Limits system). The 'secondary' care system operates through the Department for Work and Pensions and comprises long-term care benefits (Attendance Allowance, Disability Living Allowance and Carers Allowance). While decentralisation of the powers of the individual UK regions contributes in long-term care to some diversity, in reality the devolved authorities cannot follow radically different long-term care policies, because they are constrained by UK governmental decisions and legislation and by the overall structure of taxes and benefits (Bell 2010).

Long-term care services are specifically arranged into three systems: (1) domiciliary (home or non-residential) care, (2) residential care (or care in residential settings), and (3) intermediate care. Domiciliary care is supportive health and personal care provided in the client's home by professionals. It is financed through a combination of public and private spending. Supporting home care is consistent with the policy of keeping people in the community as long as possible. According to Bell (2010), this also provides a rationale for the extension of direct payments, self-directed care, and personal and individual budgets, which are the main topics of the current 'personalisation agenda'. Another distinctive trend in non-residential care is the outsourcing of local authority funded domiciliary care to the lower cost independent sector, mainly to for-profit providers. This strong trend will probably continue because local authorities have the responsibility to economise and do so by downsizing or terminating more expensive direct council provision.

Care in residential settings includes three types of institutional care facilities: residential care homes, nursing homes and long-stay hospital provision. Some residential homes are run by local authorities, but most residential care homes and all nursing homes are in the independent sector (for example private and voluntary sector) (Colombo 2011). The general policy trend tends towards the 'hotel' model of residential care, which is typical for private providers. Furthermore, the private sector has easier access to capital therefore is in a better position to build homes that provide attractive environments and meet regulatory requirements (Bell 2010). According to Laing (2012: 26), the private sector supply of care prevails (370,000 places); this is merely supplemented by the voluntary sector (67,000 places) and public sector (43,000 places) (data by April 2011).

Financing

In the UK there is a mixed economy of financing of the long-term care system: services are financed by the NHS, local authorities, charities and the older people themselves. While healthcare services are free at the point of use, social care is means-tested. Long-term care services are provided either in-kind or as cash benefits for the care recipients to hire the required services they see fit. Primarily, there is the Attendance Allowance (AA), which is focused on the social care of people over 65 years. There is also a non-means-tested disability benefit for older people with personal care needs and a benefit for carers (Comas-Herrera et al. 2010).

Care provided by local authorities and health authorities is funded through the Department Expenditure Limits (DEL) system, whereas services and benefits provided by the Department for Work and Pensions (by the central Government) are funded through Annually Managed Expenditure (AME). In 2009, the UK spent about the same amount as the OECD average on long-term care, although there is a trend to cut the amount of public and private social expenditures (including a decrease in local authority spending on social care, as fewer people are using publicly funded care than ever before (Humphries 2013).

In 2007 the government published Putting People First, whose fundamental component is personal budgets enabling an individual the allocation of funding to make choices about how best to meet personal needs, including broader health and well-being (Comas-Herrera et al. 2010). Personalisation is the crucial principal: everyone should have as much independence and control over their own care and support as is right for them (Land and Himmelweit 2010). In July 2009, the UK government issued a new Green Paper entitled '*Shaping the Future of Care Together*', which proposed more preventive care, expanding the use of cash benefits and making benefits more uniform across the country. In response to this report, the '*Future of Care*' paper of November 2009 proposed a bill guaranteeing free personal care at home to approximately 280,000 frail elderly and younger people with disabilities who require the highest level of care (Gleckman 2010).

The long-term care system is based on a statutory taxation scheme representing a pay-as-you-go system and financed by contributions and premiums (and on a minimal basis by private long-term care insurance; see Colombo 2011). Funding comes from a combination of central taxation, local taxation and user fees for social care services. Local authorities receive a finite amount of funding and determine how to distribute and set budgets for expenditure on adult social care. In April 2011, an estimated 51 per cent of independent sector home care residents were having their fees paid (in part or in full) by local authorities (Laing 2012: 14).

There are national rules on charging for residential care and national guidelines setting out principles for charging for home care ('*Fairer Charging*' *Guidance*); nevertheless, local authorities have the freedom to be more generous in the case of home care (Colombo 2011). Hence, there is a great deal of diversity in the systems operated by local authorities. In 2010, a pilot programme of personal budgets in long-term care was implemented. Evaluations of the personal budget scheme have shown evidence of cost-effectiveness in relation to social care outcomes, but weaker cost-effectiveness in respect to psycho-social well-being (Colombo 2011).

Since July 2011, a key change in the financing of care for the elderly has occurred which could affect the actual method of implementation of delivered services. The Dilnot Commission published a report in which they suggested the introduction of a '*limited liability*' model of social insurance. This is grounded on the precondition of sharing the costs of care in later life between individuals and the state, with individuals paying for their own care until they reach a 'cap', after which the state pays for their care. Currently, individuals who do not fit the means-tested criteria can be liable for unlimited costs; the means-tested threshold, above which people are liable for their full care costs, should be increased from £23,250 to £100,000 – Dilnot et al. 2011). The means-test is intended for residential (not home-based) care. This model would have the potential to create incentive for greater investment into low-level or preventative support and services. Increased attention is also placed on the importance of family and informal carers, who should be regularly assessed and regulated (CFCS 2011). However, it is obvious that the government reforms will not be introduced until 2016 (see Humphries 2013: 3–4).

One third of elder care is paid privately. As Laing (2012) shows, self-pay fees are typically £50–£100 or more per week higher than the local authority fees for a similar service and amenity basis. The government pays the remainder. However, there are some differences in financing elderly care depending on the type of service. While residential care is the domain of the market and private providers, home care is largely funded by the public sector.

Outcomes

Access to publicly funded services is possible mainly through an assessment of care needs coordinated by the local authority social services department. In recent years, elderly home care has undergone relatively extensive development. Particularly in the private and voluntary sector, the number of institutions that provide elderly care has risen (Institute of Public Care 2012). As Land and Himmelweit (2010) show, by 2008 there were nearly 5,000 home care agencies in the UK – 84 per cent in the private and voluntary sectors. This is more than double the number in 2000 when such agencies had to be registered for the first time.

There is a similar situation in residential care. On the other hand, there has been a decline in demand within the public sector and consequently public sector capacity in local authority homes and national health services long stay hospitals and nursing homes: from 532,000 beds in 2000 to 470,000 beds in 2005; in 2010 there was an increase to 481,000 beds (for more details see Laing 2012).

In 2008, 2.9 per cent of the adult population in the UK was receiving long-term care services, compared to the OECD average of 2.3 per cent. The largest proportion of provided services is performed by informal carers, especially women. In 2009, there were also around 97,500 formal personal carers working in local authority-run services, and many more working in the independent sector – this represents 0.27 per cent of the population aged between 20 and 64 (the OECD average is 1.5 per cent) (Colombo 2011). This indicates that the size of the long-term care workforce does not necessarily reflect the number of those in need. Moreover, some surveys show that long-term care services are often targeted to meet just the basic (physical or health) needs of the elderly and are less dedicated to their social and psychological needs.

The quality of long-term elderly care in the UK is assessed and measured by various regulating bodies using several methods. The large number of requirements imposed on service providers resulted in the fact that the process of assessment became very bureaucratic by 2010 (Holdsworth and Billings 2009). Quality assurance was checked at the service or organisational level and at the local level; social care services were registered and inspected by the Care Quality Commission.

The quality of care for the elderly in the UK is currently threatened by a lack of resources. For example, recent research has shown that the quality of nearly five dozen facilities surveyed has declined in the past 12 months (Appleby et al. 2013). According to Humphries (2013: 11), the obvious reason is that 'the fees paid by the councils to providers increased by only 0.9 per cent in 2012/13 – well below the rate of inflation', therefore 'this year 45 per cent of councils are planning no increase in fees to care homes for older people to cover inflation.'

As Land and Himmelweit (2010) explain, career structure and staff development is a little worse in the private sector than in the public and voluntary sectors of social services. According to them, the proportion of staff with higher qualification is much smaller in the private social care sector than the almost entirely public health and social care sector. Private sector providers of social care invest little in training staff, which results in lower quality services as well as a greater turnover in staff (see Land and Himmelweit 2010: 15).

Trends, Changes and Innovations
Summing up, population ageing along with changes in family behaviour have contributed to an increase in demand for long-term care services in the UK Many studies show that informal (unpaid) care underpins the formal (paid) care system; however, there is the assumption that the role of professional carers will increase in the future. Laing (2012) argues that the demand for paid care may be greatly increased in the future as women abandon their traditional role as provider of informal care, citing increased rates of divorce and remarriage, smaller family sizes, greater labour mobility, more employment opportunities for women combined with the increased requirements to work that are placed on them due to welfare reforms. Since 2010, there have been trends of falling public spending on elderly care and fewer people receiving services, indicating 'deeper structural imbalance between the volume of care needs, how the current system responds, and the resources available.' (Humphries 2013: 11).

Employment Services

Even though the situation on the UK labour market was at a satisfactory level in 2008 (more people were at work than ever before; claimant unemployment reached its lowest level in over 30 years), unemployment increased in the following years due to the global economic recession. However, the consequences of the crisis were not very serious. Even when the unemployment rate rose 1.6-fold between 2002 and 2011 (that is from around 5 per cent in 2002 and 2005 to 8 per cent in 2011 and the long-term unemployment rate increased from 1 per cent in 2002 and 2005 to 3 per cent in 2011), both the short-term and long-term rates were still below the EU averages (see Eurostat 2012b).

The coalition government's ambitious programme of welfare reform has been implemented since 2011 (especially new welfare-to-work programmes called 'The Work Programme' and 'Universal Credit'). Furthermore, after 2011 the Universal Jobmatch was introduced to enable the use of the Local Support Services Framework (a part of the local authorities and other organisations) and to provide help to low income people (these measures support households which have budget and debt problems, or other personal issues like numeracy skills, drug addiction or mental disease). The successive implementation of this local support is currently being scheduled in various regions for April and October 2013 (DWP 2013).

Regulation and Delivery

Labour market administration is traditionally part of the national civil service in the UK, whereby unemployment benefits are administered and paid out by local offices (JobCentre Plus). There are 11 administrative regions in the UK, each managed by a regional director who coordinates activities between the national headquarters and local JobCentre Plus offices. While the governance of JobCentre Plus is primarily a 'top-down' process characterised by a management-by-objectives system, the devolved administrations of Scotland, Wales and Northern Ireland enjoy a high level of autonomy with regard to the provision of skills and training (see Wiggan 2012).

The JobCentre Plus has traditionally worked on the principle of work-first and a performance management regime. Therefore it uses standardised, cost-effective tools that enable the quick placement of job-seekers (Cook 2008, Weishaupt 2011). Until 2010, Jobcentre Plus ensured the administration of the various New Deal programmes, place-based employment initiatives and covered three key activities: promoting an active job search (based on the Jobseeker's Agreement and Work Focused Interviews); establishing and maintaining effective relationships with employers (to attain the goal of ensuring that 80 per cent of the unemployed obtain work within 6 months); and developing partnerships with the private sector, non-profits and voluntary organisations (European Commission 2006, Cook 2008). Within the same basic structure of work incentives, the details of policy have been modified since 2010 through the introduction of the Work Programme and Universal Credit, thus consolidating most means-tested working-age benefits.

One of the most important governance reforms in UK employment services has been the privatisation which took place successively in 2000 and then from 2007 to the present in accordance with the New Public Management stream. The implementation of labour market training programmes (for example The New Deal) was newly delegated to the Learning and Skills Councils that became responsible for the distribution of resources for training and education beyond initial general education. The training programmes themselves have been delivered since 2002 by private organisations under contract to these councils (Dingeldey 2009, Tergeist and Grubb 2006). Private providers need to follow the stages of the public New Deal model (although in deprived areas with high unemployment, this was replaced by Employment Zones).

The global economic recession in the pre-2010 era prompted the UK government to implement innovations to the existing method of service provision in the area of employment: the more flexible and personalised model of Jobcentre Plus and integrating the support offered by Jobcentre Plus in partnership with other local providers (especially NGOs and local authorities; see Weishaupt 2011). Since 2010, the role of JobCentre Plus has not changed.

In response to rising unemployment in 2008, the UK government introduced several key measures dealing with extended assistance to the unemployed from public employment services. This included extra support via job-search assistance and work-focused interviews, more jobs for young people, extra training and apprenticeships (DWP 2009). In order to increase the probability of finding work, the following provisions for job-seekers reaching six months of a claim have been introduced: intensive support from personal advisers; financial support to employers who recruit job-seekers claiming job-search assistance; additional work-focused training placements; volunteering opportunities; and financial support and advice to help set up a business. Furthermore, for all those job-seekers with serious barriers to finding sustained work and who are unemployed for more than 12 months, a new personalised, individualised programme called 'The Flexible New Deal' has been offered. Finally, for people who could benefit from extra support, additional targeted help through recruitment agencies has been introduced (ibid.).

Local Employment Partnerships between job centres and local employers were already strengthened before 2010, which has allowed for pre-employment training, recruitment support and work trials to place those who might not otherwise get interviews. Employers across the country have also been encouraged to provide extra apprenticeships, internships, work experience and mentoring for young people out of work through the Backing Young Britain campaign (Tergeist and Grubb 2006, DWP 2009). After the Work Programme was launched in June 2011, many prime providers (including public and private organisations) have assembled strong partnership chains to help deliver services to participants with a wide range of needs (DWP 2012).

The Work Programme replaces previous programmes such as the New Deals, Employment Zones and Flexible New Deal and represents a new 'payment-for-results welfare-to-work programme' launched throughout the UK in June 2011. It is focused especially on people who are long-term unemployed or are at most risk of becoming so (particularly youth and those in workless households). It is delivered by a range of public, private and voluntary organisations, which are relatively free to innovate their services in an environment of low level labour market regulation and taxation (DWP 2012).

There are three main principles at the heart of the Work Programme: (1) clear incentives to deliver results of employed people (job outcomes) with higher rewards for participants who are further from the labour market; (2) freedom for service providers (in identifying the most needed people without prescription from government); (3) the long-term commitment of government and local providers (five-year contracts enabling reliable partnership and innovations of all the involved parties) (for more details see DWP 2012, compare NAO 2012).

Financing

Even though overall spending on labour market policy increased very slightly between 2005 and 2009 (from 0.62 per cent to 0.71 per cent of GDP), its contemporary level is very low compared to other EU countries. The small amount of expenditure corresponds with the fact that the British system of employment services is considered to be residual, offering mainly 'self-help' and low cost work-first measures, without investment in the sorts of training and in-depth support common in Scandinavian and some other European countries (compare Scott and Wright 2012; Wright 2011). The evaluation of the Work Programme in 2012 was critical: the programme was too quickly implemented and has had only limited success in contrast to the overoptimistic expectations. It is also considered to be confusing and inflexible in the process of implementation (different arrangements and rules across programmes). This includes divergent expectations – the Department for Work and Pensions expected that less money would be spent for less work/activities of service providers, but service providers expected that they would obtain more money to be able to provide a wide palette of services for their clients which would be of a higher quality than previously. On the other hand, the Work Programme bears a number of innovative features in design (more freedom to providers to decide how to help claimants; payment for the results providers achieve; innovative funding arrangements and payment rates for different claimant groups; and more competition among providers) (for more details see NAO 2012: 5–9).

Outcomes

Low expenditures on active labour market policies correspond to the data showing the low numbers of participants involved in active labour market measures. Although the proportion of participants using these measures was more or less constant between 2005 and 2008, it decreased from 0.35 per cent to 0.22 per cent of the labour force between 2005 and 2009. This rate of participant inflow in labour market programmes is consistently less than one tenth of the OECD average, which was about 4 per cent in 2009 and 2010 (see OECD 2012c). Improving the quality of its services should be achieved through more flexible, personalised support of JobCentre Plus advisers; the introduction of performance management structure and accreditation of their skills; developing an online job-search facility with automated job matching and an integrated system of personal accounts; involvement of local partners to have a greater influence in commissioning processes; and extended partnership between state, private and voluntary sector providers ('Total Place pilots') to ensure that services are connected and tailored to the specific needs of local communities (compare DWP 2009: 16–17, DWP 2013).

Trends, Changes and Innovations

The economic recession that began in 2008 tested the system of public employment services in the UK in terms of their ability to respond to rising unemployment and the long-term unemployment of specific groups of job seekers (especially adolescent graduates, single mothers and the disabled). The response was to increase the activation effort (Work Programme) with emphasis on individual counselling and support in job searching. Services attain a good level of quality due to the sufficient staffing of public employment services.

Until 2010 most of employment services in the UK (except outsourced training programmes) were provided solely by the public authorities – JobCentre Plus – on the principle of a 'one-stop shop'; nevertheless, after 2010, the performance management of staff and the delivery of active labour market measures changed significantly. The partnerships of local actors improved. Managers and employment advisors of JobCentre Plus received greater autonomy as of 2011, so that they could focus more on local projects (especially The Working Programmes) and the individual needs of the unemployed (compare Bellis et al. 2011). This all should assure that JobCentre Plus will be even more flexible than it was in 2010 in light of the profit sector activities.

Employment in the Health and Social Service Sector in the UK

The workforce and employment levels in HSW and social services are used in Table 11.3 to compare development in the HSW sector. Data for the whole HSW sector in the UK and member countries show all the jobs in thousands (including the self-employed); data for sub-sectors are only provided as numbers of employees. All data refer to December of the given year.

The overall trend shows growing employment (which corresponds to the LFS data presented in the appendix of Chapter 3). The number of jobs in the HSW sector increased from 3.1 million to more than 4 million, that is, by nearly one-third.

There are, however, some signs that the growth of jobs slowed down after 2006 (this is more evident in the data for Wales, Scotland and Northern Ireland). The growth of social service activities is more evident in services without accommodation, while there is some stagnation evident in residential care activities.

After government cuts of public expenditure in 2010, data on total employment in health and social services show that between 2010 and 2012 there was a similar trend, although slightly changed. Specifically, there were some further slight increases in health services from 2,030,000 to 2,052,000; in residential care from 722,000 to 790,000 (about 10 per cent); and a slight decrease in social work without accommodation from 960,000 to 942,000. Only in public administration and the defence sector do we see a more dramatic reduction of staff: from 1,870,000 to 1,772,000 (Eurostat 2012b).

**Table 11.3   Jobs in Human health and social work activities sector and
subsectors (2000–2010)**

	2000	2005	2010
WJ HSW (UK)	3 129	3 634	4 051
WJ HSW England	2 561	2 934	3 361
WJ HSW Wales	163	190	192
WJ HSW Scotland	303	391	374
WJ HSW North. Ireland	103	119	125
Residential care activities	530	616	637
SW without accommodation	640	734	891

Note: WJ HSW = Workforce jobs in Human health and social work activities, including
both the public and private sector
Source: Office for national statistics (employers' survey)

In contrast to employment growth in the social service sector as a whole (which
was due to increases of private sector services), employment in public social
services dropped considerably. Detailed data about public employment in social
services are provided separately by authorities for England, Scotland and Northern
Ireland (statistics for Wales are not available). For England (see Table 11.4) two
indicators are used for employment: head count and WTE (full time equivalent),
which are also used for all data for specific professions. The data do not include
agency staff or staff in the independent or voluntary sector (NHS 2010). The overall
trend in public social services staffing is that of decline (more in headcount than
in WTE). The decline is very severe for both domiciliary provision and residential
care staff, while employment in services for children increased. The above-
mentioned fall reflects the fact that councils are increasing the commissioning
of home care from the independent sector – 84 per cent of home care hours
in 2009–2010 compared to 67 per cent in 2003–2004 (NHS 2011). The tendency
of many councils to purchase services from the independent sector is likely to have
led to an increase in support staff needed to manage contracts over the last ten
years (NHS 2011). The downward trend in public sector employment continued
between 2010 and 2013 – the number of public sector employees decreased only
slightly in NHS from 1,592,000 (4Q 2010) to 1,566,000 (1 Q 2013) and from 347
thousand (4Q 2010) to 300,000 (1Q 2013) in other Health and Social Work not
covered by NHS, that is, by about 13 per cent (Office for National Statistics 2013).

By contrast, data for Scotland and Northern Ireland show an increased number
of staff both in headcount as well as in WTE during 2000–2010 (see Table 11.4).

Data about wages in the UK come from Annual Surveys of Hours and Earnings.
Gross annual median wages in British Pounds are used to compare wages of specific
professions (see the upper rows in Table 11.5). Rough estimates of the number of

Table 11.4   Employment in public social services in England and Northern Ireland, in thousands (2000–2010)

England Social Services	2000	2005	2010
Headcount	291 900	277 300	249 000
WTE	217 500	216 500	197 400
Area office field work[1]	109 200	116 600	110 700
Domiciliary provision	42 900	33 500	22 800
Services for children	20 800	28 500	32 400
Residential care staff[2]	56 600	47 700	39 700
For adults 65+ years	27 600	20 700	16 800
Day care staff[3]	30 800	27 900	24 500
Strategic HQ staff	19 400	21 700	20 200
Northern Ireland Social Services	**2000**	**2005**	**2010**
Headcount	:	5 008	7 521
WTE	:	4 588	6 605
Home help headcount	:	5 691	5 508
Home help WTE	:	2 100	1 951
Scotland Social Work Services	**2000**	**2005**	**2010**
Headcount	44 809	54 008	51 922
WTE	34 072	42 953	41 062

Note: Data for 2005 and 2010 in Northern Ireland are not fully comparable due to several changes in data collection and methodology. Home help = domiciliary care

[1] managers, social workers and support staff (for example home care staff) in childrens and adults services, hospitals, alcohol and drug centres etc.

[2] workers in residential care or specialist needs establishments for children, adults and older people

[3] management, care and support staff in day care setting such as nurseries and play groups, day, family and community centres and centres for people with learning, physical and mental disabilities

Sources: England – NHS (2011), Northern Ireland – DHSSPS (2010), Scotland – Scottish Government (2011)

jobs (in thousands) in specific job categories are provided in rows below the wages (in italics). Because of changes in the classifications used and the tables published, the data for specific professions are available only from 2002 (SOC classification) and 2008 (SIC classification). Some data (especially estimates of the number of jobs) are considered as less reliable by the publisher, but the differences among professions are quite coherent over time.

Innovation in Social Services

Table 11.5 **Median gross annual earnings (in £) and number of jobs (in thousands, in italics) for HSW sector and selected professions (2000–2010)**

	2000	2005	2010
Standard Industrial Classification (2003)			
All employees	15 800	18 949	21 212
	18 455	*19 114*	*21 330*
Human Health and Social Work Activities	11 969	15 494	18 466
	2 165	*2 366*	*2 926*
Residential care activities	8 639	12 228	13 704
	270	*282*	*464*
RCA activities for the elderly and disabled	Not available		13 129
			158
SWA without accommodation	11 837	13 531	14 471
	279	*287*	*457*
SWA WA for the elderly and disabled	Not available		12 708
			120
Child day-care activities	Not available		11 310
			92
Employment activities	Not available		15 715
			202
Standard Occupational Classification (2000)			
Social welfare associate professionals (323)	Not available	18 505	21 540
		204	*238*
Caring personal service occupations (61)	Not available	10 288	12 371
		1 225	*1 531*
Care assistants and home carers (6115)	Not available	10 557	12 879
		492	*616*
Childcare and related personal services (612)	Not available	8 581	10 585
		434	*586*

Note: RCA = Residential care activities, SWA = Social Work Activities, WA = without accommodation
Source: Annual Survey on Hours and Earnings (2000–2010)

The wages of typical caring professions in the social services are low, especially when compared to the median wages in the overall economy, but also when compared to wages in the HSW sector. This trend is consistent over the whole period for which data are available. The lowest wages were in 2010 in childcare professions (£10,585 – 50 per cent of the average wage), although they were low for all caring personal service occupations (£12,371 – 58 per cent of the average wage) and for jobs involving residential activities for the elderly and the disabled (£13,129 – 62 per cent of the average wage). There were somewhat higher wages in social work activities without accommodation and for workers working in employment services. The highest wages in the field of social work were in the category of social welfare professionals (£21,540 – slightly above the average wage) and professional social workers (£29,586 – 139 per cent of the average wage).

The annual gross median wage of some social services professions is close to the UK minimum wage (compare also the data on wages in Chapter 3). This can be at least partially explained by the high share of part-time work: for example in childcare and related personal services 380,000 (365,000 are women) of 586,000 workers were employed part-time and their annual wage was £8,318 (compared to £15,202 for full-time jobs and £10,585 for all jobs in the category). Nevertheless, even full-time jobs are about £5–6,000 pounds under the national median wage.

Summing up, the available data show that the number of all jobs in welfare services (that is public and private) have been increasing in the UK in the last decades (with the exception of the years of stagnation in 2006 and 2007); slight increases are shown even after 2010. By contrast, the number of public staff has decreased due to the increase of purchased services from the private sector (especially help services at home). These services are (with some exceptions) represented nearly exclusively by women, are low paid (full-time workers enhance around 60 per cent of the average wage in the economy) and two fifths of them represent a qualified workforce.

Conclusions

This chapter shows that the UK. welfare services were consistently financed (at the average level of the OECD countries between 2000 and 2010) and the UK welfare state put great emphasis on the long-term care system for the aging population, as there was sufficiently strong demand for services. However, the fees in care services increased, while out-of-pocket fees in elderly services were effectively covered by local governments. Similarly, the number of employees in social services in total increased in 2000–2010 by about one third, while the number of public staff decreased, due to the increase of purchased services from the private sector; the trend has continued since 2010, although public employment is decreasing in the sector. Social services are represented predominantly by women, are low paid and comprise of only two fifths of qualified workers.

The prices of public and private services have increased significantly in the UK since 2010 (especially for childcare). At the same time, the UK government has decided to gradually implement a reform of benefits and taxes that will result in the reduction of people eligible for benefits, tied benefits included (that is families with children, people receiving elderly care and the unemployed). This may affect access to services, although the government has committed itself to continuing in specific support to health and social services as a priority.

On the other hand, with the crisis and expenditure cuts, a trend toward informal care has been emerging. Government regulations focus on quality and good staffing. The innovations of governance in social services are bringing a larger variety of actors and marketisation. These are aiming to provide more personalised services at reasonable costs.

In the field of childcare provision, the wide variety of providers has caused the fragmentation of the provided services, which also vary from one local area to another. Although provision is determined at the central level, the coordination occurs at the local level, where private providers and non-profit organisations collaborate in a quasi-network environment.

The UK government is also focusing on improving the quality of provision and making the long-term care system more client-friendly through the implementation of government funds available for the training of social care staff, strategies to combat high staff turnover and the wider involvement of volunteers in long-term care.

Employment services are of low to middle quality, targeted at a narrow range of mostly marginalised unemployed people who are both supported and forced by activation measures and various job search techniques to find a job. Great emphasis has been placed on the greater involvement of private actors in recent years, establishing a trend for the future.

Chapter 12

Comparing the National Cases

Tomáš Sirovátka and Bent Greve

Introduction

In this chapter the national cases will be compared. The main aim is to examine the mutual links between financing, governance and employment in social services and, second, to identify the common trends as well as the differences in the four national cases.

Studies on the development of social and employment services (Ahonen 2006, Jensen 2008, 2009, Seeleib-Kaiser 2008, Dingeldey et al. 2009, Wollman and Marcou 2010, van Berkel et al. 2011) document some similarities across countries, although the welfare regimes still bear their specific traits. The trend towards marketisation has been apparent in social services since the 1980s and 1990s, accompanied by a tendency of centralisation with some exceptions in Denmark and the UK. This is because caring services (both childcare and elder care) have become too important to be left to the competence of local authorities and the risks of uneven provision must be prevented. Similar trends have been observed in employment services where re-centralisation was associated with the unification of institutions, cost containment and making services more accessible. Increasing emphasis has been put on activation, individualisation of service and cost effectiveness. Such changes have brought specific changes in governance like the implementation of New Management methods and networking (see van Berkel et al. 2011). The above trends are leading to a split of the functions of regulation, financing and delivery of services (Seeleib-Kaiser et al. 2008, Simonazzi 2008).

Nevertheless, besides these common trends, various solutions concerning the contents as well as the forms/procedures of service provision can be witnessed. The main question relates to how different approaches to regulation, financing and delivery of services might have impacted on the overall development of service provision in terms of accessibility and quality of service; similarly, how employment in social services has developed in quantitative as well as qualitative aspects.

As was already shown and discussed in the previous chapters which deal with the national case studies, we are comparing countries with very different welfare state traditions representing different welfare models: the Nordic or social-democratic (Denmark), Christian Democratic/conservative (Germany), liberal (UK) and post-communist hybrid (Czech Republic).

Table 12.1   Social protection expenditure in kind as per cent of GDP (2000–2010)

	2000	2005	2006	2007	2008	2009	2010
European Union (27)	:	8.8	8.9	8.7	8.9	9.9	10.0
Czech Republic	5,9	6.2	5.9	5.6	5.6	6.4	6.4
Denmark	10,8	11.5	11.5	11.5	12.2	13.7	13.3
Germany	9,0	9.2	9.1	9.0	9.2	10.8	10.6
United Kingdom	8,5	10.4	10.5	9.8	10.2	11.4	11.3

Source: Eurostat (2012b)

Financing of Social Services

There are substantial differences in the level and profile of financing the welfare state and social services among the four countries in focus. These differences are to a large extent determined by government revenues (that is the level and structure of taxation).

When measuring the share of social protection in kind expenditure in GDP (which indicates the amount of social services expenditure), in Denmark in 2010 it was more than twice as high compared to the Czech Republic; in the UK and in Germany the differences were not too great, but still considerable (see Table 12.1).

Germany ranks as second from the compared countries in total social protection expenditure: cash transfers are close to the level of Denmark (see Table 12.2).[1] In the Czech Republic, which represents a 'low-cost welfare state' as seen in the national chapter, expenditure on social protection in total increased slightly during 2000–2005–2010; similarly, health care expenditure increased. By contrast, expenditure on social services dropped.

Correspondingly, in the Czech Republic the total revenues in the state budget are the lowest in the last ten years, although stable. In recent years, a flat-rate income tax has been introduced and due to the crisis, VAT has been increased. Nevertheless, due to the lower ability of the population to pay for the services, the role of the state in financing social services is strong. In health care, there has been a remarkable increase in out-of-pocket fees in the last ten years: these were the highest from the compared countries by 2010 (see Table 12.3).

In Denmark, social protection expenditure was among the highest in the EU (32.4 per cent of GDP in 2010). This increased since 2005 by around 4 per cent;

---

1   In Germany, for example, elderly care is mostly financed by benefits – this is not reflected in ´in kind' expenditure by Eurostat, since the benefit recipients purchase the services. Similarly, childcare and elderly care are partly financed by specific cash benefits available for this purpose.

Table 12.2 **Social protection expenditure in total as per cent of GDP (2000–2010)**

	2000	2005	2006	2007	2008	2009	2010
European Union (27)	:	26.0	25.7	24.7	25.6	28.4	28.2
Czech Republic	18,2	17.8	17.4	17.5	17.5	19.8	19.5
Denmark	28,1	29.4	28.5	28.0	28.8	32.5	32.4
Germany	28,6	28.9	27.8	26.7	26.9	30.1	29.3
United Kingdom	25,5	25.8	25.5	22.3	25.3	28.2	27.1

Source: Eurostat (2012b)

furthermore, the level of social protection in kind increased from 11.5 per cent of GDP to 13.3 per cent – that is, by nearly 2 per cent. This level of expenditure was the highest in the EU, especially expenditure in kind (services) for old age, invalidity, childcare and employment, which grew consistently as percentages of GDP.

The level of social protection expenditure in total shows that Germany is slightly above the EU average (consistently about 29 per cent of GDP over the last ten years). This is a consequence of the traditionally high expenditure on social insurance benefits, especially in the area of social services due to the relatively high expenditure on health care services (in 2010 it increased to 8.0 per cent of GDP). Social insurance benefits cover a substantial share of care for the elderly. On the other hand, childcare is provided mainly in kind with a low level of participation by parents; this means that expenditure on family policies in kind increased from 0.8 to 1.0 per cent of GDP between 2005 and 2010, due to the modernisation of German family policy (see the national chapter).

In the UK, social protection expenditure is close to the EU average. As shown in the national chapter, the increases of expenditure on health care were evidenced in 2000–2010. Expenditure on childcare and employment services also increased,

Table 12.3 **Out of pocket fees in health care (a per cent of total HC costs) (2000–2010)**

	2000	2005	2006	2007	2008	2009	2010
Czech Republic	10.2	10.7	11.3	13.2	15.7	14.4	14.9
Denmark	14.4	14.0	13.8	13.9	13.8	13.2	13.2
Germany	11.2	13.4	13.7	13.6	13.3	13.1	13.2
United Kingdom	13.5	11.8	12.0	11.9	11.2	10.5	8.9

Source: OECD (2012b)

as did cash transfers provided to families, who could use them to purchase services. Expenditure on elderly care in kind decreased, while social transfers provided to those in need of care increased. Revenues to the state budget seem to be stable and based on the considerable tax progression, while VAT was increased in the years of crisis.

The finance available creates very different pre-conditions for the financing and service delivery in various areas of social services. In health care (compare Table 12.3), the level of user charges as percentages of total cost in the area is relatively high in all four countries compared to the other areas of social services. At the same time, other socio-cultural and political-institutional factors also play a role; therefore, there are very different patterns of governance and service provision in the four countries.

Governance of Social Services

Childcare

Family policies are directly linked to family, children, gender relations, employment and so on – in other words, to a broad complex of societal and cultural phenomena of private and public life where social values and norms are embedded. For similar reasons, Lewis and Campbell (2007: 7) claim that 'family policies are often about competition between competing values and the incorporation of values into policies, possibly to a greater extent than in other policy fields'. This is strongly reflected in the different approaches of the countries in terms of the provision of childcare services.

The Czech Republic introduced conservative re-familisation policies during the 1990s (Hantrais 2003, Saxonberg and Sirovátka 2006, Szelewa and Polakowski 2009) as a reaction to the former policies of enforced women's employment combined with persisting gender inequality in employment and family roles. Instead of pre-school care, an extended scheme of parental leave lasting until the child is four years old was implemented in the early 1990s. Financial support to nurseries for children aged 0–3 was cancelled and these facilities have nearly disappeared. Kindergartens are accessible to children aged 2–3, but only to a limited extent. Children from three to school age are the main concern. On the top of that kindergartens clearly prioritise the admission of children close to school age (five years and older).

The Czech Republic does not financially support nurseries except for the staff salaries, which may be supported by local governments, although this is not often the case. Thus expenditure on childcare for children aged 0–2 is less than 0.1 per cent of GDP.

Germany has a similarly low proportion of expenditure (0.1 per cent of GDP) while the largest spending is evident in Denmark (0.7 per cent) and then in the UK (0.5 per cent). Even though the expenditure on formal day-care services (such

Table 12.4 **Public expenditure on childcare including pre-primary education as per cent of GDP (2000–2009)**

	2000	2005	2009		
	Total	Total	Total	Childcare	Pre-school
Denmark	1.4	1.4	1.4	0.7	0.7
Czech Republic	0.3	0.3	0.4	0	0.4
Germany	0.3	0.4	0.5	0.1	0.4
United Kingdom	0.7	1.1	1.1	0.5	0.7
OECD	:	:	0.7	0.3	0.4

Note: childcare – children 0–2, pre-school – children 3–5 (inclusive)
Source: OECD (2012d)

as day-care centres and family day-care) for children aged 0–2 is relatively low in the Czech Republic, the expenditure on services for children of pre-school age (3–5) is almost at the same level as the OECD average: 0.4 per cent of GDP in 2009, when the average of the OECD countries was also 0.4 per cent. This was similar in Germany and the UK, while in Denmark it was considerably more (see Table 12.4).

For a long time, the Czech government has been passive in solving the unmet needs of childcare. Since 2007 it started to consider innovations with the aim of cheaper solutions rather than expanding the capacity of public childcare facilities. Alternative forms of childcare have been discussed like services provided at home by private child minders or neighbour help, children's groups, or private enterprise facilities. No specific measures were decided until September 2012 when the Ministry of Labour and Social Affairs submitted to the government a draft on the Act on Child Groups, which was to be supported by specific tax relief measures for working parents and employers who establish such facilities.

In many countries the percentage of children under three using formal childcare has increased since 2000 (for example in Germany from 14 per cent in 2000 to 25 per cent in 2010; in the UK from 26 per cent in 2004 to 41 per cent in 2008; in Denmark it has been traditionally high). By contrast, in the Czech Republic the percentage of children using these services increased only slightly (from 4 per cent of the population of children under three in 2001 to 7 per cent in 2005 and 2010).[2] The Czech Republic is thus a laggard (see Table 12.5). Nevertheless, the Czech enrolment rate of children between three and school age is closer to the EU average although it dropped in 2005–2010. On average parents pay low enrolment

---

2   According to Eurostat, the enrolment rate of children under three in childcare was at an average of 28.2 per cent in the EU countries in 2008.

Table 12.5   Enrolment rate of children under 3, per 100 children (2000–2011)

Country/Time	2000–2001	2005–2006	2008–2009	2010–2011
Czech Republic	4.4	7.0	6.4	7.3
Denmark	:	62.0	66.0	66.0
Germany	14.0	14.0	20.0	25.0
United Kingdom	:	25.8[2004]	40.8[2008]	:
EU (27)	:	:	28.2[2008]	:
OECD	:	22.6[2004]	30.1[2008]	:

Source: UNESCO (2013), OECD (2012d)

fees (that is monthly 10.6 per cent of the average wage) while the OECD average is 18.4 per cent (Rogers 2012 with use of OECD 2011c data).[3]

Although accessibility of childcare services is a problem due to insufficient financing by the state, the quality seems to be satisfactory; specifically, when measured as a ratio of child-to-staff, both types of service for children are at a good level. Furthermore, the hygiene and qualification standards are set by legislation, which presumably makes it difficult for non-state actors to establish new facilities given the low ability of parents to pay. Enrolment fees in nurseries, including public ones, are prohibitively high, while public kindergartens are relatively cheap for parents. For this reason, private childcare facilities constitute only a marginal segment of services: children enrolled in private pre-school facilities represented only 1.6 per cent of all enrolled children in 2010.[4]

Denmark has a well-developed system of day-care for young children: it is expected that the child's well-being be ensured through the introduction of more formal and structured learning in daycares institutions (see Gislason and Eydal 2011). In Denmark, the employment rate of women is at the highest level in Europe even of those with one or two children up to six years of age. The fertility rate is also among the highest in the EU. As Castles (2003) suggests, childcare for children aged 0–3 may be assessed as one of the key factors contributing to higher levels in fertility rates.

Childcare is a right for all children between six months and six years. The system is predominantly a public service, supervised by local authorities and funded from local taxes and central government grants. Nevertheless, there is a public-private mix of service provision in childcare. Family day-care generally consists of local-authority supported childcare/minding of children provided by

---

3   Nevertheless, these fees are higher in nurseries (children 0–3 years): since nurseries are very rare and enrolment fees in kindergarten are much lower, the total average enrolment fees are low.
4   Source: UNESCO (2013).

Table 12.6   Enrolment rates of children aged three to five years of age in pre-school educational programmes (2000–2010)

	2000	2005	2008	2010
Czech Republic	:	85.3	79.7	72.5
Denmark	87.8	89.7	91.5	92.3
Germany	82.5	74.5	92.7	92.4
United Kingdom	68.9	81.2	92.7	90.0
EU (27)	:	:	81.8	78.1
OECD	69.5	70.8	77.3	71.9

Note: The enrolment rates presented here concern formal pre-school services, and in some countries 4 and 5 year olds in primary school
Source: OECD (2011c), Eurostat (2012b)

private child-minders in their homes. Although the provision of childcare is mixed its financing and regulation is mostly a public issue. As such, 80 per cent of Danish children aged from six months to nine years have a place in a publicly-supported day-care facility and 20 per cent in a private one.

Parents pay a maximum of 25–33 per cent of the costs of the nurseries/ kindergartens from their own pockets. On average, they pay 11.2 per cent of the total costs, which is much less than the OECD average of 18.4 per cent (Rogers 2012 and OECD 2011c). The fees paid by parents for family daycares and crèches vary according to family income: lower income families pay a reduced rate, or receive the service free of charge. In addition to co-financing by parents, the high coverage of the child population in Denmark is achieved primarily due to public expenditures on childcare, which are well above the OECD and European averages.

The quality of services is higher than in most of the other countries. Statistical data from Eurostat show that even in 2000 Denmark had the lowest child-to-staff ratio of all the surveyed countries, that is, about half of that of Germany.

In Germany, support for the work-family balance has increased since the 1990s and mainly in the 2000s. Parents have to pay a variable share of between zero and 30 per cent of the total costs (Fröhlich 2006, European Commission 2009a), as an income-related fee, which differs between communities and regions; the rate is relatively lower for low-income households as compared to middle- and high-income households. Informal care arrangements are more expensive than the cost of public childcare.

Public expenditure on childcare services is at a relatively low level compared to the other countries. Expenditure on kindergarten is at the average rate for all OECD and EU countries (0.4 per cent in Germany, the OECD and EU – see Table 12.4). By contrast, expenditure on nurseries was below the average public

Table 12.7 **Pupil-teacher ratio in pre-school education (2000–2010)**

	2000	2005	2008	2010
Czech Republic	18.44	12.99	13.69	13.90
Denmark	5,42	:	:	:
Germany		11.76	11.16	1027
United Kingdom	23.21	21.14	21.46	18.29
European Union	14.96	13.77	13.28	13.11
OECD	18.28	17.01	16.36	16.51

Source: World Data Bank

expenditures in OECD in 2009: in Germany, the spending was 0.1 per cent of GDP, while the OECD average was 0.3 per cent (see Table 12.4). However, while private funding in Germany represented 40 per cent of the total funding of child care/pre-school education in 2009, in the UK it was 10 per cent and as low as 0.5 per cent in the Czech Republic (OECD 2013). In Germany, nearly two thirds of children are currently enrolled in private facilities (UNESCO 2013, own computations).

In 2005, German government initiated social innovations aimed at improving access to childcare: a law was introduced that stipulated the expansion of the provision of childcare for children under three years to the effect that local authorities be responsible for providing childcare facilities to all children under three years of age by the year 2013. Simultaneously, new steps were implemented in 2006 decreasing the parent fees for existing childcare and extending the possibilities to deduct childcare costs as expenses within the income tax system (Fröhlich 2006). Working, single parents and couples where both parents work, may deduct two thirds of childcare costs until the child's 14th birthday, that is, to a maximum of €4000 per year, per child. Thus, on average, parents pay fees in the amount of 14.1 per cent of the average wage in the country, which is below the OECD average (Rogers 2012, OECD 2011c).

In spite of the limited support and considerable but varying childcare costs for parents, according to the UNECE Statistical database, the rate of enrolled children aged up to three years increased from 14 per cent in 2005 to almost 25 per cent in 2008; this is above the EU average (compare Table 12.5). On the other hand, the enrolment rate of children from three to six years exceeds the average rate of the EU countries by over 10 per cent (see Table 12.6).

The child-to-staff ratio shows that the situation in Germany is comparatively good (OECD 2011c). The number of children per teacher was around ten in 2010, while it was 18 in the UK and 14 in the Czech Republic (see Table 12.7). In regards to child-minding services, which are not used to a great extent in Germany, the available information shows that the level of education of these workers is at a low level in Germany. According to Mühler (2010), the quality of German childcare is assessed as medium to low by international comparison, because only minimum quality standards are imposed in Germany. As such, there is great heterogeneity in the availability and quality of services among the various providers within particular regions.

Summed up, the key reforms are aiming at the universal delivery of childcare to pre-school children, strengthening the services provided to children under three, shortening the parental allowance and giving fathers access to this allowance. Since 2000, there has been great emphasis on the expansion of childcare providers operating in the market. The German childcare system is dynamic (moving towards a modernised system); however, the reforms lack strong financing and regulation from the federal government.

Like Germany, the UK government over the last 10 years has made family policy more supportive in terms of gender equality and the reconciliation of work and family life: these shifts are referred to as the 'modernisation' of the old family care model. The key measures have included the expansion of childcare and early education services; better financial support and more effective tax credits aimed at returning more parents (women) to work; better services for young children and (poor) families; and a focus on the employment activation of single parents. Unlike the Czech Republic, the UK policy-making in childcare services has been more influenced by the current EU modernisation trends. The following have become especially important: the objectives of returning parents to work and providing children with a quality early life experience in order to give them a head-start in life before they start school. Public expenditure on childcare and pre-school education increased between 2000–2009 from 0.7 per cent to 1.1 per cent of GDP, which is clearly above the OECD average both concerning early childcare (children 0–2) and pre-school (children 3–5; see Table 12.4).

Public childcare services are financed by central government (through general taxation) and organised by local authorities. Besides the Sure Start Children's Centres, there are several early education and childcare facilities that are free of charge for all three- and four-year-olds for 15 hours per week. Day nurseries are often based in workplaces and run by businesses or voluntary groups. The volume of financial support for childcare has increased in the last decade and data suggest an increase in the number of British children using the services of childcare (see Tables 12.5, 12.6). From 2006 to 2010, the share of children in public facilities increased from 71 per cent to 79 per cent of all enrolled children (OECD 2013).

Nevertheless, compared to the other countries, the UK family policies are provided mainly as cash benefits and tax credits for (poor) families. Childcare facilities are very expensive for parents, but may be partially covered by the tax credits available to working parents. Their implementation represents social innovation resulting from improved access to childcare and choice for parents. As shown in the national chapter, the cost of childcare is among the highest in the EU: on average the parents pay monthly in average 41 per cent of the average wage in the country (OECD 2011c).

Table 12.8   Public expenditure on LTC as per cent of GDP by type of care (2010)

	Total	At Home	In Institutions	Cash Benefits
Czech Republic	0,81	0,06	0,23	0,53
Denmark	4,50	1,33	1,14	2,04
Germany	1,43	0,40	0,58	0,45
United Kingdom	1,97	0,86	0,56	0,56
EU27	1,84	0,53	0,80	0,52

Source: Commission services (DG ECFIN), based on 2012 Annual Report Long-term care: need, use and expenditure in the EU-27

The quality of formal day-care services for children under five years indicated by the child-to-staff ratio is at a rather low level in the UK. In 2010, there were more than 18 children per teacher in pre/school education, which is nearly twice that of Germany (see Table 12.7). Due to the low share of public providers and wide variety of providers, a fragmentation of the provided services has emerged: there is significant variation among the regions and local areas.

Elder Care

During communism in the Czech Republic, social services including services for the elderly were heavily institutionalised and provided low quality care. Therefore, the long-term strategy of the new post-communist governments was to develop the services provided in the home environment instead of institutional care, to provide room and conditions for private and third sector providers, and to set the standards of the services.

Nevertheless, government expenditure on care social services has stagnated since 1989. The system of financing social and health services is criticised: mainly that the sources of its funding are actually random, voluntary, non-transparent, non-systematic and discretionary (Průša and Horecký 2012).

OECD statistics show that the Czech Republic spends the lowest share of GDP expenditure on (long-term) elderly care. While the average spending of the EU-27 countries was 1.8 per cent of GDP in 2010, the Czech Republic spent 0.8 per cent, which is less than half (see Table 12.8).

The Czech *Act on Social Services* of 2006 brought social innovation in the sense that clients' choice of service improved as well as the possibility to stay in a home environment as a result of better home care services. The *care allowance* is provided to the potential users of services, based on an assessment of the degree of their disability: the recipients are free to purchase a service from public bodies, NGOs, or private providers. The purpose was to increase the extent of care provided, to reduce the costs, to keep the elderly in a home environment and to

Table 12.9   Population aged 65 years and over receiving long-term care in selected countries (2010 or nearest year)

Country	Institutions	Home	Total
Czech Republic	2.2	10.9	13.1
Denmark	4.5	12.4	16.9
Germany	3.8	7.6	11.4
United Kingdom	4.2	6.9	11.1
OECD (21)	4.0	8.2	12.2

Note: data for Czech Republic and OECD from 2009, data for UK from 2004
Source: OECD (2012b)

achieve equity among service providers, thus creating a service market. In reality the new benefit did not meet the expectations, since most of the elderly do not use this option to buy the services and continue to rely on informal care: only about one-third of benefits is used to purchase formal care services.

There are differences in the scope and quality of provided services between regions and municipalities. Nevertheless, data show that the scope of elderly care in the Czech Republic slightly exceeds the EU average as well as the scope of care provided in Germany and the UK. Home care prevails greatly over care in institutions. In comparison with other EU countries, the Czech Republic uses long term care in institutions at the level of half the OECD average, while home care is about 2 per cent above the OECD average (see Table 12.9).

Even though new facilities have been constructed in the last few years, the reduction in the number of multi-bed rooms in existing facilities has caused the decrease of the overall capacity of these homes (APSS 2010).

Spatial accessibility of services is a problem: in small communities, care services are often not established at all due to lack of financial resources and political support, while large municipalities provide care services only within their boundaries. The lack of a comprehensive network of services and the unequal distribution of existing services has created a burden on informal care arrangements.

Available data reveal that the ratio of the number of beds in nursing and residential care per 1,000 people over 65 was quite similar in the countries compared, although slightly lower in the Czech Republic in 2010.

At the same time, the number of beds in Czech hospitals was slightly above the OECD average (seven beds in the Czech Republic to 5.8 beds in OECD countries). Germany is also above the average, but the UK and Denmark are below the average concerning hospital beds (see Table 12.10).

The last ten years have seen a gradual improvement in residential social service quality as well as in home care services supported by the introduction of quality standards in social services in 2007. In the case of long-term care services, quality

Table 12.10   Long-term care beds in institutions and hospitals, per 1000 population aged 65 and over (2010)

	Institutions	Hospitals	Total
Czech Republic	42.9	7.0	49.9
Denmark	51.1	0.2	51.3
Germany (2009)	50.3	8.3	58.6
United Kingdom	52.6	3.0	55.6
OECD	45.1	5.8	50.8

Source: OECD (2012b)

remains a problem. The reason is that this type of care is marginalised in the health sector, which is responsible: there is primarily a lack of staff (MLSA 2010a: 44).

Summed up, the actual capacity of services delivered in the Czech Republic is not sufficient mainly due to limited public funding. This has lead to a great extent of self-financing by the elderly themselves, even though their ability to pay is generally quite limited, especially when compared to the West European countries.

In Denmark, long-term care for the elderly is a universal system financed mostly from local taxes. The social innovations that have occurred during the last decade have emphasised the possibility of the client having a choice from a wide range of services ('free-choice model' in 2003), whose operation and quality is ensured by local municipalities either through their own local centres or through mutual agreements between the municipalities and service providers. Management reforms have also placed emphasis on standardisation and performance management, including the quality management of care services.

Although privatisation in elderly care has been made possible, the responsibility for providing and paying for care has remained within the municipality, which also makes the decisions about the type and amount of care. As in Germany, outsourcing is based on the fixed-price arrangement by municipalities with private suppliers (Höhnen 2011).

Denmark is a leader concerning the level of spending on long-term care. In 2010, these expenditures amounted to nearly twice the EU average – 4.5 per cent of GDP in Denmark, compared to 1.8 per cent of GDP in the EU (see Table 12.8 above). The costs of long-term care are financed by local authorities through block grants received from the government, local taxes and equalisation amounts received from other local authorities.

Denmark has achieved outstanding developments in care for the elderly and is consistently among those countries with the highest proportion of people over 65 who are granted long-term care (16.9 per cent in Denmark compared to the OECD average of 12.2 per cent in 2010).

Table 12.11   Population aged 65 and over as per cent to total population in selected countries (2000–2010)

	2000	2005	2010	Difference 2000–2010 (pp)
Czech Republic	13.8	14.1	15.4	1.6
Denmark	14.8	15.1	16.7	1.9
Germany	16.4	18.9	20.4	2.5
United Kingdom	15.8	16.0	16.5	0.7
OECD	13.0	13.8	14.8	1.8

Source: OECD (2013)

Danish long-term care provides comprehensive coverage for a wide-range of social services, including homecare and institutional care. Informal care-givers play a relatively small role in the Danish long-term care system.

Only a small part of the total long-term care expenses is paid by the user (out-of-pocket payments amount to about 4 per cent of total expenditure; compare Schulz 2010a, Kvist 2011, OECD 2012b). In order to encourage the elderly to stay at home for as long as possible, personal care and practical assistance is not subject to co-payments.

Although the share of skilled care workers has gradually increased (from 50 per cent in 1997 to 65 per cent in 2007), there are unskilled workers entering the sector due to the differentiation of care work, which also consists of practical help (mainly cleaning) where the unskilled often find jobs. The reform initiative on the quality of care included the reduction of the number of different assistants visiting the individual citizen, clear and measurable objectives for the services stated in the local council's contract with the care provider, the introduction of a quality fund to improve the physical infrastructure and new technology for old-age care, an accreditation model that supports staff quality through ongoing learning, and the reduction of long waiting times for places in nursing homes (compare Council of Europe 2008, Government of Denmark 2008, Schulz 2010a).

In Germany, elderly care has traditionally been provided by local authorities in cooperation with third sector organisations. Population ageing due to a decline of the fertility rate (which for more than 20 years has been below 1.4 children per woman) and an increase in the average life expectancy have lead to growth of the elderly population faster than in the other countries in focus: by 2.5 per cent in 2000–2010, that is 20.4 per cent of the total population; this is 4–5 per cent higher than that of Denmark, the UK or Czech Republic, and nearly 6 per cent more than the OECD average.

As a consequence of demographic changes, public responsibility for the provision of long-term care has grown since the 1990s. In 1995 social assistance benefits for care were replaced by the compulsory social insurance scheme (Long Term Act 1995).

The German *Social Long-term Care Insurance* (LTCI) is shaped and managed as a Bismarckian-like pay-as-you-go insurance system covering a large part of the care needs. Contributions are income-dependent and shared equally between the employee and employer. New LTCI funds were established; they are responsible for licensing the providers and establishing agreements with them, thus opening up to commercial actors. Consequently, NGOs have lost a great part of the market and local influence: in 2005 commercial providers covered 58 per cent of all the services in elderly care. A new regulatory framework laid down a rigid price system and created standard service packages for purchase. The LTCI funds are mainly responsible for capacity planning, monitoring, organising care provision and assessing long-term care, as well as for quality control. Furthermore, there are around 40 private long-term care insurance funds.

Informal care provided at home plays a significant role in elderly care, following the main priority of Germany's long-term care model. It is provided by family members or non-professional private persons and the costs of this care are covered through the cash allowances. Formal home care services are provided by licensed professionals supported by the LTCI funds (Rothgang 2010): they can substitute the informal carer, such as in cases of illness or leave (respite care), or supplement informal care (that is day and night care, short-term care).

In May 2008 a new act was passed (*Long-term Care Further Development Act*) that aims to improve the delivery of care giving (quality in particular). The major reforms included social innovations like the introduction of a new instrument called 'nursing care time'; the promotion of rehabilitation, case management and counselling; quality improvements; and adjustment of benefits.

The LTCI system is based on the principle of universality and covers most of the needs for service. The catalogue of services and the scale of charges for services are defined by governmental departments in cooperation with all the parties involved.

The quality of elderly care is monitored and controlled by social LTCI funds and the Medical Review Board of the social health insurance funds. Prior to the Act of Training Staff in Elderly Care (2002), the vocational training programmes for carers for the elderly were organised on the level of the states (*Länders*). With the introduction of the new law, the vocational training of the caregivers is standardised to a comparatively high level.

In the UK long-term care for the elderly was enacted before 1980 and provided within the social security/social assistance scheme (this is means-tested). During the 1980s, the scheme was changed into a universal system and the reforms aimed to split the role of service purchaser and provider. After 1997, the Blair government continued in the established marketised governance of social services, but public responsibility increased in the form of stricter state control of service standards and the number of services increased.

The British long-term care system can be characterised as a residual (Brodsky et al. 2003) or safety-net (Fernández et al. 2009) system that only supports those with very severe needs who are unable to meet the costs of care themselves. This organisational setting provides a rationale for the extension of direct payments, self-directed care, and personal and individual budgets within the current 'personalisation agenda'. Non-residential care is being out-sourced by local authorities to the lower cost-independent sector, mainly to for-profit providers.

There is a mixed economy of care: services are financed by the National Health Service, local authorities, charities and older people themselves. Great Britain spent on long-term care the same amount as the OECD average in 2009, but a trend to cut the amount of public and private social expenditure in the last two or three years has been observed. Since local authorities are in many areas the main purchaser of care from local providers, they have considerable market power to negotiate fees at relatively low levels. The resources that government makes available to them are very important to the care home sector, especially in less affluent areas.

In 2007 social innovation in elderly care was brought about by the government's programme *Putting People First*. Its fundamental component is personal budgets enabling the individual allocation of funding to make choices about how best to meet personal needs. Since 2008 the UK has introduced measures to support family carers, including support for carers to (re-)enter the job market and training opportunities for them (Colombo et al. 2011).

In recent years, elderly home care has undergone relatively extensive development. The number of agencies in the private and voluntary sector has doubled since 2000, when such agencies had to be registered for the first time. Some surveys, however, show that long-term care services are often targeted at meeting only the basic (physical or health) needs of the elderly and are less dedicated to their social and psychological needs (Little 2012). One-third of elderly care is paid privately (Laing 2012).

Private-sector providers of social care invest little in training staff, thus resulting in lower quality services as well as a greater turnover of staff. Laing (2012: 3) argues that the demand for paid care may be greatly increased in the future as women abandon their traditional role as providers of informal care, due to increased rates of divorce and remarriage, smaller family sizes, greater labour mobility and more employment opportunities for women.

Employment Services

Employment services are becoming an increasingly important institution of the welfare state: they are expected to contribute substantially to employment growth, competitiveness and social (active) inclusion. These expectations have been growing in recent years in correspondence with the increasing labour market insecurities, pressures on welfare state finance and diminishing workforce due to the ageing of the population.

Table 12.12   Unemployment rate in selected countries (per cent) (2002–2011)

	2002	2005	2009	2010	2011
Czech Republic	7.3	7.9	6.7	7.3	6.7
Denmark	4.6	4.8	6.0	7.4	7.6
Germany	8.4	11.2	7.8	7.1	5.9
United Kingdom	5.1	4.8	7.6	7.8	8.0
EU27	8.9	9.0	9.0	9.7	9.7

Source: Eurostat (2012b)

Most countries in Europe have implemented a series of reforms in recent years in order to make their employment services more effective. These policy reforms concern both governance and the substance of employment and social policies. The governance reforms aim at the *coordination* of minimum income support schemes and unemployment compensation with active labour market policies, tax-benefit schemes and services of different kinds; the *integration* of social policy functions and institutions: cross-field (for example one-stop shops), levels of public administration (national, regional and local); the *cooperation* of various actors and agencies responsible for specific policies; and improving *implementation conditions*: personnel, professional, managerial, institutional (van Berkel et al. 2012). Hence, several new trends have emerged in the EU countries with these reforms: marketisation and contractualisation, New Public Management, individualisation, network governance, inter-agency cooperation and organisational innovation at the local level (ibid.).

Most of these changes have also been observed in the countries compared in this chapter, however, in various extents and forms as shown in the national chapters. The countries compared here belong to those in the EU where the unemployment rate is below the EU average: all had 7–8 per cent in 2010 against the EU average of 9.7 per cent. The crisis increased the unemployment rate more in Denmark and in the Czech Republic than in the UK; only in Germany did it remain stable in spite of the crisis (see Table 12.12).

Similarly, the long-term unemployment rate was below the EU average (3.9 per cent in 2010) in all the countries in focus. In Germany, this rate is the highest of the compared countries (3.4 per cent), while in Denmark it is the lowest (1.5 per cent). In the Czech Republic it was 3.0 per cent and in the UK 2.5 per cent. Germany, however, shows decreasing figures of long-term unemployment (2.8 per cent in 2011) perhaps also due to the reforms of employment services, while in the other countries it was on the increase due to the crisis.

In spite of the similarity in the level of unemployment rates, the substance of employment services and policies as well as their governance show differences. Expenditure on active labour market policies in the Czech Republic (0.23 per cent

Table 12.13 Labour market policy expenditure by type of action as share of GDP (2002–2010)

	2002				2005				2009(UK)/2010		
	Total	1	2–7	8–9	Total	1	2–7	8–9	1	2–7	8–9
Czech Republic	0.46	0.07	0.12	0.28	0.50	0.13	0.13	0.24	0.72	0.12	0.23	0.38
Denmark	4.14	0.10	1.74	2.31	3.77	0.16	1.27	2.34	3.37	0.38	1.41	1.58
Germany	3.39	0.21	1.03	2.14	2.91	0.29	0.61	2.01	2.26	0.38	0.56	1.33
United Kingdom	:	:	:	0.24	0.62	0.39	0.05	0.18	0.71	0.35	0.04	0.31
EU27	:	:	:	:	2.0	0.22	0.51	1.27	2.17	0.24	0.54	1.36

Notes: Special values: – not applicable or real zero or zero by default; 0 less than half of the unit used; not available; 1 Labour market services; 2 Training; 3 Job rotation and job sharing; 4 Employment incentives; 5 Supported employment and rehabilitation; 6 Direct job creation; 7 Start-up incentives; 8 Out-of-work, income maintenance and support; 9 Early retirement

Source: Eurostat (2012b)

of GDP in 2010; see columns 2–7 in Table 12.13) was well below the average of the EU (0.54 per cent), as well as expenditure on employment service (0.12 per cent compared to 0.24 per cent; see column 1). The other countries spent about three times more on employment services. Great variations are seen in the expenditures on ALMPs, which are much higher than the EU average in Denmark (1.41 per cent of GDP), average in Germany (0.56 per cent), below average in the Czech Republic (0.23 per cent of GDP) and the UK (0.04 per cent).

In the Czech Republic, there were several legislative and institutional changes implemented in 2003–2008, such as compulsory bidding of individual action plans to the unemployed after five months of unemployment, transition to the New Management practices associated with the use of ESF projects, and an increasing number of non-governmental organisations and actors involved in ALMP delivery. Nevertheless, appropriate implementation conditions (staffing and training) were not created for the introduction of individualised service: the Czech Public Employment Services in the long-term are understaffed and under-financed (Sirovátka et al. 2007, Sirovátka 2008). This has become even worse recently due to the crisis and the increasing numbers of the unemployed; Kalužná (2008) calculates 202 clients per front-line staff in 2006. This number increased to about 300 during the crisis.[5] The reform aimed to save money by stream-lining the overall management, administration and payment of social benefits with the unemployment benefits, while cutting the numbers of staff, including front-line staff, assuming that job mediation might be outsourced to private agencies.[6]

Under these circumstances the changes adopted may be labelled as unfinished innovations and did not bring more effectiveness in meeting the needs of the clients. Nevertheless, many small-scale examples of social innovation may be found in the form of individual projects of active labour market policies financed from ESF. They are typically carried out by private agencies or NGOs and often provide better treatment to the clients than is possible from Public Employment Services. This is because the projects typically combine several tools like diagnostics, counselling, training and job creation.

Danish labour market policy aims at both flexibility and security. Public employment services and other actors in ALMPs have a role in this: implementing active labour market policies combined with relatively generous unemployment benefits. These are based on a strict work ethic: the duty of the unemployed to actively seek work or actively participate in mandatory full-time activation programmes. Furthermore, there is a variety of related welfare state services, such as life-long education programmes, adult vocational training and education,

---

5   Own estimates based on the fact that unemployment went up by about 50% and the number of staff was cut by 12 per cent in 2011.

6   This assumption has not become true since the rigid legislation did not involve sufficient incentives for private agencies.

childcare and health care, which are mostly financed through the tax system (Hendeliowitz 2008).

The delivery of labour market services falls largely within the public domain, although elements of marketisation have been introduced. Even though spending on active labour market policies declined slightly after 2002, in 2010 it was three times the EU average (see Table 12.12). The recent governance reform has created a more decentralised multi-level governance system, which is matching the public agencies at the national and local levels with a corresponding network involving key stakeholders. Municipalities are responsible for the activation of all unemployed, with and without insurance, and the state is responsible for benefits for unemployed people with insurance. The new one-stop Job Centres are anchored in Local Employment Councils, which bring together interdependent policy actors who engage in institutionalised negotiations that produce public value in terms of policy advice, policy surveillance, and the initiation and funding of projects (Sørensen and Torfing 2007), although strict central rules must be followed. Vocational training programmes take place mainly in educational institutions, which form part of the public labour market training system and which are the product of cooperation between the organisations of social partners and public authorities operating together within a tightly structured network (Dingeldey 2009).

The share of participants in labour market programmes as a percentage of the labour force is among the highest in Denmark (6.5 per cent of the labour force) – more than twice as high as the OECD average in 2010. The ratio of clients to front-line staff is good in Denmark – between 62 to 74 in 2006 (Winter 2008). Summing up, the role of ALMPs within the flexicurity strategy creates good pre-conditions for employment in this field of social service.

The German reforms of employment services were much more substantive than those of the other countries compared. Previously, separated labour market activation and benefit streams for the long-term unemployed were integrated. Germany has also implemented a number of components of activation strategies aimed both at more intensive contact, counselling and the follow-up of the unemployed in collaboration with private providers.

The Hartz reforms brought a modernisation of public employment services along the lines of New Public Management (based on performance targets), increased accountability of local employment offices, outsourcing of many services and open competition between private service providers. At the same time, activation of the unemployed was given priority and sanctions for their inactivity were introduced. Both the level of unemployment benefits and their durations were reduced and eligibility for subsistence allowances/social assistance was reduced.

The Federal Employment Agency was transformed into a service provider with private management structures which include target agreements between the different layers of the PES. Further, over 40 per cent of staff was shifted to placement and counselling functions in order to improve the staff/client ratio; new intervention strategies were based on jobseeker profiling and integration

Table 12.14   Participant inflow in labour market programmes as a per cent of the labour force (2–7) (2002–2010)

	2002	2003	2005	2009	2010
Czech Republic	1.54	1.77	1.16	0.98	1.06
Denmark	-	5.25	5.20	5.5	6.54
Germany	7.35	5.18	4.67	3.68	3.59
United Kingdom	-	-	0.30	0.22	-
OECD average	-	-	3.51	3 .89	4.12

Notes: 2 Training; 3 Job rotation and job sharing; 4 Employment incentives; 5 Supported employment and rehabilitation; 6 Direct job creation; 7 Start-up incentives
Source: OECD Employment Outlook

agreements. Client to front-line staff ratios improved with the reform to a level of 86 for youth and 158 for adults (OECD 2011f).

Due to the above reforms in 2002–2010, the expenditure on ALMPs dropped from 1.03 per cent of GDP to 0.56 per cent (close to the OECD average); nevertheless, expenditure on public employment services increased from 0.21 per cent of GDP to 0.38 per cent (see Table 12.13).

The number of participants inflowing into the active labour market measures declined with the reform until 2006 (from around 7 per cent of the German labour force in 2002 to 6 per cent in 2006 and 4 per cent in 2007) and has remained at a constant level until now. These numbers are around the average level of the OECD countries (see Table 12.14).

The problem discussed in studies is that the two-tier system composed of PES for the short-term unemployed and ARGE for the long-term unemployed are too complex: although the quality of individual counselling and job mediation has improved at PES, the overall coordination of the employment services provided has not. Nevertheless, more intensive casework and individualised service to most of the clients have brought some social innovation in terms of the adequacy and quality of service, as well as efficiency.

The UK represents the case of the liberal welfare state approach in employment services and labour market policies. Support to job search and counselling is traditionally given first priority while expenditures on active labour market policies are among the lowest in the EU; similarly low is the proportion of the participants in the ALMP measures (see above). The UK has been recognised as a deliberate marketiser in the governance of activation (van Berkel et al. 2012) due to the explicit emphasis on outsourcing and quasi-markets in employment services and New Public Management business-like methods (target-setting and a monitoring-oriented governance system).

Employment services are provided through JobCentre Plus, private providers and the voluntary sector. In response to rising unemployment in 2008, the British government introduced some new measures. Activation measures like job search reviews and work-focused interviews were applied to a great extent. Furthermore, for those job seekers reaching six months of a claim, it became possible to obtain intensive support from personal advisers as well as financial support to employers who recruit them. There were additional work-focused training places, volunteering opportunities, and more financial support and advice to help set up a business (DWP 2009: 35). The British JobCentre Plus has no policy-making authority; however, all decisions are made in consultation with the chief executive officer of JobCentre Plus and its board (Weishaupt 2011).

The reforms of governance included the integration of benefits, their coordination with financial incentives in the tax system and the use of personal accounts; however, other areas like vocational training have been rather neglected. The gains in the quality of employment services are observed in the individualisation of treatment provided to jobseekers in general, and to those disadvantaged in the labour market in particular. However, the staffing of PES is assessed as insufficient for the relatively intensively mandated schedule of interventions: the client to front-line-staff ratio was 80 for Job Seeker Allowance recipients but 1,000 for clients receiving non-employment benefits (Tergeist and Crubb 2006).

In summary, the British system of public employment services is highly centralised. Financing and related rules are subject to strong central regulation, tools of management by objectives and cost effectiveness. Services like job mediation and counselling achieve variable quality due to what is only partially sufficient staffing of public employment services.

Employment in Social Services

The countries compared differ very much concerning the level of employment in social services. As data by Labour Force Survey have shown, the share of employment in the HSW sector in total employment was the highest of the EU in Denmark in 2010 (19.1 per cent); in the UK it was 13.1 per cent; in Germany 12.1 per cent; and in the Czech Republic 6.9 per cent. In the UK and Germany, there was an increase of 2.2 percentage points and 2.1 percentage points, respectively, between 2000 and 2010; in Denmark, 1.6 per cent and in the Czech Republic only 0.8 percentage points (see Table 3.2 in Chapter 3).

In human health activities employment (NACE 2 Q 76), the shares are almost identical in Denmark, Germany and the UK (about 7 per cent of the overall employment or slightly more), but in the Czech Republic it is less (5.1 per cent). However, there are great differences in the level of employment in social services. In 2010 the shares of employment in residential care and social work without accommodation were 4.6 per cent and 7.5 per cent in Denmark, respectively; 2.5

per cent and 3.4 per cent in the UK; 2.7 per cent and 2.3 per cent in Germany; and 1.2 per cent and 0.7 per cent in the Czech Republic. In employment services, the share of employment was very similar in Denmark (0.7 per cent), the UK (0.8 per cent) and Germany (0.9 per cent), while in the Czech Republic it was only 0.1 per cent of total employment. This indicates that the different national paths of the development of social services as characterised in the above section have considerable consequences on employment in social services. In this perspective, Denmark appears to be the most developed compared to the UK, Germany and especially the Czech Republic, the laggard.

Nevertheless, the countries also differ in part-time work in the HSW sector: about 40 per cent in Denmark, in Germany and UK, while in the Czech Republic it is 9.1 per cent. This means that the differences in employment as equivalents of full-time employment between the Czech Republic and the other countries are actually less polarised than the data on total employment indicate. The above differences in part-time employment in the HSW sector are not sector-specific, but mirror the overall employment patterns in the countries.

Data from the national statistics give more insight into the recent developments. In the Czech Republic, the growth of HSW employment was about 20 per cent in 2000–2010. In the same period, there was a shift from pedagogical and medical employee categories to social care employees and social workers. This trend was due to the strategy of the Ministry of Labour and Social Affairs, which expanded the number of services for the growing senior population, and the Ministry of Health, which streamlined the existing medical services in healthcare by reducing their number to the conditions of cost containment. The number of jobs in employment services and social security has also grown, although more slowly. In addition, this was merely artificial growth due to the reform of social benefits administration – social assistance was transferred from the municipalities to employment offices, but at the same time, the numbers of staff in social assistance administration were actually cut. Evidently, budget constraints have limited the growth of employment in the sector.

Denmark has the highest share of HSW sector employment of total employment in the EU-27 (19 per cent in 2010). Employment in the HSW sector still grew by 8 per cent between 2000 and 2010 (although most of the employment growth was in part-time work). These figures are clearly related to the central role of social services in the Danish welfare state. Social services employment prevails in the HSW sector, in which the health sector constituted only 37 per cent. This high employment figure in social services implies a more heterogeneous employment structure ranging from highly specialised and skilled professions to workers with minor skills providing services like cleaning and cooking.

According to national data, employment in health and social services grew by 8–10 per cent in the specific subsectors, but more rapidly in medical and dental practice activities (13.5 per cent); growth was much smaller (1 per cent) in social institutions for children (where it was already high).

According to Eurostat data, the HSW sector is highly dominated by women (more than 80 per cent of workers). As in other countries in focus, the workforce is ageing rather rapidly – the share of workers over 50 increased from 24 per cent in 2000 to 31.4 per cent in 2010.

In Germany there is a clear trend of rapid growth in the number of workers employed in the HSW sector for the whole 2000–2010 period, most apparently in social care, especially elderly care. Between 2005 and 2010, there was 34 per cent growth in the number of workers caring for the elderly and 18 per cent growth in the number of educators. In total the number of employees in the HSW sector grew from 3,568 thousand to 4,329 thousand, that is, by 21 per cent between 2000 and 2010.

The development of employment in specific social service professions shows substantial growth. For example, the total number of workers in residential care and social work grew from 1,020.8 thousand to 1,426.6 thousand, that is, by 40 per cent. The number of employees in kindergartens from 367,000 in 2000 to 459,000 in 2010, that is, by 25 per cent. Finally, the number of social workers and carers grew from 358,000 to 538,000 in the same period, that is, by 50 per cent. In the future, the continuation of the trend might only be expected especially in elderly care, due to the considerable trend of ageing.

The decline in the number of workers in childcare facilities between 2002 and 2005 was reversed by a trend of growth of employment in day childcare facilities between 2006 and 2010. Similarly, there was at first stagnation and then strong growth of employment in the Agency for Work (from approximately 95,000 in 2002 to 124,000 in 2010), due to the modernisation of the German welfare state putting more emphasis on services for the elderly, children and the unemployed.

In the UK, the overall trend was the fast growth in the number of jobs in the HSW sector. According to data by an employer survey, the number of jobs in the HSW sector increased from 3.1 million to more than 4 million, that is, by nearly one-third. In contrast to the employment growth in the social service sector as a whole (which was due to increases of private sector services), employment in public social services dropped considerably. On the other hand, the purchase of services from the independent sector is likely to have lead to an increase in support staff in the municipal councils, which have needed to manage contracts over the last 10 years (NHS 2011).

The problems of future labour supply are indicated by the ageing of the workforce in social services. In all four countries the labour force in health and social services has grown older in the past ten years. In all the countries compared, more than 30 per cent of employees were above the age of 50 in 2010, the highest share in Denmark (34.4 per cent). At the same time, the share of employees under 25 is around 10 per cent, the lowest being in the Czech Republic (4.6 per cent) and the highest in Germany (11.5 per cent).

When comparing employment in the HSW sector by education, the structure is more differentiated in Denmark (42.8 per cent high education and 21.1 per cent low education) and in the UK (48.7 per cent and 13.8 per cent, respectively). Fewer highly educated workers and a less differentiated employment structure is observed in Germany (34.2 per cent and 13 per cent) and in the Czech Republic (25.9 per cent and 5 per cent). The difference is mainly due to the high share of social services in Denmark and in the UK to some extent. In all the countries the educational levels of the labour force in HSW in the 15–29, 30–49 and 50+ age groups have seen improvements. There is a better educational structure in the 15–29 age group in the Czech Republic (fewer of those with a low level and more of those with a high level of education). In Denmark and Germany, there has been a reduction in the share of highly educated workers in the youngest age group. In Denmark there has been a decrease of low educated employees, whereas in Germany an increase in this age group. In the UK, the share of highly educated workers is relatively stable across the age groups and the share of the low educated is decreasing.

Nevertheless, in countries where the educational structure has been improving, the problems are indicated by the low pay in social services, which may be an obstacle to providing sustainably good quality services in the future. The wages in the HSW sector are well above the average wages in manufacturing in Denmark and Germany – by 22.5 per cent and 19 per cent, respectively; in the UK it is only by 5.5 per cent above the average of manufacturing. By contrast, in the Czech Republic wages in the HSW sector are 7.1 per cent lower than in manufacturing.

Still, in Denmark social services workers are relatively low paid compared to the average wage and the wages of other selected professions (20–28 per cent below the national average wage). In Germany the wages of all social care professions are substantially lower, while the lowest wages are found in employment services and residential nursing care. Compared to the average in the total economy in 2010, they represented 51.5 per cent and 64.5 per cent of the average wage. Lastly, in the UK the lowest wages were in 2010 in childcare professions (50 per cent of the average wage); they were also low for all the caring personal service occupations (58 per cent of the average wage) and for residential activities for the elderly and the disabled (62 per cent of the average wage).

Conclusions

Employment in the HSW sector shows very different national cases: it was very high in Denmark in 2010 (19.1 per cent of total employment), at a middle level in the UK (13.1 per cent) and Germany (12.1 per cent), and low in the Czech Republic (6.9 per cent). When focusing only on the selected social services, the differences are even greater: 12.8 per cent of total employment in Denmark, 6.6 per cent in the UK, 5.9 per cent in Germany and 2 per cent in the Czech Republic. The level of public financing of the welfare state, especially social protection in kind (services) corresponds very well to the above levels of employment in social services.

The wages in the HSW sector are above the average wages in industry in Denmark and Germany (about 20 per cent), only by 6 per cent in the UK, but 7 per cent lower in the Czech Republic. This all indicates possible problems in the UK and Czech Republic for the future labour supply.

Although there are differences in the level of employment in social services, which are to a large extent due to the previous development of social services (path dependency) and due to the financial base of the welfare state, there are also some common trends of development. First, we see a tendency of mixing the resources for financing social services: public and private resources. The share of private co-financing by the service user is not negligible, specifically in child and elderly services in all countries, Denmark included. Nevertheless, the countries differ in the extent to which they support the entitled population through specific benefits or tax relief measures: this support is better in Denmark and to some extent in the UK, but worse in Germany and the Czech Republic.

Second, there is a trend towards the modernisation of the welfare state by putting more emphasis on services than on transfers, except in the Czech Republic where the communist legacy caused delay or even reversed these trends. Specifically, some of the identified modernisation trends are as follows: a shift towards universalism in the provision of social services or even in the formulation of the 'right' to services, as in Denmark. Another trend is the increasing role of public administration (state and municipalities) in regulation and financing: service delivery was split from the regulation and financing of the service and shifted to non-state providers. Regulation is focused mainly on the rules of prices and quality of service, although market competition is the binding principle, however with differences among the countries. The growing trend towards New Public Management methods in the regulation and financing of social services is associated with this tendency.

Third, there is a trend towards individualising service and strengthening the options of choice by clients of the services (that is empowerment). Lastly, all the countries have implemented several social innovations in social services concerning the access, quality, service delivery and efficiency. Very often they aim for improved client choice and empowerment. These innovations are very dependent on the stage of the previous development of social services. This means that in countries like Denmark, where social services are well developed, advanced social innovations are understood as 'systemic change' supported by sufficient financing and regulation by public administration. On the other hand, in some cases where social services are less developed and less sufficiently financed, like in the Czech Republic, there are evidently only some (often failed) attempts at innovation, with rather varying and unreliable effects.

Chapter 13

Conclusions

Tomáš Sirovátka and Bent Greve

Introduction

The previous chapters have dealt with the issue of how modern welfare states are solving the challenge of financing and ensuring social services and sufficient employment in social services even in conditions of economic crisis and the consolidation of public finance. This is a central issue with regard to the modernisation of the welfare state as 'employment friendly' or as a social investment welfare state, since health and social services contribute in many ways to employment growth, the productivity of labour and a growing economy. This further leads to stable and equitable societies.

In this book, different methodological approaches have been applied which use the knowledge of numerous previous studies, various documents and statistical data that provide evidence about financing and employment in health and social services in Europe. In-depth analyses have been carried out concerning the financing, regulation and delivery of selected social services in the four countries chosen as representatives of liberal, corporatist, social democratic and post-communist welfare regimes. This has made it possible to assess changes in the patterns of financing, governance and employment in social services since 2000; this period includes times of rapid economic development as well as downturn after the financial crisis.

This chapter is structured so that, firstly, conclusions about employment, financing and innovation in social services are presented. This is followed by a discussion on convergence and divergence in the developments of social services. Finally, some recommendations are presented for a new typology of social services in Europe.

Employment in Social Services

Coherent analyses of employment patterns and employment characteristics in health and social services are relatively rare. For this reason, one of the goals of this book has been to investigate the recent developments. As the analysis for the 10-year period between 2000 and 2010 has shown, there has been substantial growth of employment in the health and social services (HSW) in most European countries, continuing even in times of economic crisis. There are substantial differences between countries in the level of health and social service employment: the highest level is in the North European countries and the Netherlands, while South-Eastern and Central Europe represent low levels. Part-time employment has comprised an important part of employment growth, but with substantial differences among countries.

There are several problems related to social service employment:

- rapidly ageing labour force in the HSW sector
- signals in some countries of de-skilling in some segments of social services
- some aspects of working conditions in HSW are challenging, for example those related to working schedule, stress and health-related risks resulting in high turnover in some of the professions
- hard working conditions contrast with low wages in some HSW professions and segments.

The dualisation of employment in social services is emerging in many countries in regards to the type of contract, remuneration/pay, skill level and professional standards required.

The segment of the formal, more standardised, high quality services provided by a relatively highly qualified workforce is co/existing with a segment of hidden, semi-formal, unknown-quality services provided by family or civil society with less qualified people who are often neighbours or immigrant workers. Although service quality frameworks including qualification standards are set by policy-makers, there may be a problem in meeting them if job quality in the social services is too low and unsustainable.

Social services require innovations that would attract younger as well as older workers to the sector. This should entail systematic education to meet higher standards of quality and sustainability. Working conditions and wages are crucially important in this process.

A broad range of factors influence the development of employment in social services in the EU countries. First, there are general factors associated with societal development that influence the development of social services and employment in social services mostly in the long-term perspective. Above all, the already established welfare state models imply a certain path dependency which is best identified in the level and sources of financing like government revenues and expenditure on social services. In international comparison, public expenditure on social services is closely associated with the level of employment in social services. In contrast to orthodox economic thinking, the current reality shows that a higher level of employment in social services is not linked to greater public debt. Those countries which are ahead in social service employment (as well as overall employment) are also more successful in maintaining sound public finances.

Another important factor is the change in family roles, indicated by female employment. Higher levels of employment in social services are clearly associated with the higher employment rate of women (and higher fertility rates at the same time). This appears as the most consistent and strongest driver of employment in social services. This is due to the fact that the development of social services opens new job opportunities for women and enables parents to balance work and family life.

The ageing of society, indicated by the old-age dependency ratio, has not yet proven to be significantly correlated with social service employment. Nevertheless, the impacts of ageing on the demand of social services will be greater in the future due to the expected rapid change in demographic structure. Second, there is due to be an advancement of gender equality in those countries which currently prefer familialisation policies (post-communist and South-Europe welfare states). These welfare states have so far primarily relied on the alternative or informal caring options, although there are consequences like a lower female employment rate and a lower level of formal employment in social services.

There are other important factors. Above all, politics matters: a higher employment rate in social services is associated with lower unemployment rates. This is mainly due to the overall better performance of the labour market, as well as to a deliberate strategy of fostering public sector employment in times of economic slowdown, both issues being influenced by political considerations (Cussack et al. 1989, Tepe 2009). In recent years social service employment growth has been positively associated with GDP growth, although dependencies work in both directions. It seems that economic recession has been forcing governments to reduce growth in social service employment. It is evident that during and after a crisis, it is difficult to increase public investment into social services despite the increasing demand for services. This might particularly be the case in countries where expenditure used to be low for a long period of time and in countries which are facing huge and increasing public deficits and/or a high level of public sector debt. Political actors can gain more electoral support if they reduce public employment and expenditure. In such cases, it would be preferable that innovations in regulation, financing and delivery of social services be used as instruments for coping with the pressures emerging from fiscal consolidation.

Financing of Social Services

Given the financial crisis and expected fiscal pressures on the welfare states, the core issue is how to proceed in order to develop long-term sustainability in the financing of the welfare state. Fiscal pressure due to globalisation and change in demography is one issue; another is the expected outcome of the fiscal crisis, which is leading to an even more prudent fiscal policy than before, at least for a certain period of time. Thus, another central policy issue is how to deal with this development.

The Economic and Monetary Union of the EU has set targets of maximum levels: 3 per cent public sector deficits, 60 per cent public sector debt and 0.5 per cent of GDP in structural deficits. This poses challenges for future financing.

The question is whether these are sufficient criteria when related to other types of sustainability (for example environment, jobs, demographics and equity issues). Furthermore, it is important to see how different ways of using the financial system might have an impact on growth in the economy.

The debate on sound public finance is not new and includes the impact of both spending and taxation components, from both automatic stabilisers and balanced budget multiplicator effects. The possible negative impacts on the overall economy as a result of taxes on work and savings have also been classical issues in public sector financing. Financing should not only be judged upon the overall effects or on sound finance, as the impact of changes on the public sector economy and the level of activities also depends on the overall economic situation in a country and its level of unemployment.

In relation to ensuring economic growth, another issue is how to choose financial instruments so as far as possible that both financing and economic growth are achieved. This is further due to the fact that economic growth will have a positive impact on financial sustainability; this typically has an impact on both the overall level of public sector spending and income. In this sense, an OECD study has pointed to the general rules that the raising of taxes on immovable property has the least impact on economic growth, whereas increasing taxes on corporations has the highest impact (Johansson et al. 2008).

The pressure on financing has also increased the focus on more efficient and lean government spending, so that welfare state efforts produce the highest possible outcome. This infers the welfare state as a social investment state; for example, it establishes care for children to enable both the mother and father to be on the labour market. This has been evident in most EU countries, corporatist and liberal welfare regimes (which have previously been perceived as service-lean states; Fleckenstein (2010)) as well as in the post-communist and South-Europe welfare states. Whether to focus on sustainable *social* development over simply sustainable development (that is more focus on investment in social issues than in the financial sector) is an important normative question (Tangian 2010). However, social policies can be seen as having an impact on the ability to reduce risk in modern societies and to influence economic development through a more extensive welfare state.

The way to ensure sustainable finance is therefore through several different however often interlinked, channels, including more efficient use of public sector spending; nevertheless, it is also true that 'given the magnitude of fiscal consolidation required, the spending cuts will most likely have to be accompanied by revenue raising measures' (Koske 2010: 18). Furthermore, phasing out tax concessions and changes towards a better structure for the tax base as well as increasing environmental taxes and duties could also be elements of fiscal consolidation.

The ability to ensure compliance within the tax system is also an important aspect of creating a sustainable tax system. The lack of compliance, even within what are in principle the same tax-rates, implies an overall lower level of public sector income. The recent tendencies in Europe to combat fraud and ensure that tax-havens are reduced as well as the fact that information can be exchanged more easily among the tax-authorities are all aspects related to ensuring sustainable public sector financing.

Chapter 4 has shown that so far no further convergence in the way revenues are generated within the EU countries has taken place over the last ten years. The level of revenue has remained relatively stable as a proportion of the overall economy, making the financial situation less stable given the increase in spending as well as the financial crisis. At the same time, trends towards creating a broader tax-base and lower tax rate, especially for corporate income tax and taxation of the highest income earners, has actually taken place. This will be a challenge for welfare states in the future. This also raises the issue of the need, at least on the European level, to agree on some common tax-rates, as is the case within the VAT system.

Overall, it seems that a variety of measures is needed to ensure fiscal sustainability with regard to long-term stability in public finances, while also taking environmental issues into consideration. Sustainable financing will include measures to reduce the level of deficit and debt, as does the type within the EU-finance pact, as well as those types of instruments that can best ensure long-term sustainability in the financing of the welfare states.

Those measures already implemented show that there could be a rule enacted even for the structural deficit. A limit to the structural deficit should in principle not be a hindrance for active fiscal stimulus in times of crisis. Unless there has been a focus on ensuring a surplus in good times, there may be a stronger focus on public sector spending, despite the fact that deficits in public sector finance can be changed both by variations in expenditure and income.

A continuous focus on the tax base and broadening it by reducing loopholes and tax concessions also seem to be ways to ensure sustainable revenue for the public sector, as has been the trend in recent years. Europe's strategy to reduce the use of tax-havens and better information and compliance with the tax-system also point in this direction. The sustainable financing of the welfare state could further enhance the option of sustainability in the provision of social services, as this would imply a lower risk of cuts and reductions in services being needed to ensure balance in public sector finances.

Social Innovation

Social innovation has become an important topic of discussion in the social sciences and on the EU agenda. Basically, the innovations in social services should better meet the needs of people and societal development. Given the pressures on the public budgets, the innovative approaches and practices are expected to be further developed, implying a more effective public sector.

The increasing role of innovation in social services is due to several interrelated changes:

- the shift towards a knowledge economy
- new social risks such as outdated skills in the labour market
- need for the combination of work and family life
- the ageing of society
- social exclusion due to insufficient access to social services
- increasing financial pressure on public budgets
- the lack of adequate financing of social services
- changing forms of governance
- the public-private mix and post-New Public Management measures.

Several governance reforms in the welfare states and social services are aiming to solve these challenges.

The positive effects of service innovation (for example the use of IT) might involve improved user access to information, greater user satisfaction, more targeted services, faster delivery of services, simplified administration, improved working conditions or employee satisfaction and cost reductions (see European Commission 2011b).

Social innovations better meet social needs in new ways which are more effective than the existing solutions by enhancing the capacity to act for the broad range of actors involved and by empowering the users of services. From a more general perspective, social innovation may be seen as the changing relationship among state, market and family within the process of service provision ensuring more adequate service to the clients and/or more effective service delivery.

The analyses in the national case studies, on the one hand, looked at the relationship between the governance reforms in social services. On the other hand, they analysed the innovations as improvements in the provision of social services in substance aimed at meeting client needs. More effective service provided with respect to individual and/or local needs at a reasonable cost is becoming a key concern. At the same time, the individualisation of service and economic efficiency are also the main objectives.

Various types of innovations have appeared in the last decades in social services. The process of the rearrangement of the relationships among state, market and family in service provision has brought a broad trend of splitting the functions of regulation, financing and service delivery as well as the pluralisation of actors. The state as direct service provider is diminishing its role, while the market and NGOs are becoming more important. This process includes several innovations which can be summarised as follows:

- marketisation (outsourcing of service delivery to private providers, more competition, increasing role of private resources in the form of co-payments/fees for service)

- increasing emphasis on the complementary relationship between formal (professional) and informal (family) service provision
- stronger state regulation (quality standards of services, price limits)

All three elements have an impact on the sustainability and development of social services. The various ways of enhancing work and family life and the use of market-type mechanisms in the public sector raise issues concerning the relation between state and market, as well as the importance that public sector demand and financing can have for private companies in many countries. The last aspect seems to be central for achieving the synergy in the state/market/family relationship.

While reforms in governance bring less state involvement in service delivery, there is greater emphasis on more effective regulation and control. This change in the public-private mix, partnership and networking is combined with New Management practices in social services (i.e. management by objectives, monitoring and incentivising the actors).

These changes are leading to the individualisation (for example often tailor-made provisions) of service with increasing attention to the needs of clients, their choice and empowerment. This is seen in various methods of their involvement or empowerment within the process of service delivery. Either their choice is larger (through the use of vouchers, or they are becoming direct purchasers of services) and/or their rights are better guaranteed (rights to service, service quality standards). The regulation of service quality through output (service) standards or process (professional and performance) standards is an essential condition for individualisation and choice. Technological progress is another form of social innovation. This includes the use of information technologies in the public sector services and new welfare technologies in care – typically in elderly care.

Governance reforms and social innovations are only partly overlapping areas. It is only possible to understand the changes in policies as social innovations if their objectives and/or effects/impacts (process, product or outcome effects) correspond to the criteria set for the categories of social innovation like adequacy, quality, effectiveness and efficiency of the services, empowerment and/or increased capacity of the actors involved to act (see Chapter 5). By contrast, the reforms which only aim at cost containment, irrespective of the other aspects of social innovation, do not belong in this category.

There are great differences in the scope, character and impact of social innovation, as was seen in the chapters on particular countries. In Denmark, where social services are the most developed and best regulated, social innovations approximate the model of the systemic innovation of the complex state/market/family relationship. By contrast, in the Czech Republic, we only find attempts at social innovation, which appear as rather partial, with ambiguous effects concerning the adequacy and efficiency of the service provided.

National Case Studies: Convergence or Divergence?

The case studies have shown that the four countries are very different concerning the level of employment in the HSW sector: it is very high in Denmark (19.1 per cent of total employment in 2010), at the middle level in the UK (13.1 per cent) and Germany (12.1 per cent), and low in the Czech Republic (6.9 per cent). When focusing only on social services, the differences are even greater: 12.8 per cent of total employment in Denmark, 6.6 per cent in the UK, 5.9 per cent in Germany and 2 per cent in the Czech Republic.

Similarly, the level of jobs in the HSW sector indicated by the level of wages is diverse. The wages in the HSW sector are above the average wages in industry in Denmark and Germany (by about 20 per cent), 6 per cent higher in the UK, but 7 per cent lower in the Czech Republic.

Table 13.1   **Financing of social services and employment in social services in four countries (key facts) (2000, 2010)**

	2000				2010			
	DK	**CZ**	**GER**	**UK**	**DK**	**CZ**	**GER**	**UK**
Financing (% GDP)								
Total social protection expenditure	28.1	18.2	28.6	25.5	32.4	19.5	29.3	27.1
Social protection expenditure in kind	10.8	5.9	9.0	8.5	13.3	6.4	10.6	11.3
Employment rates (%)								
Employment rate	76.4	64.9	65.3	71.0	73.4	65.0	71.1	69.5
Employment rate women	72.1	56.8	57.8	64.5	71.1	56.3	66.1	64.6
Child (0–6) employment gap women 20–40 (2009)	..	41.0	22.2	21.2	..	41.0	16.0	21.1
Employment in social services (%)								
Employment share of HSW sector in total employment	17.5	6.1	10.0	11.0	19.1	6.0	12.1	13.2
Employment in social services (residential + without accommodation), and employment services	..	..	..	..	12.8	2.0	5.9	6.7
Educational level in HSW sector (ratio high/low education)	..	..	..	..	2.0	5.2	2.6	3.5
Wage level in HSW sector (difference in % to manufacturing sector)	..	..	..	..	22.5	- 7.1	19.0	- 4.7

Source: Data by Eurostat, compiled by the authors

The countries analysed do not seem to have serious problems with the de-skilling of the labour force in social services; nevertheless, in Denmark and Germany the educational level is somewhat decreasing in the younger age group and there are increasing numbers of workers in social services, especially cleaning. Some differentiation is evidenced between the personal carers (better wages) and other assisting professions which provide, for example, simple housework tasks.

Although there are differences in the level of employment in social services, which are to a large extent due to the previous development of social services (path dependency) and due to the financial base of the welfare state (see Table 13.1), there are also some common trends of development.

First, there is a trend towards the modernisation of the welfare state by putting more emphasis on services than on transfers, except in the Czech Republic where the communist legacy caused a delay of this or even reversed the trends. The common modernisation trend has been identified as a shift towards universalism in the provision of social services, or even in the provision of the 'right' to service for citizens, as in Denmark. Nevertheless, the level of service can vary, or may even be dissimilar in some service areas.

The other trend is the increasing role of state public administration in regulation and financing focused on prices and quality of service; however, market competition is the binding principle, even though there are differences among the countries in focus.

Third, there is a tendency to change within the public-private mix, not only in service delivery, but also in the mixing of resources for financing social services between the public and private. The share of private co-financing by the service user is sometimes relatively high. The countries differ in the extent to which they support the entitled service users through specific benefits or tax relief methods: this support is better in Denmark and to some extent in the UK, but worse in Germany and the Czech Republic.

Fourth, there is a trend towards the individualisation of services and the strengthening of options for the clients of the services (through empowerment). Lastly, several innovations in social services have taken place in all the countries concerning the scope, quality, modes of financing and service delivery. In Denmark, where social services are well developed, social innovations which are understood as a 'systemic change' and supported by the sufficient financing and regulation of public administration do occur. Where social services are less developed and less sufficiently financed, there seem to be mere attempts at innovation.

This analysis has shown that there is some convergence across the EU countries concerning the principles and instruments used in social services. At the same time, path dependency of the welfare states is strong: policies based on similar principles vary in the scope/coverage and quality of services and in how they are provided. Similarly, different levels of quality in social services employment are emerging.

The common trends and differences are summarised below (see Box 13.1).

Development in childcare and employment services seems to be more dependent on the specific welfare state model than that of elderly care, which is more influenced by demographic change and increasing demand for professional formal services. Denmark represents a country where childcare services are among the most developed in Europe, including services for children 0–3 years. They are financed by the public sector and by parents through fees, which are progressively derived from their incomes. There is a right to care and the services are well regulated in terms of quality standards and staffing.

During the last decade, the United Kingdom and Germany have modernised their approach to childcare by putting much more emphasis on childcare for children aged 0–3. Thus, the childcare employment gap for women has effectively been closed in Germany to the level of the UK (see Table 13.1). Moreover, since 2013 the obligation of providing childcare has been imposed on municipalities. In the Czech Republic, the emphasis is still put on informal family care for children aged 0–3 years, which is somewhat supported through parental benefits and tax relief for caring parents, but with negative consequences for women's employment.

In Denmark, Germany as well as in the UK, strong tendencies towards the pluralisation of childcare alternatives and the marketisation of childcare have emerged since 2000. The share of the costs of childcare covered by parents in all these countries reaches about 25–30 per cent of the total cost (in the case of Denmark, this depends on the level of household income). However, in Denmark and to a lesser extent in Germany, the rest of these expenses are covered by public sources (that is communes, municipalities). In the UK, targeted tax relief can help parents from the low income brackets. The trend towards the universal provision of child care, in combination with targeted financial support to parents, has enabled an increase in the coverage of childcare in the UK and Germany. Nevertheless, the UK still suffers from rather high costs for parents and a lower quality of childcare. In Germany the problem is mainly the relatively high cost of childcare for low income families, as targeted support is lacking. These problems may hamper the future development of childcare and employment (in childcare and in general) in both countries. In the Czech Republic, the reasons for the underdeveloped childcare for the 0–3 age group and for the women's child employment gap are complex: the lack of social investment in childcare is the main reason, however.

In elderly care, there is a shared commitment to providing care to the elderly in all countries since informal/family care is less available due to the breakdown of the extended or even nuclear family and to the increasing pension age of the potential family member-carer. However, the approaches of the countries are different in several respects.

In the Czech Republic after 1989, the trend towards the humanisation of elderly care as well as the pluralisation of service providers has been evident, with increasing emphasis on home care and de-institutionalisation. Public expenditure on elderly care, however, remains relatively low, while the share of informal care is still about 20 per cent of the care provided to the elderly. The main problems include the insufficient coverage of home care, low quality of institutional care and high cost of care in institutions. A new benefit provided to entitled recipients of care – the care allowance – has not significantly increased the extent of professional care, as the level of the benefit seems to be rather low for this purpose as well as for paying for institutional care.

In Denmark, elderly care is understood as a right; the coverage of elderly care is high, but underpinned with sufficient financing. Home care is well developed and free of charge, while targeted financial support is provided for the rather costly institutional care. The share of informal and private providers (not including family) is quite low. Great emphasis is placed on providing choice for clients. This is combined with the responsibility of the state in regulation (quality standards and professionalisation).

In Germany, the rapid ageing of the population caused a shift towards universalism in elderly care in the mid 1990s: this was provided within a social insurance scheme which ensured benefits for those elderly who need care. Nevertheless, the costs of care are high, especially in institutions, and there is little targeted financial help available to the clients. The share of private providers of care has increased, while the role of traditional providers like NGOs has decreased in the last decade. A rigid price system has been implemented as key regulation. Another emerging problem is the quality of care, which is variable depending on the region, municipality and their specific adopted standards.

In the UK, marketisation is a strong strategy for ensuring elderly care, accompanied by the regulation of quality standards from the central level. The goal is to change the targeted system of elderly care to a universal one. Market competition has pushed the cost of care down and increased choice for clients. Home care has developed in scope and quantity. On the other hand, the quality of care is often unsatisfactory, ranging from local systems where only basic needs seem to be met and where professional standards are not guaranteed well to systems with higher quality and broader coverage of needs.

In employment services, differences in policy objectives and measures are very much dependent on the specific welfare and labour market regime. There are great differences in financing active labour market policy measures: in Denmark the financial support to ALMPs is high; in Germany it is above OECD average; in the Czech Republic it is low; and in the UK, very low. The differences in the numbers of participants in the ALMP measures vary correspondingly. More similarity is found in the financing of employment services, although in the Czech Republic the support is very low compared to the other three countries in focus. Consequently, in the Czech Republic, the poor implementation conditions (under-staffing of public employment services combined with low accessibility to ALMPs) (Sirovátka and Winkler 2011) has caused the failures of the new regulation of the individual action plans. The centralisation reform of 2010/2011, which accompanied the marketisation of labour market policies, has led to cuts in public budgets and Public Employment Services staff numbers, but without improvement in the performance of employment services.

In the other countries, modernisation trends in employment services have brought marketisation in service delivery accompanied by stronger regulation by the state and the implementation of New Public Management methods. The most transparent of these trends have been in the UK and to a large extent in Germany; in Denmark to a lesser extent. Another trend is the individualisation of services with more emphasis on counselling and mediation in Public Employment Services (casework); there has been an increasing capacity of private agencies in this respect.

These trends are nevertheless situated in very different national policy contexts. In Denmark, Germany and the UK, the scope of the measures of active labour market policy have dropped and work-first measures have been the most preferred option. Denmark remains close to the 'human resources development' model of activation with great emphasis on labour market training and job entry promotion. The UK is clearly following the 'work first' model with emphasis on counselling and incentivising the unemployed. Germany inclines towards the work-first model as well, but applies a more balanced approach.

Box 13.1   Comparison of governance (regulation, financing and delivery of social services) and outcomes in four countries

	DK	CZ	GER	UK
Regulation				
Universalism vs. Targeted service	Explicit universalism, services as a right	Targeted services	Shift to universalism but accessibility/cost problems	Targeted services, some shift to universalism
Quality standards	Strong regulation	Medium to weak regulation (except childcare)	Medium regulation but variable (decentralisation)	Medium to weak regulation
New Public Management methods	More general approach applied within good/responsible public governance	Not applied; bureaucratic governance	Selective application (employment services)	Strong application
Choice for clients	High emphasis	Low emphasis	Medium emphasis	Medium emphasis

	DK	CZ	GER	UK
Financing				
User fees	Rather low	Rather low, high in private facilities	Medium and variable (decentralisation)	Rather high (except in employment services)
Targeted financial support	Very accessible and generous	Less accessible, rather low, selective	Less accessible (selective), medium level	Rather accessible, low to medium level
Delivery				
Marketisation	Medium, strongly regulated	Rather strong, least regulated	Strong, regulated	Very strong, less regulated
Innovation	Systemic approach, complex changes	Partial attempts	Mainly public-private mix in delivery, mixing formal-informal service	Public-private mix in delivery, mixing public-private resources, formal-informal
Outcomes in service provision				
Coverage/ accessibility	Very high in all fields	Consistently rather low (except elderly care – medium)	Medium, increasing in care services	Medium in LTC and in childcare, low in employment services
Price/cost of service	Mostly low	Mostly high (except childcare 3– school age)	Medium to high	High (except employment services)
Quality of service	Workloads low	Workloads medium in childcare, elderly care, high in employment services	Workloads medium	Workloads high in childcare, medium in elderly care, medium to high in employment services

Source: Compiled by authors

Employment growth in social services was at least 20 per cent or even higher in the Czech Republic (although from a much lower base), Germany and the UK (from an average base), while in Denmark it was lower but from a substantially higher base. In this respect, some convergence is evident.

The ageing of the workforce in social services is the apparent trend in the countries studied as well as in the EU overall. In all the countries the composition of employees in social services documents an overall trend of increasing qualifications. However, in some sub-sectors like personal home care the situation is worse: this is apparent in Denmark, for example, where the spectrum of professions involved in care is quite large, including assistance with simple domestic tasks. The qualification standards required by the public bodies responsible for regulation play a positive role in all countries and work to guarantee professional service.

The quality of employment indicated by wages is very different in the HSW sector. In Denmark and Germany, wages on average are about 20 per cent or more above the wages in manufacturing. In the UK, the average wage is slightly higher than that of manufacturing; however, in the Czech Republic, this figure is lower. Some categories of social workers in caring professions earn about half the average wage in the UK and Germany, and little more in the Czech Republic. Their position is more advantageous in Denmark, where the sector is more professionalised and better financed.

Typology of Social Service Models

The findings of the preceding chapters indicate a possible typology of social service models, by using three key dimensions of comparisons which characterise the most important trends in development since 2000, as described above and summarised in Box 13.1:

1. movement towards social investments and servicing indicated by expenditure on social services, scope of employment in social services
2. the regulatory role of public authorities in this process indicated by service quality and professional standards, price control and the guarantee of rights to service and choice for clients
3. marketisation and pluralisation of the actors in service delivery indicated by the share of private providers and open competition

The typology suggested is based on the analysis of the key features and trends in 'governance' of social services. When using the above dimensions, Denmark may be labelled as a 'regulated, social investment welfare mix', the UK as a 'regulated marketiser', the Czech Republic as an 'unregulated marketiser' and Germany as a 'state managed modernising welfare mix' (see Box 13.2).

Box 13.2   Typology of governance in social services according to three dimensions

	CZ	DK	GER	UK
Modernisation (social services)	Weak	Strong	Medium	Medium
Regulation (state)	Weak	Strong	Medium/ strong	Medium
Marketisation	Medium/ strong	Medium	Medium/ Strong	Strong

Source: Compiled by authors

Reflection on the first and third trends which we use in our typology has previously lead to similar typologies – those designed by Pollitt and Bouckaert (2000) and Ahonen et al. (2006), who distinguished 'marketisers' and 'modernisers' in social services, and similarly van Berkel et al. (2012). The addition of the 'regulation dimension' seems to be crucial in several respects like accessibility and quality of social service, scope and quality of employment in social services, as documented in the book. Stoy (2012) has elaborated typology of welfare services by using variables characterising the quantity of the services, kind of services and how they are organised (using data on employment patterns in social services and expenditure on social services) for 25 countries. His findings confirm the traditional typology as elaborated by Esping-Andersen (1990, 1999) and cluster Czech Republic with rudimentary regime, Denmark with social democratic, Germany with conservative and UK with liberal regime. Our findings fit quite well to this typology while the aspects of regulation are more elaborated and represent key distinguishing feature.

This typology reflects the current situation. From the perspective of dynamics, the differences would be less strong since there are some convergence trends found in the studied countries. This mirrors the promotion of similar goals and principles, in spite of the various instruments and levels of finance.

When reflecting on the consequences for employment in social services, it seems that the modernisation trend (indicated by the volume and profile of public finance) plays a role mainly in the level of employment in social services, while the balance between regulation and marketisation somewhat influence the quality of employment in social services. The question is to what extent the convergence in principles is influenced by EU regulations.

The Open Method of Co-ordination (OMC) has been central since the Amsterdam Treaty and has served as an attempt to move forward with a supranational impact also in development in the core welfare state areas. These theoretical underpinnings have been building upon new institutionalism on path-dependency and the impact of learning effects to alter beliefs and practices. This was seen early on as the best approach to coping with this complex issue involving many actors and countries (Roth and Schmidt 2000). Since then, this complexity has not been reduced due to the enlargement of the EU.

The real impact of the OMC has often been questioned, as has the direction from which it came (that is whether the impact has been from below or from above). Another issue concerned how strong the pressure has been, ranging from very mild in most programs, such as the European Employment Strategy (EES), to stronger pressure concerning issues in the EMU.

The impact of the EES on national active labour market policy has been questioned. Armingeon thus argued that there has been an impact on ALMP from a higher level of spending as a result of the EU strategy (Armingeon 2007). This is confirmed in a study from 2011 that OMC had an impact through the mutual learning of the peer-review program, although not supporting the arguments that recommendations have an impact (Vliet and Koster 2011, Mailand 2009).

A possible explanation for the variation of impact is that the EES has several different types of governance objectives. They include the promotion of learning and convergence (although maintaining respect for diversity), the integration of separate policy areas and increasing participation (Trubek and Mosher 2003).

There has been movement towards a larger role for the EU in the core area of welfare state services, although the way to a higher impact on welfare policies has been very diverse. In some areas, this has been achieved through court cases (for example Laval); in others through agenda-setting as part of the communication of viewpoints and the OMC (active labour market policy); still other areas have used gradual economic integration, implying a gradually weaker role for individual member states in the field of social policy. Generally, the EU impact has been stronger where there have been directives or court decisions.

However, given the financial crisis pressures from convergence and tendencies towards it (compare Chapter 4), the role of the EU (taken more as a common set of options and possibilities rather than as a specific entity) can imply further development towards welfare state models moving in the same direction. The demand for fiscal consolidation thus acts as pressure on the decision-makers also in relation to social services.

The Future of Employment in Social Services

The changing employment structures and the ageing of society are leading to an overall increase in the demand for social services. However, it is not clear how this expansion of demand for social services will affect employment in social services, since re-familisation and re-commodification may imply an increase in the provision of informal/family services, instead of formal services. The central question is whether this trend will continue under the conditions of the recent economic crisis, or whether it will change again when Europe is back on track. It seems that the key factor influencing the future is the awareness of the central role of social services as a part of a social investment strategy and political commitment to support the development of social services, including the use of innovative approaches to deliver in a financially viable way.

The public sector deficit in several countries is likely to negatively affect public expenditure on social services. The processes of marketisation and trends toward a new public-private mix, with more emphasis on private than public, are apparent in most social service sectors. Nevertheless, the active role of the state in regulating and financing social services is beneficial: it supports innovations in social services (improving the services and/or the capacity of the actors to provide the services) and helps to mobilise resources, either public (local, regional, national, European) or private.

Those forming policy in the regulation, financing and delivery of social services face many choices in how to solve the various issues related to social service provision and employment in the social services. The central role that social services have within the concept of sustainable development, both for meeting the needs of people and generating sustainable employment, should be recognised.

The sustainable financing of social services requires that the necessary levels of tax and duty are decided and that compliance is ensured. This will further depend on the commitment of governments to long-term social investments, also to help in achieving a better work-family life balance.

Governance that is responsive to the current demand for social services and pressures on public expenditure presupposes diversity in service supply and delivery (public-private mix, marketisation, decentralisation, networking and New Public Management). However, sufficient regulation by public authorities (including the setting of adequate standards of services) should be in place. Among other things, this relates to who the service providers are as well as what the forms of public support are.

A variety of measures is needed to ensure fiscal sustainability with regard to having long-term stability in public finances while also taking environmental issues into consideration. Given the continued pressure on the welfare states, it can be important to have automatic stabilisers in place to reduce the change in the level of unemployment over the business cycle. In the future, employment in social services could thus be an important factor in how to make it possible to reduce the level of unemployment.

Measures already implemented show that there could be a rule enacted even for a structural deficit. A limit to the structural deficit should in principle not be a hindrance to active fiscal stimulus in times of crisis; however, unless there has been emphasis on ensuring a surplus in prosperous times, it might imply a stronger focus on public sector spending. Nevertheless, a deficit in public sector finance can be changed both by a variation in expenditures and income.

A continuous focus on the tax base and broadening it by reducing loopholes and tax concessions also seem to be ways to ensure sustainable revenue for the public sector; this has also been in line with the trends in recent years. It emphasises that simply looking at tax-rates – whether for persons or companies – is not necessarily going to provide the full information in a comparative perspective. Moving towards a higher reliance on non-movable assets, including property, can also contribute to more stable development.

In the context of the crisis and fiscal consolidation, it is difficult to expect increased public investment in social services: the problem is that many countries must develop most social services in times of economic austerity and fiscal pressure on the welfare states that are not only temporary (due to crisis), but rather long-term (ageing and increasing pension system costs). Innovations in governance (that is regulation, financing and delivery of social services) may help to overcome the pressures emerging from fiscal consolidation by mobilising available national and local resources – public and private, formal and informal.

Social innovation plays an increasing role in social services, especially when understood and implemented as systematic change which could include several elements: focus on consumer needs and service quality standards; mobilising resources and combining different ways of financing social services – public and private; sufficient levels of public expenditure (dependent on sound public finance); a suitable governance framework which creates room for the participation of a broader range of actors and synergy of their actions.

Lastly, there is a growing concern about ensuring a sufficient labour supply in social services, especially in care services and promoting opportunities for employment in this sector for groups with low levels of employability. This means expanding job opportunities and attracting new employees to the sector from a variety of backgrounds (young graduates, disadvantaged groups, older workers, migrants and male workers). Thus the crucial issues include the profile and professional status of the jobs in the sector and the creation of a more age-balanced workforce by attracting young people. This is closely related to working conditions, investing in training and skills and developing lifelong learning and on-the-job training for employees in social services.

References

Adam, S. and Browne, J. 2011. *A Survey of the UK Tax System, Briefing Note No. 9*. The Institute for Fiscal Studies.

Adema, W. and Ladaigue, M. 2005. Net Social Expenditure. More Comprehensive Measures of Social Support. *OECD Social, Employment and Migration Papers 29*. Paris: OECD.

Adema, W., Fron, P. and Ladaique. M. 2011. Is the European Welfare State Really More Expensive? Indicators on Social Spending, 1980–2012; and a Manual to the OECD Social Expenditure Database (SOCX). *OECD Social, Employment and Migration Working Papers 124*. Paris: OECD.

Agnolucci, P. 2009. The effect of the German and British environmental taxation reforms: A Simple assessment. *Energy Policy*, 37: 3043–3051.

Ahonen, P., Hyyryläinen, E. and Salminen, A. 2006. Looking for governance configurations of European welfare states. *Journal of European Social Policy*, 16(2): 173–184.

Allan, J.P. and Scruggs, L. 2004. Political partisanship and welfare state reform in advanced industrial societies. *American Journal of Political Science*, 48: 496–512.

Albrecht, J. 2006. The use of consumption taxes to re-launch green tax reforms. *International Review of Law and Economics*, 26: 88–103.

Alsasua, J., Bilbao-Ubillos J. and Olaskoaga J. 2007. The EU integration process and the convergence of social protection benefits at national level. *International Journal of Social Welfare*, 16: 297–306.

Andersen, J.G. and Pedersen, J.J. 2007. *Continuity and Change in Danish Active Labour Market Policy: 1990–2007, CCWS Working Paper No. 2007-54*. Aalborg: Aalborg University.

Andersen, L.B., Christensen J.G. and Pallesen, T. 2008. The political allocation of incessant growth in the Danish public service, in *The State at Work: Public Sector Employment in Ten Western Countries* (Vol. 1), edited by H.-U. Derlien and B.G. Peters. Cheltenham/Northampton: Edward Elgar, pp. 249–267.

Andersen, T.M. 2011. *A flexicurity labour market in the great recession – the case of Denmark*. Paper prepared for CPB-ROA conference on flexibility of the labour market, Den Haag, January 2011. Available at: http://www.cpb.nl/sites/default/files/paper-flex-andersen_0.pdf [accessed: 22 November 2012].

Anderson, K.M. and Meyer, T. 2006. New social risks and pension reform in Germany and Sweden, in *Industrial Welfare States: Adapting Post-war Social Policies to New Social Risks*, edited by K. Armingeon and G. Bonoli. London and New York: Routledge, pp. 171–191.

Appleby J., Humphries R., Thompson J, and Galea A. 2013. *How is the Health and Social Care System Performing? Quarterly Monitoring Report*, 3 February. London: The King's Fund.

APSS – Asociace poskytovatelů sociálních služeb 2010. *Komparace služeb sociální péče o seniory.* [Online: Asociace poskytovatelů sociálních služeb České republiky, o.s.]. Available at: http://www.apsscr.cz/files/projekty/island_komparace.pdf [accessed: 21 May 2013].

APSS – Asociace poskytovatelů sociálních služeb 2013. *O projektu E-Qualin v sociálních službách v ČR.* [Online: Asociace poskytovatelů sociálních služeb České republiky, o.s.]. Available at http://www.apsscr.cz/cz/projekty/e-qalin [accessed: 21 May 2013].

Armingeon, K. 2006. Reconciling competing claims of the welfare state clientele, in *The Politics of Post-industrial Welfare States: Adapting Post-war Social Policies to New Social Risks*, edited by K. Armingeon and G. Bonoli. London: Routledge, pp. 100–122.

Armingeon, K. 2007. Active Labour Market Policy, International Organizations and Domestic Politics. *Journal of European Public Policy*, 14(6): 496–512.

Audit Commission 2007. *Seeing the Light: Innovation in Local Public Services.* Northampton: Belmont Press.

Aust, A. and Bönker, F. 2004. New Social Risks in a Conservative Welfare State: The Case of Germany, in *New Risks, New Welfare: The Transformation of the European Welfare State*, edited by P. Taylor-Gooby. New York: Oxford University Press, pp. 29–53.

Bahle, T. 2003. The Changing Institutionalization of Social Service in England and Wales, France and Germany: Is the Welfare State on the Retreat? *Journal of European Social Policy*, 13(1): 5–20.

Barr, N. 2012. *Economics of the Welfare State.* 5th Edition. Oxford: Oxford University Press.

Baumol, W.J. 1967. The macroeconomics of unbalanced growth. *American Economic Review*, 57: 415–426.

Bell, D. 2010. *The Impact of Devolution. Long-term Care Provision.* UK: Joseph Rowntree Foundation. [Online: JRF]. Available at: http://www.jrf.org.uk/sites/files/jrf/impact-of-devolution-long-term-care.pdf [accessed 13 December 2012].

Bell, D. and Bowes, A. 2012. Free Personal Care in Scotland (Almost) 10 Years On, in *Universal Coverage of Long-Term Care in the United States*, edited by D.A. Wolf and N. Folbre. New York: Russell Sage Foundation, pp. 79–102. [Online: RSF]. Available at: https://www.russellsage.org/sites/all/files/Wolf_LTC/Wolf_Universal-LTC_Chapter-5.pdf [accessed: 9 April 2013].

Bellis, A., Oakley, J., Sigala, M. and Dewson, S. 2011. *Identifying claimants' needs: Research into the capability of Jobcentre Plus advisers. Research Report No 748.* London: Department for Work and Pensions. Available at: https://www.gov.uk/government/uploads/system/uploads/attachment_data/file/214522/rrep748.pdf [accessed: 16 August 2013].

Bernhard, S. and Wolff, J. 2008. Contracting out placement services: Is assignment to private providers effective for needy job-seekers?, *IAB Discussion Paper 5/2008*. Available at: http://doku.iab.de/discussionpapers/2008/dp0508. pdf [accessed: 10 November 2012].

Beuermann, C. and Santarius, T. 2006. Ecological Tax Reform in Germany: handling two hot potatoes at the same time. *Energy Policy*, 34: 917–929.

Blackburn, P. 2011. *Children's Nurseries UK Market Report 2011*. London: Laing and Buisson. Available at: http://www.laingbuisson.co.uk/Portals/1/ PressReleases/ChildrensNurseries_11_PR.pdf [accessed: 12 August 2013].

Blank, R. 2000. When Can Policy Makers Rely on Private Markets? The Effective Provision of Social Services. *The Economic Journal*, 110(462): 34–49.

Bloch, C. 2010. *Towards a conceptual framework for measuring public sector innovation. Module 1 – Conceptual Framework*. The joint Nordic research project Measuring innovation in the public sector in the Nordic countries (MEPIN).

BMFSFJ – Bundesministerium für Familie, Senioren, Frauen und Jugend. 2013. *Vierter Zwischenbericht zur Evaluation des Kinderförderungsgesetzes*. Paderborn: Bonifatius GmbH. [Online: BMFSJF]. Available at: http://www. bmfsfj.de/RedaktionBMFSFJ/Broschuerenstelle/Pdf-Anlagen/Kif_C3_B6G-Vierter-Zwischenbericht-zur-Evaluation-des-Kinderf_C3_B6rderungsgese tzes,property=pdf,bereich=bmfsfj,sprache=de,rwb=true.pdf [accessed: 25 May 2013].

Bode, I. 2006. Disorganised welfare mixes. *Journal of European Social Policy*, 16(4): 346–359.

Bonoli, G. 2006. New social risks and the politics of post-industrial social policies, in *The Politics of Post-Industrial Welfare States. Adapting Post-war Social Policies to New Social Risks*, edited by K. Armingeon and G. Bonoli. London/ New York: Routledge, pp. 3–26.

Bonoli, G. 2007. Time Matters: Postindustrialization, New Social Risks and Welfare State Adaptations in Advanced Industrial Democracies. *Comparative Political Studies* 40: 495–520.

Bönker, F., Hill, M. and Marzanati, A. 2010. Towards marketization and centralization? The changing role of local government in long-term care in England, France, Germany and Italy, in *The Provision of Public Services in Europe*, edited by H. Wollman and G. Marcou. Cheltenham/Northampton: Edward Elgar, pp. 97–119.

Borghi, V. and van Berkel, R. 2007. Individualised service provision in an era of activation and new governance, *International Journal of Sociology and Social Policy*, 27(9/10): 413–424.

Börzel, T. and Risse, T. 2007. Europeanization: The Domestic Impact of European Union Politics, in *Handbook of European Union Politics*, edited by K.E. Jørgensen, M. Pollack, and B. Rosamond. London: Sage, pp. 483–504.

Bosch, G. and Lehndorff, S. 2001. *New Forms of Employment and Working Time in the Service Economy (NESY)*. Final Report. TSER Programme of the European

Commission, Directorate General for Science, Research and Development. Wissenschaftzentrum Nordhein-Westfalen, Institut Arbeit und Technik (IAT).

Bredgaard, T. and Larsen, F. 2007. Implementing public employment policy: what happens when non-public agencies take over? *International Journal of Sociology and Social Policy*, 27(7/8): 287–300.

Brewer, M., Emmerson, C. and Miller. H. (eds) 2011. *The IFS Green Budget.* London: The Institute for Fiscal Studies.

Brodsky, J., Habib, J. and Hirschfeld, M. 2003. *Key Policy Issues in Long-term Care.* Geneva: World Health Organisation.

Bruttel, O. 2005a. *New Private Delivery Arrangements: An Initial Evaluation Using Institutional Economics*, in: *Contractualism in Employment Services*, edited by E. Sol and M. Westerveld. Brussels: Kluwer Law International, pp. 209–230.

Bruttel, O. 2005b. *Contracting-out and Governance Mechanisms in the Public Employment Services, WZB Discussion Paper SP I 05-109.* Available at: http://www.econstor.eu/bitstream/10419/44013/1/501168788.pdf [accessed: 30 November 2012].

Brys, B., Matthews, S. and Owens, J. 2011. Tax Reform Trends in OECD Countries. *OECD Taxation Working Papers, No. 1.* Paris: OECD.

Caluori, J. 2009. *Childcare and the Recession – Summary. Policy Insight Paper 3.* UK: Daycare Trust. National Childcare Campaign. Available at: http://www.daycaretrust.org.uk/data/files/Policy/childcare_and_the_recession__summary.pdf [accessed: 12 November 2012].

Carmel, E. and Papadopoulos, T. 2003. The new governance of social security in Britain, in *Understanding Social Security: Issues for Social Policy and Practice*, edited by J. Millar. Bristol: Policy Press, pp. 31–52.

Castles, F.G. 2003. The world turned upside down: below replacement fertility, changing preferences and family-friendly public policy in 21 OECD countries. *Journal of European Social Policy*, 13(3): 209–227.

Castles, F.G. 2004. *The Future of the Welfare State.* Oxford: Oxford University Press.

Caulier-Grice, J., Davies, A., Patrick, R. and Norman, W. 2012. *Social Innovation Overview: A Deliverable of the Project: The Theoretical, Empirical and Policy Foundations for Building Social Innovation in Europe (TEPSIE).* European Commission – 7th Framework Programme. Brussels: European Commission, DG Research, The Young Foundation.

CCCABC. 2007. *Good Governance of Child Care: What does it mean? What does it look like? Introduction, Denmark Model.* Vancouver: Coalition of Child Care Advocates of BC. Available at: http://www.cccabc.bc.ca/cccabcdocs/governance/ggcc_denmark_model.pdf. [accessed: 5 October 2012].

CEDEFOP 2010. *Quality assurance in the social care sector: the role of training.* Luxembourg: Publications Office of the European Union.

CEDEFOP 2011. Assuring quality in vocational education and training. The role of accrediting VET providers. *Cedefop Reference series, 90*, Luxembourg:

European Centre for the Development of Vocational Training. Available at: http://www.cedefop.europa.eu/EN/Files/3061_en.pdf [accessed: 3 November 2012].

Cerami, A. 2006. *Social Policy in Central and Eastern Europe. The Emergence of a New European Welfare Regime*. Berlin: LIT Verlag.

CFCS 2011. *Briefing note on the Report of the Commission on Funding of Care and Support*. London: Commission on Funding of Care and Support. Available at: http://webarchive.nationalarchives.gov.uk/20130221130239/http://www.dilnotcommission.dh.gov.uk/files/2011/09/Technical-Briefing-Note.pdf [accessed: 13 August 2013].

Choe, R., Emmerson, C., Miles, D. and Shaw, J. 2007. *The IFS Green Budget*. London: Institute for Fiscal Studies.

Christensen, T. and Lægreid, P. (eds) 2007. *Transcending New Public Management: The Transformation of Public Sector Reforms*. Aldershot: Ashgate.

Christensen, T. and Lægreid, P. 2010. Increased Complexity in Public sector Organizations – the challenges of Combining NPM and Post-NPM, in *Governance of Public Sector Organizations: Proliferation, Aautonomy and Performance*, edited by P. Lægreid and K. Verhoest. Basingstoke: Palgrave Macmillan, pp. 255–275.

Christensen, J. G. and Pallesen, T. 2008. Public employment trends and the organization of public sector tasks, in *The State at Work: Public Sector Employment in Ten Western Countries* (Vol. 2), edited by H.-U. Derlien, and B.G. Peters. Cheltenham/Northampton: Edward Elgar, pp. 7–32.

Citi, M. and Rhodes, M. 2007. New Modes of Governance in the European Union: A Critical Survey and Analysis, in *Handbook of European Union Politics*, edited by K.E. Jørgensen, M. Pollack, and B. Rosamond. London: Sage, pp. 463–482.

Clinch, J.P., Dunne, L. and Dresner, S. 2006. Environmental and wider implications of political impediments to environmental tax reform, *Energy Policy*, 34: 960–970.

Colombo, F., Llena-Nozal, A., Mercier, J. and Tjadens, F. 2011. *Help Wanted: Providing and Paying for Long-Term Care*. Paris: OECD.

Comas-Herrera, A., Wittenberg, R. and Pickard, L. 2010. The Long Road to Universalism? Recent Developments in the Financing of Long-term Care in England. *Social Policy and Administration*, 44(4): 375–391.

Cook, B. 2008. *National, regional and local employment policies in Sweden and the United Kingdom. Working Paper No. 08-05*. Callaghan: Centre of Full Employment and Equity.

Council of Europe 2008. *European Social Charter, 28th Report of the Implementation of the European Social Charter submitted by the Government of Denmark*. Strasbourg: Council of Europe Secretariat.

Crespy, A. 2010. When 'Bolkenstein' is trapped by the French anti-liberal discourse: a discursive-institutionalist account of preference formation in the realm of European Union multi-level politics. *Journal of European Public Policy*, 17(8): 1253–1270.

Crespy, A. and Gajewska, K. 2010. New Parliament, New Cleavages after the Eastern Enlargement? The Conflict over the Service Directives as an Opposition between the Liberals and the Regulators? *Journal of Common Market Studies*, 48(5): 1185–1208.

Cusack, T.R., Notermans, T. and Rein, M. 1989. Political-economic aspects of public employment, *European Journal of Political Research*, 17: 471–500.

ČSÚ/CZSO (Czech Statistical Office) 2008. *Dlouhodobý vývoj předškolního vzdělávání v České Republice*. Publication of CZSO 3310-08. Praha: CZSO.

ČSÚ/CZSO (Czech Statistical Office) 2011. *Česká republika od roku 1989 v číslech*. Praha: CZSO.

ČSÚ/CZSO (Czech Statistical Office) 2012. *Trh práce v ČR 2000–2011*. Praha: CZSO.

Daguerre, A. 2006. Childcare policies in diverse European welfare states, in *Industrial Welfare States: Adapting Post-war Social Policies to New Social Risks*, edited by K. Armingeon and G. Bonoli. London and New York: Routledge, pp. 211–226.

Daly, M. 2010. Shifts in family policy in the UK under New Labour. *Journal of European Social Policy*, 20(5): 433–443.

Damgaard, B. and Torfing, J. 2010. Network governance of active employment policy: the Danish experience. *Journal of European Social Policy*, 20(3): 248–262.

Derlien, H.-U. 2008. The German public service: between tradition and transformation, in *The State at Work: Public Sector Employment in Ten Western Countries* (vol. 1), edited by H.-U. Derlien and B.G. Peters. Cheltenham/Northampton: Edward Elgar, pp. 170–195.

Di John, J. 2011. Taxation, development state capacity and poverty reduction. *International Journal of Social Welfare*, 20: 270–279.

Dilnot, A, Warner, N. and Williams, J. 2011. *Fairer Care Funding: The Report of the Commission on Funding of Care and Support*. London: Commission on Funding of Care and Support.

Dingeldey, I. 2009. Changing Forms of Governance as Welfare State Restructuring. Activating Labour Market Policies in Denmark, the UK and Germany, in *Governance of Welfare State Reform: A Cross National and Cross Sectoral Comparison of Policy and Politics*, edited by I. Dingeldey, and H. Rothgang. Cheltenham: Edward Elgar, pp. 69–93.

Dingeldey, I. and Rothgang, H. (eds) 2009. *Governance of Welfare State Reform, A Cross National and Cross Sectional Comparison of Policy and Politics*. Cheltenham: Edward Elgar.

Dingeldey, I. 2011a. Fragmented Governance Continued. The German Case, in *The Governance of Active Welfare States in Europe*, edited by R. van Berkel, W. de Graaf and T. Sirovátka. Basingstoke: Palgrave Macmillan, pp. 62–85.

Dingeldey, I. 2011b. Moving towards Integration whilst Maintaining Segmentation, in *Unemployment Protection Systems and Labour Market Change in Europe*, edited by J. Clasen and D. Clegg. Oxford: Oxford University Press, pp. 55–75.

Donberger, S. and Jensen, P. 1997. Contracting out by the public sector: theory, evidence, prospects. *Oxford Review of Economic Policy*, 13(4): 67–78.

Dresner, S. et al. 2006. Social and political responses to ecological tax reform in Europe: an introduction to the special issue. *Energy Policy*, 34: 895–904.

DT 2013. *Childcare Costs Survey 2013*. London: Daycare Trust and Family and Parenting Institute. Available at: http://www.daycaretrust.org.uk/data/files/Research/costs_surveys/Childcare_Costs_Survey_2013.pdf [accessed; 13 August 2013].

DWP 2009. *Britain's Recovery: Achieving Full Employment*. London: Department for Work and Pensions.

DWP 2010. *Universal Credit: Welfare that Works*. London: Department for Work and Pensions. [Online: Department for Work and Pensions]. Available at: https://www.gov.uk/government/uploads/system/uploads/attachment_data/file/181145/universal-credit-full-document.pdf [accessed on 13 August 2013].

DWP 2012. *The Work Programme*. [Online: Department for Work and Pensions]. Available at: https://www.gov.uk/government/uploads/system/uploads/attachment_data/file/49884/the-work-programme.pdf [accessed: 13 August 2013].

DWP 2013. *Universal Credit. Local Support Services Framework*. [Online: Department for Work and Pensions]. Available at: https://www.gov.uk/government/uploads/system/uploads/attachment_data/file/181395/uc-local-service-support-framework.pdf [accessed: 16 August 2013].

Elias, P. 1997. Occupational Classification (ISCO-88): Concepts, Methods, Reliability, Validity and Cross-National Comparability. *OECD Labour Market and Social Policy Occasional Papers, No. 20*. Paris: OECD.

Entwistle, T. and Martin, S. 2005. From Competition to Collaboration in Public Service Delivery: A New Agenda for Research. *Public Administration* 83(1): 233–242.

Esping-Andersen, G. 1990. *The Three Worlds of Welfare Capitalism*. Princeton, NJ: Princeton University Press.

Esping-Andersen, G. 1999. *The Social Foundations of Postindustrial Economies*. Oxford: Oxford University Press.

Esping-Andersen, G. 2008. *The Incomplete Revolution: Adapting to Women's New Roles*. Malden, MA: Polity Press.

Eurochild 2010. *Family policies that work best for children — fighting child poverty and promoting child well-being. The Family and Parenting Support Thematic Working Group study visit to Sweden and Denmark, 26–30 April 2010*. Brussels: EC. Available at: http://www.eurochild.org/fileadmin/Events/2010/04_Study_Visit/FPS%20Study%20Visit%202010_REPORT1%262.pdf [accessed; 10 April 2012].

Eurofound – European Foundation for the Improvement of Living and Working Conditions 2006. *Employment developments in childcare services for school-age children*. Luxembourg: Office for Official Publications of the European Communities.

Eurofound – European Foundation for the Improvement of Living and Working Conditions 2007a. *Fourth European Working Conditions Survey.* Luxembourg: Office for Official Publications of the European Communities.

Eurofound – European Foundation for the Improvement of Living and Working Conditions 2007b. *Working time flexibility in European companies.* Luxembourg: Office for Official Publications of the European Communities.

Eurofound – European Foundation for the Improvement of Living and Working Conditions 2007c. *Extended and unusual working hours in European companies,* Luxembourg: Office for Official Publications of the European Communities.

Eurofound – European Foundation for the Improvement of Living and Working Conditions 2008. *Employment security and employability: A contribution to the flexicurity debate.* Luxembourg: Office for Official Publications of the European Communities.

Eurofound – European Foundation for the Improvement of Living and Working Conditions 2010. *European Company Survey 2009: An overview.* Luxembourg: Office for Official Publications of the European Communities.

Eurofound – European Foundation for the Improvement of Living and Working Conditions 2012. *Fifth European Working Conditions Survey: Overview Report.* Luxembourg: Publications Office of the European Union.

European Commission 2006. *Implementing the Community Lisbon programme: Social services of general interest in the European Union.* COM (2006) 177 final. Brussels: European Commission.

European Commission 2007a. *Services of general interest, including social services of general interest: a new European commitment.* COM (2007) 724 final. Brussels: European Commission.

European Commission 2007b. *White Paper. Together for Health: A Strategic Approach for the EU 2008-13.* Brussels: European Commission.

European Commission 2008a. *Biennial Report on social services of general interest.* Commission staff working document. Brussels: European Commission.

European Commission 2008b. *Long-term care in the European Union.* Brussels: European Commission.

European Commission 2009a. *The provision of childcare services A comparative review of 30 European countries.* Brussels: European Commission.

European Commission 2009b. *Structures of Education and Training Systems in Europe. Denmark. 2009/10 Edition.* Brussels: European Commission.

European Commission 2010. *Second Biennial Report on social services of general interest. Commission Staff Working Document, SEC (2010) 1284 final.* Brussels: European Commission.

European Commission 2011a. *Taxation trends in the European Union.* Brussels: European Commission.

European Commission 2011b. *Innovation Union Scoreboard 2010. The Innovation Union's performance scoreboard for Research and Innovation,* 1 February 2011. Brussels: European Commission. Available at: http://www. proinno-europe.eu/metrics [accessed: 21 January 2013].

Eurostat 2012a. *Statistics in Focus 55/2012.*

Eurostat 2012b. *Statistical database.* [Online: Eurostat]. Available at: http://epp.eurostat.ec.europa.eu/portal/page/portal/statistics/themes [accessed: various dates in 2012–2013].

Eurostat. 2012c. *European Union Statistics on Employment of women.* [Online: Eurostat]. Available at: www.appsso.eurostat.ec.europa.eu [accessed: March 23 2013].

Evers, A., Lewis, J. and Riedel, B. 2005. Developing child-care provision in England and Germany: problems of governance. *Journal of European Social Policy*, 15(3): 195–209.

Fagnani, J. and Math, A. 2010. Recent reforms in French and German family policies. Similar challenges, different responses. *Sociologia, problemas e práticas* 64: 11–35.

Falkner, G. 2000. The Council or the Social Partners? EC Social Policy between diplomacy and collective bargaining. *Journal of European Public Policy*, 5(5): 705–724.

Farnsworth, K. 2004. Welfare through Work: An Audit of Occupational Social Protection at the turn of the New Century. *Social Policy & Administration*, 38(5): 437–455.

Fernández, J.-L., Forder, J., Truckeschitz, B., Rokosova, M. and McDaid, D. 2009. *How can European states design efficient, equitable and sustainable funding systems for long-term care for older people? Policy Brief No. 11.* Copenhagen: World Health Organisation Europe.

Finch, N. 2008. Family policies in the UK, in *Family Policies in the Context of Family Change*, edited by I. Ostner and C. Schmitt. Wiesbaden: VS Verlag, pp. 129–154.

Fleckenstein, T. 2010. Party Politics and Childcare: Comparing the Expansion of Service Provision in England and Germany. *Social Policy & Administration*, 44(7): 789–807.

Forstater, M. 2006. Green Jobs. Public Service Employment and Environmental Sustainability. *Challenge*, 49(4): 58–72.

Fröhlich, K. 2006. *An Evaluation of Recent Child Care Reforms. Discussion Paper. DIW Berlin and IZA.* Berlin and Bonn: DIW and IZA. Available at: http://www.diw.de/documents/dokumentenarchiv/17/44655/20060905_wrohlich_paper_vfs.pdf [accessed: October 7, 2012].

FOA – Fag og arbejde 2009. *Family day-care in Denmark.* Copenhagen: The Danish Trade Union FOA – Trade and Labour. Available at: http://applikationer.foa.dk/Publikationer/pjecer/Paedagogisk/FamilyDayCareInDenmark.pdf [accessed: 4 November 2012].

Fujisawa, R. and Colombo, F. 2009. The Long-Term Care Workforce: Overview and Strategies to Adapt Supply to a Growing Demand. *OECD Health Working Papers, No. 44.* Paris: OECD Publishing.

Gathmann, Ch. and Sass, B. 2011. *Female Labour Supply and Childcare: An Evaluation of Germany's New Childcare Subsidy.* Vienna: Vienna University.

Available at: http://econ.univie.ac.at/uploads/tx_cal/media/gathmann.pdf. [accessed: 10 October 2012].

Giddens, A. 1998. *The Third Way. The Renewal of Social Democracy.* Oxford: Oxford University Press.

Gíslason, I.V. and Eydal, G.B. (eds). 2011. *Parental leave, childcare and gender equality in the Nordic countries.* Copenhagen: Nordic Council of Ministers.

Gleckman, H. 2010. *Long-term care financing reform: lessons from the U.S. and abroad.* The Urban Institute. Available at: http://www.commonwealthfund. org/~/media/Files/Publications/Fund%20Report/2010/Feb/1368_Gleckman_ longterm_care_financing_reform_lessons_US_abroad.pdf. [accessed: 20 October 2012].

Gough, I. 2011. From financial crisis to fiscal crisis, in *Social Policy in Challenging Times. Economic crisis and welfare systems*, edited by K. Farnsworth and Z. Irving. Bristol: Policy Press, pp. 49–64.

Gough, I. and Sharkh, M.A. 2011. Financing welfare regimes: mapping heterogeneous revenue structures, *International Journal of Social Welfare*, 20: 280–291.

Government of Denmark. 2008. *National Strategy Report 2008–2010 (NSR).* Copenhagen.

Government 2012. [Online: Official website of British Governments called]. Available at: www.direct.gov.uk [accessed: 12 April 2013].

Graefe, P. 2004. Personal Services in the Post-industrial Economy: Adding Nonprofits to the welfare mix. *Social Policy & Administration*, 38(5): 456–469.

Greer, S. 2011. The weakness of strong policies and the strength of weak policies: Law, experimentalist governance, and supporting coalitions in European Health Care Policy. *Regulation and Governance*, 5: 187–203.

Greve, B. 1996. Indication of Social Policy Convergence in Europe. *Social Policy & Administration*, 30(4): 348–367.

Greve, B. 2002. *Vouchers. Nye styrings- og leveringsmåder i velfærdsstaten.* København: DJØF's forlag.

Greve, B. 2004. *The Times They Are Changing? Crisis and the Welfare State.* Wiley: Blackwell.

Greve, B. 2006. Is There a Demographic Time-bomb?, in *The Future of the Welfare State. European and Global Perspectives*, edited by B. Greve. Aldershot: Ashgate.

Greve, B. 2007a. *Occupational Welfare – Winners and Losers.* Cheltenham: Edward Elgar.

Greve, B. 2007b. What Characterises the Nordic Welfare State Model. *Journal of Social Sciences*, 3(2): 43–51.

Greve, B. 2008. What is Welfare? *Central European Journal of Public Policy*, 2(1): 52–75.

Greve.B. 2009. Can Choice in Welfare States Be Equitable? *Social Policy & Administration*, 43(6): 543–556.

Greve, B. 2010. Taxation, equality and social cohesion. European experiences, in *Challenges of social cohesion in times of crisis: Euro-Latin American Dialogue*, edited by M. Zupi, and E. Puertas. Madrid: FIIAPP.

Greve, B. 2011. Editorial Introduction: Overview and Conclusion. *Social Policy & Administration*, 45(4): 333–337.

Greve, B. (ed.) 2013. *Routledge Handbook of the Welfare State*, Oxford: Routledge.

Grossman, E. and Woll, C. 2011. The French Debate over the Bolkenstein directive. *Comparative European Politics*, 9(3): 344–366.

Habart, P. 2007. Týrání a zanedbávání seniorů v zařízeních ústavní péče v České republice. [Online]. Available at: http://www.cspv.cz/dokumenty/kongres2006/HP%2013/Pavel%20Habart.pdf [accessed: 3 October 2012].

Hagemann, R. 2012. Fiscal Consolidation: Part 6. What Are the Best Policy Instruments for Fiscal Consolidation? *OECD Economics Department Working Papers, No. 937*. OECD Publishing.

Hantrais, L. 2003. *Family Policy Matters*. Bristol: Policy Press.

Heichel, S., Pape, J. and Sommerer, T. 2005. Is there convergence in convergence research? An overview of empirical studies on policy convergence, *Journal of European Public Policy* 12(5): 817–840.

Heinemann, S. 2008. Women's employment and part-time employment in the public service, in *The State at Work: Public Sector Employment in Ten Western Countries* (vol. 2), edited by H.-U. Derlien, H.-U. and B. G. Peters. Cheltenham/Northampton: Edward Elgar, pp. 85–121.

Heinicke, K. and Thomsen, S. 2010. *The Social Long-term Care Insurance in Germany: Origin, Situation, Threats and Perspectives. Discussion paper No. 10-012*. Center for European Economic Research. Available at: ftp://ftp.zew.de/pub/zew-docs/dp/dp10012.pdf [accessed: 19 October 2012].

Heise, A. 2008. European Economic governance: what is it, where are we and where do we go? *International Journal of Public Policy*, 3(1/2): 1–19.

Hemerijck, A. 2002. The Self-Transformation of the European Social Model(s), in *Why we Need a New Welfare State*, Esping-Andresen. G. et al. Oxford: Oxford University Press, pp. 173–213.

Hendeliowitz, J. 2008. *Danish Employment Policy. National Target Setting, Regional Performance Management and Local Delivery*. Roskilde: Employment Region Copenhagen & Zealand.

Hiilamo, H. 2008. *Promoting Children's Welfare in the Nordic Countries. Reports of the Ministry of Social Affairs and Health*. Helsinky: Yliopistopaino. Available at: http://www.policyalternatives.ca/sites/default/files/uploads/publications/National%20Office/2009/04/Promoting%20Children%27s%20Welfare%20in%20the%20Nordic%20Countries.pdf [accessed: 5 October 2012].

Hill, M. and Hupe, P. 2002. *Implementing Public Policy. Governance in Theory and in Practice*. Sage: London.

HM Treasury 2010. *Spending review 2010*. [Online: HM Treasury]. Available at: https://www.gov.uk/government/uploads/system/uploads/attachment_data/file/203826/Spending_review_2010.pdf [accessed: 8 July 2013].

HMRC 2013. *What are tax credits?* [Online: HM Revenue and Customs]. Available at: http://www.hmrc.gov.uk/taxcredits/start/who-qualifies/what-are-taxcredits. htm#8 [accessed: 13 August 2013].

Hoffmann, F. and Leichsenring, K. 2011. *Quality management by result-oriented indicators: Towards benchmarking in residential care for older people. Policy Brief.* Wien: European Centre for Social Welfare Policy and Research.

Hogwood, B.W. 2008. Public employment in Britain: from working in to working for the public sector, in *The State at Work: Public Sector Employment in Ten Western Countries* (vol. 1) edited by H.-U. Derlien and B.G. Peters. Cheltenham/Northampton: Edward Elgar, 19–39.

Höhnen, P. 2011. *Elderly Care in Denmark. Walqing social partnership series 2011.10.* Roskilde: Roskilde University.

Holdsworth, L. and Billings, J. 2009 (with update of appendix on March 2011). *Quality in Long Term Care. United Kingdom (England).* [Online: Canterbury, Interlinks]. Available at: http://interlinks.euro.centre.org/sites/default/files/ WP4_UK_NationalReport_final.pdf [accessed: 25 October 2012].

Holman, D. and McClelland, C. 2011. *Job Quality in Growing and Declining Economic Sectors of the EU, Walqing working paper 2011.3.* Manchester: Walqing.

Hora, O. and Sirovátka, T. 2012. *Srovnání efektů aktivní politiky zaměstnanosti v České republice v období růstu (2007) a během první fáze krize (2009).* Praha: VÚPSV – výzkumné centrum Brno.

Horák, P. and Horáková, M. 2009. Role liniových pracovníků ve veřejné politice. *Sociologicky casopis/Czech Sociological Review,* 45(2): 369–395.

Horák, P. 2010. Možnosti a aktuální způsoby realizace aktivační politiky na trhu práce ve dvou regionech ČR: výpovědi expertů z úřadů práce a z nestátních organizací., in *Nová sociální rizika na trhu práce a potřeby reformy české veřejné politiky,* edited by Winkler, J. and Klimplová, L. Brno: Masarykova univerzita, 186–198.

Horák, P. 2011. Stabilita a flexibilita organizací zainteresovaných do administrace a realizace aktivních programů a sociálních služeb na lokálních trzích práce, in *Institucionální změna a veřejná politika. Analýza politiky zaměstnanosti,* edited by J. Winkler. and M. Žižlavský. Brno: Masarykova univerzita, pp. 75–122.

Horák, P. 2012. Realizace veřejných programů a sociálních služeb na regionálních trzích práce optikou stability a flexibility státních a nestátních organizací. *Fórum sociální politiky,* 6(2): 9–17.

Howard, Ch. 1997. *The Hidden Welfare State. Tax Expenditures and Social Policy in the United States.* Princeton: Princeton University Press.

Højlund, H. 2009. Hybrid inclusion – the new consumerism of Danish welfare services. *Journal European Social Policy,* 19(5): 421–431.

Hübenthal, M. and Ifland, A.M. 2011. Risks for children? Recent developments in early childcare policy. *Childhood,* 18(1): 114–127. Available at: http://chd. sagepub.com/content/18/1/114 [accessed: 22 October 2012].

Huber, E. and Stephens, J.D. 2006. Combatting Old and New Social Risks, in *The politics of post-industrial welfare states: adapting post-war social policies to new social risks*, edited by K. Armingeon and G. Bonoli. London: Routledge, pp. 143–168.

Huber, M., Maucher, M. and Sak, B. 2006. *Study on Social and Health Services of General Interest. Final Synthesis Report.* Prepared for DG Employment, Social Affairs and Equal Opportunities. DG EMPL/E/4 VC/2006/0131. Vienna: European Centre for Social Welfare Policy and Research.

Hubert, A. et al. 2010. *Empowering people, driving change: Social innovation in the European Union.* Brussels: European Commission.

Humphries, R. 2013. *Paying for social care. Beyond Dilnot.* London: The King's Fund. Available at: http://www.kingsfund.org.uk/sites/files/kf/field/field_publication_summary/social-care-funding-paper-may13.pdf [accessed: 14 August 2013].

IAQ (Institut Arbeit und Qualifikation) 2007. *Women in Low-Skill Work.* Study for the European Parliament's committee on Women's Rights and Gender Equality. Brussels, European Parlament: Universität Duisburg-Essen.

Institute of Public Care 2012. *People Who Pay For Care: An analysis of self-funders in the social care market.* Oxford: Institute of Public Care at Oxford Brookes University. Available at: http://ipc.brookes.ac.uk/publications/index.php?absid=646 [accessed: 14 August 2013].

Jacobi, L., and Kluve, J. 2007. Before and After the Hartz Reforms: The Performance of Active Labour Market Policy in Germany. *Journal for Labour Market Research* 40: 45–64.

Jacquot, S., Ledoux, B. and Palier, B. 2011. A Means to Changing European Resources: The EU and Reconciliation of Paid Work and Private Life. *European Journal of Social Security*, 13(1): 26–46.

Jak do školky 2013. [Online: *Internetový portal Jakdoskolky.cz.*]. Available at: http://www.jakdoskolky.cz/soukrome-jesle/. [accessed: 7 January 2013].

Jeřábek, H. 2005. Péče o staré lidi v rodině (východiska, klasifikace, kritické momenty, in *Rodinná péče o staré lidi.* edited by Jeřádek, H. Praha: Karlova Univerzita, pp. 9–19.

Jensen, C. 2008. Worlds of welfare services and transfers. *Journal of European Social Policy*, 18(2): 151–162.

Jensen, C. 2009. Determinants of welfare services provision after the Golden Age. *International Journal of Social Welfare*, 20: 125–134.

Jesle-jesličky 2013. Available at: http://www.jesle-jeslicky.cz/tag/jesle-praha/page/2/ [Accessed 7 January 2013].

Jessop, B. 1995. Towards a Schumpeterian Workfare Regime in Britain? Reflections on Regulation, Governance, and Welfare State. *Environment and Planning*, 27(10): 1613–1626.

Jessop, B. 1999. The Changing Governance of Welfare: Recent Trends in its Primary Functions, Scale and Modes of Coordination, *Social Policy & Administration*, 33(4): 348–359.

Johansson, Å. , Heady, C., Arnold, J., Brys, B. and Vartia, L. 2008. Taxation and Economic Growth. *OECD Economic Department Working Papers, No. 620*. Paris: OECD.

Jordan, A. 2005. Policy convergence: a passing fad or a new integrating focus in European Union studies? *Journal of European Public Policy*, 12(5): 944–953

Kalužná, D. 2008. *Main features of the public employment service in the Czech Republic. OECD social, employment and migration papers No. 74*. Paris: OECD.

Keman, H., van Keersbergen, K. and Vis, B. 2006. Political parties and new social risks: The double backlash against Social Democracy and Christian Democracy, in *The Politics of Post-Industrial Welfare States. Adapting Post-war Social Policies to New Social Risks*, edited by K. Armingeon and G. Bonoli. London and New York: Routledge, pp. 27–51.

Kemmerling, A. and Bruttel, O. 2005. *New Politics in German Labour Market Policy? The Implications of the Recent Hartz Reforms for the German Welfare State. Discussion Paper SP1, No. 2005-101*. Berlin: Wissenschaftszentrum Berlin fuer Sozialforschung,

Klein, J.-L. and Harrison, D. 2007. *L'innovation sociale. Émergence et effects sur la transformation des sociétés*. Montréal: Press de L'Université du Québec.

Klok, J., Larsen, A., Dahl, A. and Hansen, K. 2006. Ecological Tax Reform in Denmark: history and social acceptability. *Energy Policy*, 34: 905–916.

Knill, Ch. and Lehmkuhl, D.1999. How Europe Matters: Different Mechanisms of Europeanization, *European integration online papers (EIoP)*, ISSN-e 1027-5193, No. 3.

Koch, P. and Hauknes, J. 2005. *On Innovation in the Public Sector.* Publin Report D20. Oslo: NIFU STEP.

Kolářová, J. 2007. *Klíč k jeslím*. Praha: Gender Studies.

Konle-Seidl, R. 2008. *Changes in the governance of employment services since 2003. IAB Discussion Paper No. 6/2008*. Nürnberg. IAB.

Korpi, W. 1999. *Gender, Class and Patterns of Inequalities in Different Types of Welfare States*, Conference of RC 10 of the International Sociological Association, Prague, September 9–12, 1999.

Korpi, W. 2003. Welfare-State Regress in Western Europe, Institutions, Globalization, and Europeanization. *Annual Review of Sociology*, 29: 589–609.

Korpi, W. and Palme, J. 2003. New politics and class politics in the context of austerity and globalization: Welfare state regime. *American Political Science Review* 97: 425–446.

Koske, I. 2010. After the crisis: Bringing German Public Finances back to a sustainable path. *Economics Department Working Paper No. 766*. Paris, OECD.

Kristiansen, J. 2011. Arbejdsgiveres frie valg af arbejdskraft og produktionssted, in *Frit valg. Velfærd i Den Europæiske Union*, edited by Poulsen, S. and Jørgensen, S. København: Jurist- og Økonomforbundets Forlag, pp. 49–66.

Kuchařová, V., Bareš, P., Höhne, S., Nešporová, O., Svobodová, K., Šťastná, A., Plasová, B. and Žáčková, L. 2009. *Péče o děti předškolního a raného školního věku.* Praha: VÚPSV.

Kuchařová, V. and Svobodová, K. 2006. *Síť zařízení denní péče o děti předškolního věku v ČR.* Praha: VÚPSV.

Kühnle, S. 1999. *Survival of the European Welfare State. Working Paper No. 9.* Oslo: Arena.

Kumlin, S. 2010. Claiming Blame and Giving Credit: Unintended Effects of How Government and Opposition Frame the Europeanization of Welfare. *QoG Working Papers Series, 2010: 26.* Gothenburg: Quality of Government Institute, University of Gothenburg.

Kvist, J. 2011. *Pensions, Health Care and Long-term Care – Denmark. ASISP Annual Report 2011 prepared for EC.* Brussels: EC.

Kvist, J. and Saari, J. (eds) 2007. *The Europeanisation of Social Protection.* Bristol: Policy Press.

Kvist, J. and Greve, B. 2011. Has the Nordic Welfare Model been Transformed? *Social Policy & Administration*, 45(2): 146–160.

La Cour, A. and Højlund, H. 2007. Voluntary Social Work as Paradox. *Acta Sociologica* 68(4): 41–55.

Laing, W. 2012. *Care of Elderly People UK Market Survey 2011/2012.* London: Laing and Buisson.

Land, H. and Lewis, J. 1998. Gender, Care and the Changing Role of the State in the UK, in *Gender, Social Care and Welfare State Restructuring in Europe*, edited by J. Lewis. Aldershot: Ashgate, pp. 51–84.

Land, H. and Himmelweit, S. 2010. *Who cares, who pays? A report on personalization in social care prepared for UNISON.* London: UNISON. Available at: http://www.unison.org.uk/acrobat/19020.pdf [accessed: 5 October 2012].

Larsen, T. P. and Taylor-Gooby, P. 2004. New Risks at the EU Level; Spillover from Open Market Policies ?, in *New Risks, New Welfare: The Transformation of the European Welfare State*, edited by P. Taylor-Gooby. New York: Oxford University Press, pp. 181–208.

Later Life in the United Kingdom 2012. [Online: London: Age UK]. Available at: http://www.ageuk.org.uk/Documents/EN-GB/Factsheets/Later_Life_UK_factsheet.pdf?dtrk=true [accessed 5 October 2012].

Lefresne, F. 2010. A comparative overview of unemployment benefit: striving to provide security for employees in their career paths, in *Unemployment benefit systems in Europe and North America: reforms and crisis source*, edited by F. Lefresne. Bruxelles: ETUI.

Lerner, A. 1943. Functional finance and the Federal Debt. *Social Research*, 10: 38–51.

Leitner, S. 2003. Varieties of Familialism. The caring function of the family in comparative perspective. *European Societies: The Official Journal of the European Sociological Association.* 5(4): 353–375.

Lewis, J. and Campbell, M. 2007. Work/Family Balance and Gender Equality 1997–2005. *Social Politics* 14(1): 4–30.

Lipsky, M. 1980. *Street-Level Bureaucracy. Dilemmas of the Individual in Public Services.* New York: Russell Sage Foundation.

Little, D. 2012. *Britain Fails On Quality Of elderly care.* [Online: Sky News – Friday, 25 May 2012]. Available at: http://uk.news.yahoo.com/britain-fails-quality-elderly-care-013526861.html [accessed 24 April 2013].

Lødemel, I., and H. Trickey (eds) 2001. *An offer you can't refuse. Workfare in international perspective.* Bristol: The Policy Press.

Longley, M., Riley, N., Davies, P. and Hernández-Quevedo, C. 2012. *United Kingdom (Wales): Health System Review. Health Systems in Transition 14 (11).* Copenhagen: World Health Organization. Available at: http://www.euro.who.int/__data/assets/pdf_file/0006/177135/E96723.pdf [accessed on 9 April 2013].

Magnusson, L. and Ottosson, J. (eds) 2001. *Europe – One Labour Market?* Berlin: Peter Lang.

Mailand, M. 2009. North, South, East, West: The implementation of the European Employment Strategy in Denmark, the UK, Spain and Poland, in *Changing European Employment and Welfare Regimes: The influence of the open method of co-ordination on national reforms*, edited by M. Heidenreich, M. and J. Zeitlin. London: Routledge, pp. 133–137.

Martínez-Vázquez, J. and Yao, M.H. 2009. *Fiscal decentralization and public sector employment: a cross country analysis.* Madrid: Instituto de Estudios Fiscales Working Paper 13/09.

Martinsen, D.S. 2005. The Europeanization of Welfare. *Journal of Common Market Studies*, 43(5): 1027–1054.

Martinsen, D.S. and Vrangbæk, K. 2008. The Europeanization of Health Care Governance: Implementing the Market Imperatives of Europe. *Public Administration*, 86(1): 169–184.

Matland, R.E. 1995. Synthesising the implementation literature. The ambiguity-conflict model of policy implementation. *Journal of Public Administration Research and Theory*, 5(2): 145–174.

Matthews, S. 2011. What is a "Competitive" Tax System? *OECD Taxation Working Papers, No. 2.* Paris: OECD Publishing. Available at http://dx.doi.org/10.1787/5kg3h0vmd4kj-en. [accessed 8 October 2012].

Mau, S. and Verweibe, R. 2010. *European Societies, Mapping Structures and Change.* Bristol: Policy Press.

McDonald, P. Sustaining fertility through public policy: The range of options. *Population*, 2002/3(57): 417–446.

Mejstřík, M. et al. 2011. *Rámec strategie konkurenceschopnosti*, Praha: Úřad vlády České republiky, Národní ekonomická rada vlády. Available at: http://www.vlada.cz/assets/ppov/ekonomicka-rada/aktualne/Ramec_strategie_konkurenceschopnosti.pdf [accessed 12 October 2012].

Mishra, R. 1984. *The Welfare State in Crisis: Social Thought and Social Change.* Sussex: Wheatsheaf Books Ltd.

MLSA/MPSV 2012. Analýza vývoje zaměstnanosti a nezaměstnanosti v ČR. [Online: MPSV/MLSA] Available at: http://portal.mpsv.cz/sz/politikazamest/trh_prace [accessed 5 September 2012].

MLSA/MPSV 2010a. Diskusní materiál k východiskům dlouhodobé péče v České republice. [Online: MPSV/MLSA]. Available at: http://www.mpsv.cz/files/clanky/9597/dlouhodoba_pece_CR.pdf. [accessed 5 September 2012].

MLSA/MPSV 2006, 2007, 2008, 2009, 2010b, 2011. *Statistická ročenka z oblasti práce a sociálních věcí 2005, 2006, 2007, 2008, 2009, 2010.* (Statistical yearbook on labour and social affairs). MLSA: Praha.

Mooney, G. and Wright, S. 2009. Introduction: Social policy in the devolved Scotland: Towards a Scottish welfare state? *Social Policy and Society*, 8(3): 361–365.

Morel, N. 2006. Providing coverage against new social risks in Bismarckian welfare states: the case of long term care, in *Industrial Welfare States: Adapting post-war social policies to new social risks*, edited by K. Armingeon and G. Bonoli. London and New York: Routledge, pp. 227–247.

Moreno, L. 2004. Spain's Transition to New Risks: A Farewell to Superwomen, in *New Risks, New Welfare: The Transformation of the European Welfare State*, edited by P. Taylor-Gooby. New York: Oxford University Press, pp. 133–157.

Morgan, H. 2005. Disabled People and Employment: the potential impact of European Policy, in *Working Future?, Disabled People, policy and social inclusion*, edited by A. Roulstone and C. Barnes. Bristol: Policy Press, pp. 47–62.

Moulaert, F., Martinelli, F., Swyngedouw, E. and Gonzalez, S. 2005. Towards Alternative Model(s) of Local Innovation. *Urban Studies*, 42(11): 1669–1990.

Mosley, H. 2005. Job-Centers for Local Employment Promotion in Germany, in *Local Governance for Promoting Employment – Comparing the Performance of Japan and Seven Countries*, edited by S. Giguére and Y. Higuchi. Tokyo: The Japan Institute for Labour Policy and Training, pp. 165–178.

Mühler, G. 2008. *Institutional Childcare. An Overview on the German Market. Discussion Paper No. 08-077.* Mannheim: Centre for European Economic Research (ZEW).

Mühler, G. 2010. *Consequences of Mixed Provision of Child Care – An Overview on the German Market. Discussion Paper No. 08-077.* Mannheim: Centre for European Economic Research (ZEW).

Musgrave, R. and Musgrave, P. 1976. *Public Finance in Theory and Practice, 2nd edn.* London: McGraw-Hill.

NAO – National Audit Office. 2012. The Introduction of the Work Programme. London: The Stationery Office. Available at: http://www.nao.org.uk/wp-content/uploads/2012/01/10121701.pdf [accessed: 10 April 2013].

NHS – National Health Service 2011. *Personal Social Services Staff of Social Services Departments at 30 September 2010, England.* Leeds: The NHS Information Centre.

Next Generation Service for Older and Disabled People 2010. Final report, 13th September 2010. Advisory Committee on Older and Disabled People. Available at: http://www.ofcom.org.uk/files/2010/09/ACOD-NGS.pdf [accessed 5 October 2012].

Nies, H. et al. 2010. *Quality Management and Quality Assurance in Long-Term Care. European Overview Paper.* [Online: Utrecht and Vienna: Interlinks]. Available at: http://interlinks.euro.centre.org/sites/default/files/WP4_Overview_FINAL_04_11.pdf [accessed 25 September 2012].

Novotná, M. 2012. *Finanční analýza: současné a budoucí možnosti financování provozu jeslí.* [Online: Praha: Gender Studies, o.p.s.]. Available at: http://www.feminismus.cz/download/financni_analyza.pdf [accessed 9 June 2013].

Nygard, M. 2012. *The financial crisis and recent family-policy changes in Finland, Germany and the United Kingdom – toward workfare or social investment?* Abo Akademi University, Finland. Available at: http://www.vasa.abo.fi/users/minygard/The%20financial%20crisis%20and%20recent%20family%20policies%20%28final%20paper%29.pdf [accessed 18 March 2013].

O'Connor, J. 1973. *The Fiscal Crisis of the State.* New York: St. Martin's Press.

OECD 1981. *The Welfare State in Crisis.* Paris: OECD.

OECD 2005a. *Oslo Manual: Guidelines for Collecting and Interpreting Innovation Data. 3rd Edition.* Paris: OECD.

OECD 2005b. *Social expenditure database 1980-2001.* Paris: OECD.

OECD 2006. *Starting Strong II: Early Childhood Education and Care.* Paris: OECD, Available at: http://www.oecd.org/newsroom/37425999.pdf

OECD 2007. Consumption Taxes: the way of the Future? *OECD Policy Brief.* Paris: OECD.

OECD 2011a. *OECD Economic Outlook.* Volume 1. Paris: OECD.

OECD 2011b. *OECD's Current Tax Agenda.* Paris: OECD.

OECD 2011c. *OECD Family database.* [Online]. Available at http://www.oecd.org/document/4/0,3746,en_2649_34819_37836996_1_1_1_1,00.html.

OECD 2011d. *OECD Factbook.* Paris: OECD. [Online: OECD]. Available at: http://www.oecd.org/publications/factbook/oecdfactbook2011-2012.htm [accessed: 2 January 2013].

OECD 2011e. Building Flexibility and Accountability Into Local Employment Services: Country Report for Denmark. *OECD Local Economic and Employment Development (LEED) Working Papers, 2011/12.* Paris: OECD.

OECD 2011f. *G20 Country Policy Briefs GERMANY, Reinforced public employment services* (Meeting of Labour and Employment Ministers, 26–27 September 2011, Paris).

http://www.oecd.org/els/48724053.pdf [accessed: 20 October 2012].

OECD 2012a. *Re-thinking elderly care: realizing the potentials of new welfare technologies and user-driven innovation.* Paris: OECD.

OECD 2012b. *Health policies and data.* [Online: OECD] Available at: http://www.oecd.org/health/health-systems/oecdhealthdata2012.htm [accessed: 21 January 2013].

OECD 2012c. *Employment Outlook*. Paris: OECD.

OECD 2012d. OECD family database. [Online: OECD]. http://www.oecd.org/els/family/oecdfamilydatabase.htm [accessed: 18 January 2013].

OECD 2013. *OECD Factbook 2013. Economic, Environmental and Social Statistics*. Paris: OECD. [Online: OECD]. Available at: http://www.oecd-ilibrary.org/economics/oecd-factbook-2013_factbook-2013-en [accessed on 14 August 2013].

Office for National Statistics 2013. *Public Sector Employment, Q1 2013. Statistical Bulletin*. [Online]. Available at: http://www.ons.gov.uk/ons/dcp171778_314151.pdf [accessed: 12 August 2013].

Österle, A. 2010. Long-term Care in Central and South-Eastern Europe: Challenges and Perspectives in Addressing a 'New' Social Risk. *Social Policy & Administration*, 44(4): 461–480.

Pavolini, E. and C. Ranci 2008. Restructuring the welfare state: reforms in long-term care in Western European countries. *Journal of European Social Policy*, 18(3): 246–259.

Pennings, F. 2009. Introduction: Regulation 883/2004 – The Third Coordination Regulation in a Row. *European Journal of Social Security*, 11(1–2): 3–7.

Perrini, F. 2005. Social entrepreneurship domain: setting boundaries, in *The New Social Entrepreneurship: What Awaits Social Entrepreneurial Ventures?*, edited by F. Perrini. Cheltenham/Northampton: Edward Elgar, pp. 1–25.

Pfau-Effinger, B. 2004. *Development of Culture, Welfare States and Women's Employment in Europe*. Aldershot: Ashgate.

Phills, J.A. J., Deiglmeier, K. and Miller, D.T. 2008. Rediscovering social innovation. *Social Innovation Review*, Fall. Stanford: Stanford Graduate School of Business.

Pierre, J. and Peters, B.G. 2000. *Governance, Politics and the State*. New York: St. Martin's Press.

Pierre, J. 2008. The welfare state is female: trends in public sector employment in Sweden, in *The State at Work: Public Sector Employment in Ten Western Countries* (Vol. 1), edited by H.-U. Derlien and B.G. Peters. Cheltenham/Northampton: Edward Elgar, pp. 268–282.

Pierson, P. 1994. *Dismantling the Welfare State? Reagan, Thatcher and the Politics of Retrenchment*. Cambridge: Cambridge University Press.

Pierson, P. 1996. The path to European political integration: A historical institutionalist analysis. *Comparative Political Studies*, 29: 123–163.

Pierson, P. 2005. *The New Politics of The Welfare State*. Oxford: Oxford University Press.

Plantenga, J. and Remery, Ch. 2009. *The provision of childcare services: A comparative review of 30 European countries*. Luxembourg: Office for Official Publications of the European Communities.

Princová, I. 2009. *Poskytování postakutní péče v Nemocnici P. a její kvalita*. Praha: UK FHS.

Productivity Commission 2011. *Early Childhood Development Workforce, Research Report. Part D – Early childhood development systems and workers in other Countries.* Melbourne: Australian Government. Available at: http://www. pc.gov.au/_data/assets/pdf_file/0010/113896/23-early-childhood-appendixd. pdf [accessed: 14 August 2012].

Pollitt, C. and G. Bouckaert 2000. *Public Management Reform. A Comparative Analysis.* Oxford: Oxford University Press.

Průša, L. 2010. *Poskytování sociálních služeb seniorům a osobám se zdravotním postižením.* Praha: VÚPSV.

Průša, L. 2011. *Model efektivního financování a poskytování dlouhodobé péče.* Praha: VÚPSV.

Průša, L. and Horecký, J. 2012. *Poskytování služeb sociální péče pro seniory v České republice a ve Švýcarsku: mezinárodní komparace.* Tábor: APSS.

Radaelli, C.M. 2003. The Europeanization of Public Policy, in *The Politics of Europeanization,* edited by K. Featherstone and C.M. Radaelli. Oxford: Oxford University Press, pp. 27–56.

Radaelli, C.M. 2004. Europeanisation: Solution or problem? *European Integration online Papers (EIoP),* 8(16).

Radaelli, C.M. 2005. Diffusion without Convergence: How Political Context Shapes the Adoption of Regulatory Impact Assessment, *Journal of European Public Policy,* 12(5): 924–943.

Räisänen, H., Alatalo, J., Krüger Henriksen, K., Israelsson, T. and Klinger, S. 2012. *Labour market reforms and performance in Denmark, Germany, Sweden and Finland.* Helsinki: Publications of the Ministry of Employment and the Economy. Employment and entrepreneurship, 19/2012. Available at: http://www.tem.fi/files/32993/TEMjul_19_2012.web.pdf [accessed: 20 October 2012].

Reinhard, H.-J. 2010. Towards a European Pension Policy? *European Journal of Social Security,* 12(3): 200–215.

Rhodes, R.A.W. 1992. Beyond Whitehall: Researching local governance. *Social Sciences,* 13: 2.

Rogers, S. 2012. Child care costs: how the UK compares with the world. *The Guardian, 21 May.* Available at: http://www.guardian.co.uk/news/datablog/2012/ may/21/child-care-costs-compared-britain. [accessed: 2 March 2013].

Room, G. et al. 2005. *The European Challenge. Innovation, policy learning and social cohesion in the new knowledge economy.* University of Bristol: The Policy Press.

Rosamond, B. 2009. Supranational Governance, in *The Sage Handbook of European Studies,* edited by C. Rumford. London: Sage, pp. 89–109.

Roth, C. and Schmid, J. 2000. Multi-Level Governance in the European Employment and Labour Market Policy: A Conceptual Outline and Some Empirical Evidence. *Global Policy Studies,* 1: 92–130.

Rothgang, H. 2010. Social Insurance for Long-term Care: An Evaluation of the German Model. *Social Policy and Administration,* 44(4): 436–460.

Rouban, L. 2008. The French paradox: a huge but fragmented public service, in *The State at Work (Vol. 1): Public Sector Employment in Ten Western Countries*, edited by H.-U. Derlien and B.G. Peters, B.G. Cheltenham: Edward Elgar, pp. 222–248.

Rüling, A. 2010. Re-Framing of Childcare in Germany and England: From a Private Responsibility to an Economic Necessity. *German Policy Studies*, 6(2): 153–186.

Salamon, L. M. 2005. *The New Governance. Getting Beyond the Right Answer to the Wrong Question in Public Sector Reform. The J. Douglas Gibson lecture.* School of Policy Studies, Queens University.

Salamon, L.M. (ed.) 2002. *The Tools of Government: A Guide to New Governance.* New York: Oxford University Press.

Saxonberg, S. and Sirovatka, T. 2006. Failing Family Policies in Eastern Europe. *Journal of Comparative Policy Analysis*, 8(2): 185–202.

Saxonberg, S. and Sirovatka, T. 2009. Neo-liberalism by Decay? The Evolution of the Czech Welfare State. *Social Policy & Administration*, 43(2): 186–203.

Schettkat, R. and Yocarini, L. 2003. *The Shift to Serivce: A review of the literature.* IZA Discussion Paper Series, No. 964. Nürnberg: Forschungsinstitut zur zukunft der Arbeit – Institute for the Study of Labour.

Scott, W. and Wright, S. 2012. Devolution, social democratic visions and policy reality in Scotland. *Critical Social Policy*, 32: 440–453.

Schulz, E. 2010a. The long-term care system for the elderly in Denmark. *Discussion Papers 1038*. Berlin: DIW. [Online: DIW]. Available at: http://www.diw.de/documents/publikationen/73/diw_01.c.359021.de/dp1038.pdf [accessed: 11 November 2012].

Schulz, E. 2010b. *The Long-Term Care System.* Berlin: Deutsches Institut für Wirtschafsforschung. [Online: DIW]. Available at: http://www.diw.de/documents/publikationen/73/diw_01.c.359024.de/dp1039.pdf [accessed: 11 November 2012].

Schulz, E. 2012. *Determinants of Institutional Long-Term Care. Enepri Research Report No. 115.* European Network of Economic Policy Research Institutes. Available at: http://www.ceps.eu/book/determinants-institutional-long-term-care-germany [accessed: 8 March 2013].

Seeleib-Kaiser, M. 2008. Welfare State Transformations in Comparative Perspective: Shifting Boundaries of Public and Private Social Policy, in *Welfare State Transformations: Comparative Perspectives*, edited by M. Seeleib-Kaiser. Basingstoke: Palgrave Macmillan, pp. 1–13.

Seeleib-Kaiser, M. (ed.) 2008. *Welfare State Transformations: Comparative Perspectives.* Basingstoke: Palgrave Macmillan.

Simonazzi, A. 2008. *Care regimes and national employment models, Working Paper n. 113.* Universita Degli Studi di Roma 'La Sapienza', Dipartmento di Economia Publica.

Simonazzi, A. 2010. Reforms and job quality: The case of the elderly care sector. *Work Organisation Labour and Globalisation*, 4(1): 41–56.

Sinfield, A. 2007. Tax Welfare, in *Understanding the Mixed Economy of Welfare*, edited by M. Powell. Bristol: Policy Press, pp. 129–148.

Sirovátka, T. 2007. New Social Risks and Social Exclusion as a Challenge to Czech Social Policy. *European Journal of Social Security*, 9(1): 55–77.

Sirovátka, T., Greve, B. and Hora, O. 2011. *Public/private mix and social innovation in service provision, fiscal policy and employment*. [Online: web portal of NEUJOBS project, Brussels, NEUJOBS WP 7 State of the art report No. 2]. Available at: http://www.neujobs.eu/publications/state-art-reports/ [accessed: 12 June 2012].

Sirovátka, T. 2008. Activation Policies under Conditions of Weak Governance: Czech and Slovak cases compared. *Central European Journal of Public Policy*, 2(1): 4–29.

Sirovátka, T., Horák, P. and Horáková, M. 2007. Emergence of new modes of governance in activation policies: Czech experience. *International Journal of Sociology and Social Policy*, 27(7/8): 311–323.

Sirovátka, T., and Kulhavý, V. 2008. *Implementation of the new policies of activation and their effects for labour market inclusion of the vulnerable groups in the Czech Republic*. Paper prepared for the IAB / DGS conference 'Activation policies on the fringes of society', May 15/16, 2008, Nürnberg.

Sirovátka, T. and Winkler, J. 2011. Governance of Activation Policies in the Czech Republic: Uncoordinated Transformation, in *The Governance of Welfare States in Europe*, edited by R. van Berkel, W. de Graaf and T. Sirovátka. Houndmills, Basingstoke: Palgrave Macmillan, pp. 173–194.

Sirovátka, T. and Šimíková, I. 2013. *Politika zaměstnanosti a další opatření na trhu práce v dlouhodobé perspektivě a v průběhu krize*. Praha: VÚPSV.

Sokačová, L. 2010. Zařízení péče o děti, in *Rodinná politika: rodičovská a mateřská v kontextu slaďování rodinného a pracovního života a rovných příležitostí žen a mužů*, 16–21, edited by L. Sokačová. [Online: Gender studies, Praha,]. Available at: http://aa.ecn.cz/img_upload/8b47a03bf445e4c3031ce32 6c68558ae/Rodinna_politika.pdf [accessed: 7 March 2013].

Sol, E. and Westerveld, M. (eds). 2005. *Contractualism in employment services. A new form of welfare state governance*. The Hague: Kluwer.

Sørensen, E. and Torfing, J. (eds.) 2007. *Theories of Democratic Network Governance*. Basingstoke: Palgrave Macmillan.

Statistics Denmark 2012. *Quality Declaration – Earnings statistics on central and local government employees*. Available at: www.dst.dk/declarations/862 [accessed: 20 August 2018].

Statistics Denmark 2013. *Quality Declaration – Register-based labour force statistics (RAS statistics)*. Available at: www.dst.dk/declarations/848 [accessed: 20 August 2018].

Statistisches Bundesamt 2005–2011. *Mikrozensus: Bevölkerung und Erwerbstätigkeit Beruf, Ausbildung und Arbeitsbedingungen der Erwerbstätigen (Band 2: Deutschland)*, Wiesbaden: Statistisches Bundesamt.

Statistisches Bundesamt 2007–2010. *Verdienste und Arbeitskosten: Arbeitnehmerverdienste (2007–2010)*, Wiesbaden: Statistisches Bundesamt.

Stoy, V. 2012. Worlds of Welfare Services: From Discovery to Exploration. *Social Policy & Administration* 46, early view online. Available at: http://onlinelibrary. wiley.com/journal/10.1111/(ISSN)1467-9515/earlyview [accessed: July 2013].

Strategie mezinárodní konkurenceschopnosti ČR 2011. [Online: Úřad Vlády ČR]. Available at: http://www.vlada.cz/cz/media-centrum/aktualne/premier-predstavil-plan-posileni-konkurenceschopnosti-cr-86002/ [accessed: 20 December 2012].

Sure Start Children's Centres Census 2012. *Developments, trends and analysis of Sure Start Children's Centres over the last year and the implications for the future.* [Online: 4children organisation web portal]. Available at: http://www.4children. org.uk/Resources/Detail/Sure-Start-Childrens-Centres-Census-2012 [accessed: 26 March 2013].

Szelewa, D. and Polakowski, M. 2008. Who cares? Changing patterns of childcare in Central and Eastern Europe, *Journal of European Social Policy*, 18(2): 115–131.

Taleb, N. 2010. *The Black Swan. The Impact of the Highly Improbable.* London: Penguin.

Tangian, A. 2010. Not for bad weather: macroanalysis of flexicurity with regard to the crisis. *Working Paper, 2010-06.* Brussels: ETUI.

Tangian, A. 2007. *Is work in Europe decent? A study based on the 4th European survey of working conditions 2005.* Düsseldorf, Germany: Institute for Economic and Social Sciences (WSI).

Taylor-Gooby, P., (ed.) 2004a. *New Risks, New Welfare.* Oxford: Oxford University Press.

Taylor-Gooby, P. 2004b. New risks and social change, in *New Risks, New Welfare: The Transformation of the European Welfare State*, edited by P. Taylor-Gooby. New York: Oxford University Press, pp. 1–28.

Taylor-Gooby, P. 2008. The New Welfare Settlement in Europe, *European Societies*, 10(1): 3–24.

Taylor-Gooby, P. 2012. Root and Branch Restructuring to Achieve Major Cuts: The Social Policy Programme of the 2010 UK Coalition Government, *Social Policy & Administration*, 46(1): 61–82.

Teague, P. 2001. Deliberative Governance and EU Social Policy. *European Journal of Industrial Relations*, 7(1): 7–26.

Tepe, M. 2009. Public administration employment in 17 OECD nations from 1995 to 2005. *Working Papers on the Reconciliation of Work and Welfare in Europe 12/2009.*

Tepe, M. and Vanhuysse, P. 2013a. *Parties, Unions, and Activation Strategies: The Context-Dependent Politics of Active Labor Market Policy Spending, Political Studies*, 61(3): 480–504.

Tepe, M. and Vanhuysse, P. 2013b. Cops for Hire: The Political Economy of Police Employment across German States, *Journal of Public Policy*, 33(4): 165–199.

Tergeist, P. and Grubb, D. 2006. Activation Strategies and the Performance of Employment Services in Germany, the Netherlands and the United Kingdom, *OECD Social, Employment and Migration Working Papers*. Available at: http://www.oecd.org/els/emp/37848464.pdf [accessed: 4 September 2012].

The Clearinghouse on International Developments in Child, Youth and Family Policies. United Kingdom 2008. Columbia University. [Online]. Available at: http://www.childpolicyintl.org/countries/uk.html.

Theobald, H. 2004. *Care Services for the Elderly. Infrastructure, access and utilization from the perspective of different user groups*. Berlin: Veröffentlichungsreihe der Arbeitsgruppe Public Health. Available at: http://bibliothek.wzb.eu/pdf/2004/i04-302.pdf [accessed: 12 September 2012].

Timonen, V. 2004. New Risks – Are they still New for the Nordic Welfare States?, in *New Risks, New Welfare: The Transformation of the European Welfare State*, edited by P. Taylor-Gooby. New York: Oxford University Press, pp. 83–110.

Trubek, D. and Mosher, J. 2003. New Governance, Employment Policy, and the European Social Model, in *Governing Work and Welfare in a New Economy*, edited by J. Zeitlin and D. Trubek. Oxford: Oxford University Press, pp. 33–58.

Truss, E. 2012. *Affordable Quality: New Approaches to Childcare*. [Online: Centre Forum, London]. Available at: http://www.centreforum.org/assets/pubs/affordable-quality.pdf [accessed: 14 August 2013].

ÚIV 2012. *Statistická data o předškolní výchově*. [Online: Ústav pro informace ve vzdělávání]. Available at: http://www.uiv.cz/clanek/729/2009 [accessed 5 December 2012].

UNECE – United Nations Economic Commission for Europe 2012. *Statistical database. Indicator employment rates by the number of children (till 2 chd)*. [Online: UNECE]. Available at: http://w3.unece.org [accessed: 15 June 2013].

UNESCO 2013. *United Nations Educational, Scientific and Cultural Organization. On-line database*. Available at: http://stats.uis.unesco.org/unesco/TableViewer/tableView.aspx?ReportId=175 [accessed: 19 August 2013].

UNICEF 2007. *Innocenti Report Card 7*. [Online: UNICEF]. Available at: www.unicef-irc.org/publications/pdf/rc7_eng.pdf [accessed 5 May 2012].

UNIFEM 2006. *Women and employment in central and eastern Europe and the western commonwealth of independent states*. Bratislava: Unifem.

ÚZIS ČR 2011. *Aktuální informace Ústavu zdravotnických informací a statistiky České republiky*. [Online: ÚZIS]. Available at: http://www.uzis.cz/system/files/18_11.pdf [accessed 8 May 2012].

van Berkel, R., de Graaf, W. and Sirovátka, T. (eds) 2011. *The Governance of Welfare States in Europe*. Basingstoke: Palgrave, Macmillan.

van Berkel, R. de Graaf, W. and Sirovátka, T. (eds) 2012. Governance of the activation policies in Europe: Introduction. *International Journal of Sociology and Social Policy*, 32(5/6): 260–272.

van Vliet, O. and Koster, F. 2011. Europeanisation and the Political Economy of Active Labour Market Policies. *European Union Politics*, 12(2): 217–239.

Veggeland, N. 2011. *Taming the Regulatory State. Politics and Ethics.* Cheltenham: Edward Elgar.

Verschraegen, G., Vanhercke, B. and Verpoortenert, R. 2011. The European Social Fund and domestic activation policies: Europeanization mechanism. *Journal of European Social Policy*, 21(1): 55–72.

Verdier, D. and Breen, R. 2001. Europeanization and Globalization. Politics Against Markets in the European Union. *Comparative Political Studies*, 34(3): 227–262.

Vis, B., van Kersbergen, K. and Hylands, T. 2011. To What Extent Did the Financial Crisis Intensify the Pressure to Reform the Welfare State? *Social Policy & Administration*, 45(4): 338–353.

Vláda 2011. *Analýza podmínek a možností zařazení dětí od dvou let věku do mateřských škol a vyhodnocení dalšího řešení rozšíření péče o děti do tří let.* Praha: Úřad vlády ČR. Available at: http://www.vlada.cz/assets/media-centrum/aktualne/Analyza-podminek-a-moznosti-deti.pdf [accessed 9 October 2012].

Vláda ČR 2012. *Analýza podmínek a možností zařazení dětí od dvou let věku do mateřských škol a vyhodnocení dalšího rozšíření péče o děti do tří let.* Praha: Úřad vlády ČR. Available at: http://www.vlada.cz/assets/media-centrum/aktualne/Analyza-podminek-a-moznosti-deti.pdf [accessed 23 March 2013].

Wagner, A. 1911. Staat in nationalökonomischer Hinsicht in *Handwörterbuch der Staatswissenschaften*, edited by J. Conrad, L., Elster, W. Lexis, and E. Loening, 7, pp. 727–739.

Weishaupt, J.T. 2011. *Social Partners and the Governance of Public Employment Services: Trends and Experiences from Western Europe. Working Document No. 17.* Geneva: ILO.

Wessels, W. 2001. The Amsterdam Treaty in Theoretical Perspectives: which dynamics at work, in *European Union After the Treaty of Amsterdam*, edited by W. Wessels and J. Monar. New York: Continuum, pp. 760–783.

Winter, D. 2008. *Employment Service Delivery in Denmark.* Copengahen: The Danish National Centre for Social Research.

Wiggan, J. 2012. A kingdom united? Devolution and welfare reform in Northern Ireland and Great Britain. *Policy & Politics*, 40(1): 57–72.

Wollman, H. and Marcou, G. (eds) 2010. *The Provision of Public Services in Europe: Between State, Local Government and Market.* Cheltenham: Edward Elgar.

Wright, S. 2011. Steering with sticks, rowing for rewards: The new governance of activation in the UK, in *The Governance of Active Welfare States in Europe*, edited by R. van Berkel, W. de Graaf, and T. Sirovátka. Basingstoke: Palgrave Macmillan, pp. 85–109.

Index